Eloquent Reticence

Eloquent Reticence

Withholding Information in Fictional Narrative

Leona Toker

THE UNIVERSITY PRESS OF KENTUCKY

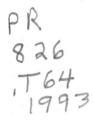
Copyright © 1993 by The University Press of Kentucky

Scholarly publisher for the Commonwealth,
serving Bellarmine College, Berea College, Centre
College of Kentucky, Eastern Kentucky University,
The Filson Club, Georgetown College, Kentucky
Historical Society, Kentucky State University,
Morehead State University, Murray State University,
Northern Kentucky University, Transylvania University,
University of Kentucky, University of Louisville,
and Western Kentucky University.

Editorial and Sales Offices: Lexington, Kentucky 40508-4008

Library of Congress Cataloging-in-Publication Data

Toker, Leona.
  Eloquent reticence : withholding information in fictional
narrative / Leona Toker.
    p.   cm.
  Includes bibliographical references and index.
  ISBN 0-8131-1811-5 (alk. paper)
  1. English fiction—History and criticism.   2. Silence in
literature.   3. Narration (Rhetoric)   4. Fiction—Technique.
I. Title.
PR826.T64   1992
823.009'23—dc20   92-16175

To Gregory

Contents

Preface

This book suggests an ethically oriented method of narratological analysis and applies it to seven classical novels—five English and two American. The new points made about these exquisite and much discussed texts on the pages below are either the direct yield of the approach proposed or a result of thoughts that have been prompted by it in the context of issues raised by prior scholarship. Conversely, the application of the method to individual texts has contributed to its refinement.

I refrain, as much as possible, from entering into polemics with other scholars. My references to critical opinions different from my own stem from the wonder at the versatility of a text's meaning and its refractions. In general, I refer mainly to those theoretical and critical studies that have either stimulated my thinking (sometimes by way of disagreement) or covered important ground lying beyond the scope of this book.

Work on this project began many years ago, when my first steps in Western literary criticism were encouraged and guided, with a great deal of patience and without compromise, by Professor H.M. Daleski, whose disciple, albeit somewhat deviant, I have always remained. Since then I have always had the benefit of his advice, generous attention, constructive criticism, and encouragement with this and other projects. My constantly increasing debt to him is beyond acknowledgment.

It grieves me that Dorothea Krook, to whom I owe special gratitude, is no longer here to accept it. She was one of the first readers of the manuscript, and both her criticism and her praise have been of great value.

I thank Professor Wolfgang Iser, whose work in reception theory has exerted considerable influence on the theoretical basis of this book, for important timely consultations, and for numerous acts of kindness.

I am grateful also to the people who have read, or listened to, and commented on, different parts of this work—in particular, to Alexander Gelley of the University of California, Irvine, and my Hebrew University colleagues Emily and Sanford Budick, Baruch Hochman, Elizabeth Freund, Ruth Nevo, Shlomith Rimmon-Kenan, and Ora Segal.

My parents, Nedda and Aba Strazhas, and my husband, Gregory, have always given me much needed support.

In the early stages of this work I received financial help from the Association of Lithuanian Immigrants and from the Jewish Agency, for which I thank them. The final version was produced during my stay at Constance University; I am grateful to the Alexander von Humboldt Foundation for the fellowship that made possible this particularly fruitful visit.

My thanks go to research assistants Ilana Rosberger and Barbara Hall. Their help was of particular importance during my work on the book about Nabokov published in 1989, but they have also contributed to the present project.

An early version of chapter 5 was published in a special issue of *Hebrew University Studies in Literature* in honor of A.A. Mendilow (Jerusalem, 1982), 57-79. A version of chapter 2 has appeared in *College Literature* 15 (1988): 111-35; and of chapter 3 in *Conradiana* 21 (1989): 183-202. I thank *HSLA*, West Chester University, and *Conradiana* for permissions to reprint these materials.

CHAPTER ONE

Introduction

speak silence with thy glimmering eyes
   —Blake, "To the Evening Star"

By all means place the "how" above the
"what" but do not let it be confused with
the "so what."
   —Vladimir Nabokov, *Strong Opinions*

In information theory the absence of a message is a message in its own right; in politics reticences and omissions are clues of major significance; in personal relationships evasions are signs more loaded than words. Silence speaks: "Day unto day uttereth speech, and night unto night sheweth knowledge" (Psalms 19:2); silence, as in Blake's "To the Evening Star," is also spoken. In poetry silence can speak, technically, through pauses, obscure images, tropes, and other channels of psychedelic appeal. In the novel, the most voluble heteroglot genre,[1] it speaks through manipulative informational gaps. The present book is devoted to the study of the rhetoric of such gaps in seven eloquently reticent novels.

Russian formalism, French structuralism, and American narratology have developed precision tools for the rhetorical and structural analysis of prose fiction. The makers and the users of these tools have, however, always been aware that descriptive analysis begs questions of the "so what" type and is insufficient as an end in itself rather than as a means to other ends such as thematic analysis, semiotics of culture, metaphysical inquiry, study of the force and self-reflexivity of language, study of reader response, and numerous unclassifiable insights into individual texts. The method developed below relates descriptive analysis, through the discussion of audience response, to the inquiry into what in recent critical conversation has been called "the ethics of form." It stops short of probing the ethical theory worked out in individual novels but maps a narratological avenue of approach to it.

As is now widely recognized, ethical concerns are not merely a matter of issues raised in the content of literary works or of authors' proclaimed or implied attitudes. In the case of what John Gardner regards as genuinely moral fiction, philosophical issues are explored and attitudes tested and refined not prior to but during and through the work of imagination (fiction is a "mode of thought"[2]), and the narrative, in its turn, creates conditions for a specific moral-intellectual experience of the reader. These conditions are shaped not only by the content but also by genre features, style, narrative techniques—whatever is commonly associated with "form." The formal features of a work therefore have an ethical significance.

The ethics of literary form is one of the central concerns of Martha Nussbaum's *The Fragility of Goodness*. Nussbaum believes that an author's choice of genre and style is not "content neutral";[3] she demonstrates this on the material of Greek tragedies, Plato's dialogues, and Aristotle's treatises. The formal issues that her study deals with, from the philosophical vantage point, are mainly genre features, choice of metaphors, and framing. Wayne Booth's *The Company We Keep* approaches ethical problematics from the positions of critical theory and focuses on the significance of figurative language, the ethics of instrumental "weapon" metaphors, and mythopoeic macro-metaphors as well as on questions of scope and balance.[4] By contrast, Meir Sternberg's *The Poetics of Biblical Narrative* proceeds, as my study does, from narratological positions. Sternberg shows the role of a wide range of narrative techniques in promoting the single overall ethical tendency of the text through the "drama of knowledge" in which the Old Testament engages the reader.[5] My book examines a smaller set of narrative techniques, yet in a way that opens up to discussions of the different kinds of moral-intellectual experiences in which seven classical novels involve the audience. The passage from rhetorical analysis to such discussions is, as noted above, via the effects of the techniques in question on the dynamics of audience response.

I speak of "audience" rather than "reader response" because the latter term has become too loaded.[6] It frequently suggests against-the-grain readings of texts from the point of view of different interest groups. The term "audience response" does not presuppose an analogy with the theatrical framework, yet such an analogy is not entirely out of place.

Indeed, when Pushkin's Eugene Onegin makes his way, long after the curtain has risen, to his seat in the theatre (stepping, rather unethically, on people's feet), the audience, "breathing criticism, is ready to applaud an *entrechat*, hiss Phaedra, Cleopatra, call out Moëna—for the purpose merely of being heard."[7] "Breathing criticism" is Vladimir Nabokov's translation of the original "breathing liberty." Most literary study is the liberties that we take with texts—within limits. My self-imposed restrictions here exclude the *anre rem* ideological scrutiny: a temporary submission to the sway of the text is held to be in order before one reasserts one's freedom. Rhetorical analysis focuses only on the response that the texts "foresee," though its task often lies in determining the very limits of its field of inquiry.

"Audience response" may be viewed as one part of this wide field. It consists in our automatic estimation of the completeness or incompleteness of the information available at any given moment of reading and our attempts to correlate the presented and the assimilated data, to arrange and rearrange the material, extrapolate, make gap-filling conjectures, form and adjust expectations. It entails the emotions aroused by *our own information-processing performance* rather than the *vicarious* emotions aroused by the experience of the characters.

Hence this study is not primarily concerned either with the text's appeal to vicarious emotions (what D.H. Harding calls "feeling with" the characters) or with the text's influence on our subliminal moral evaluations (what Harding calls "feeling for" the characters[8])—which is not to deny the importance of both. These aspects of response are here considered only insofar as they are affected by ways in which the stream of ludic information (the "make-believe" or "play information," like "play money" in the Monopoly game) is monitored in the text.

In the ideal absence of what information theory calls "noise," audience response could, in principle, approximate the common denominator of sundry individual readings. In practice, however, its intensity varies in inverse proportion to the individual reader's ability to respond to a greater number of textual irritants simultaneously and to experience moments of disinterested aesthetic contemplation that temporarily silences the wish to pursue the mysteries of the plot.

In some novels the elements of audience response are analogous, or parallel, to elements of the characters' experience. Thwarting of a character's ambitions can be reenacted—often in a different part of the novel—by our frustration at being denied the information we want; a character's obsessive hope can be reenacted by an intensification of our suspense caused by an enigma. In Nabokov's *Pnin*, for instance, there is an abrupt shift from the story of Victor Wind's visit with Pnin to a much later episode in which Victor does not participate. Our vivid interest in the Pnin-Victor friendship is not satisfied (the relationship develops away from the limelight): this frustration, as it turns out, reenacts Pnin's own eventual disappointment when Victor is suddenly summoned away.

As the subject of the novel narrows down from a record of multiple experience (picaresque novel) to an analytic account of a single human situation, parallel experience gains importance. By placing us in an intellectual predicament analogous to that of the characters, parallel experience can turn into a direct means of conveying to us the specific emotional climate of the novel's world, without the mediation of overt didactics, fictional brainstorms, or "vicarious" emotion. Yet it can perform a variety of other functions as well. In some works, in most of Conrad's novels, for instance, analogies between the "dramas of knowledge" in which the reader and the characters find themselves involved reduce the importance of the differences between them in other spheres of experience; as a result, cognitive issues are privileged and to a large extent universalized. In other works, for example, in the stories of Varlam Shalamov, who is known (insufficiently) to the English speaking public as the author of *Kolyma Tales* and *Graphite*,[9] such analogies further emphasize the difference between the reader's situation and that of the Gulag prisoners described; as a result, a warning is issued against hastily judging the characters according to conventional norms. In some works, of course, parallel experience has no special significance—in detective fiction, for example, our reenactment of a Dr. Watson's gropings is a means rather than the end or even a by-product of mystification.

Parallel experience is of the greatest interest when it is isomorphic with a novel's themes—a theme here being understood not as a semantic field that accommodates multiple recurrent motifs but as a latent statement that can be regarded as the organizing principle of the work. However, though the reader may be aware of the mental operations performed in piecing together the data of the text, he or she seldom registers the analogy between these operations and the experience of the characters: parallel experience is not among the notions that underlie our reading conventions. My references to it are meant to be consciousness-raising: I believe that analysis of parallel experience can be a useful interpretive strategy, a way of thinking that can yield new insights into familiar texts. Accordingly, the seven "reticent" novels discussed have been chosen because they bring into bold relief tendencies that also appear, in a less salient form, in numerous other works.

The reticence in question is not to be measured against the plenitude of extratextual reality. It consists not in the presumed inadequacy of the mimetic model provided by the text but in the suppression of information concerning the model itself, the fictional world whose spatial and causal-temporal relationships constitute the so-called *fabula* of a novel. I shall attempt to show how gaps in the *fabula* information open upon mirrors that the novels hold up to the audience.

What, then, are the gaps in the *fabula* information?

The term *fabula* was first used by Russian formalist critics of the turn of the century. It refers to the sum total of fictional events in their chronological and logical order and may be understood to include all the available circumstances and details of those events. The counterpart of the *fabula* is the *sjuzhet*, the sequence in which the fictional events are presented in the narrative. In a broader sense, the *sjuzhet* is the totality of devices and techniques used in the telling of the story.[10] The audience is supposed to reconstruct the *fabula* from the *sjuzhet* in the process of reading.

Reconstruct or construct? Post-formalist critical positions deny the preexistence of the *fabula*[11] and reject the possibility of "extracting" a meaning from the signs on the page[12] or even of separating the "brute facts" of the texts (including grammatical, metrical, or phonetic features) from systems of interpretation.[13] Strictly speaking, the *sjuzhet* is the immediate given; the *fabula* is an abstraction from the *sjuzhet* rather than the material to which the latter gives form;[14] and the fictional narrative *imitates* rather than constitutes the flow of information. Its sentences do not present accounts of fictional events but create the facts that they purport to communicate.[15] Thus any sentence in a fictional narrative is a performative speech act, an act which, like "I name this ship Queen Elizabeth" or "I apologize," is made possible by a verbal formulation that describes that which it performs.[16]

This act, however, properly "takes place" only when it is perceived, or "concretized," by a comprehending reader. The text may be regarded as containing not so much information as instructions for the reader, instructions as to how the *fabula* should be built and what attitude should be taken to its different parts.[17] Even when the reader has the impression of being engaged in a dialogue with the narrator or novelist (in, for instance, Fielding's *Tom Jones*), narrative units can still be interpreted not as the novelist's contribution to this dialogue but as "instructions" for the reader to conjure up the interlocutor in his or her imagination.

The instructions can never be exhaustive: a text cannot present all the humanly perceptible features of an object described or all the details of an action. It is always characterized by a degree of indeterminacy, but when it presents a sufficient number of features (instructions) to cause instant pattern recognition, the missing details are supplied by the reader's imagination.[18] This cooperation of the reader with the text is automatic and instantaneous. It is indeterminate and idiosyncratic but does not constitute a misreading so long as it does not conflict with the "instructions" of the text. This is what distinguishes blanks, or spots of indeterminacy, practically infinite in any text, from definite and relatively infrequent informational gaps—bearing in mind that in some narratives there are camouflaged gaps perceived as blanks on the first reading. However incomplete the instructions presented by the text to the audience may be, in the case of mere blanks they contain sufficient data for pattern recognition. In the case of gaps, on the other hand, the information offered by the text is felt to be incomplete: it does not immediately congeal into a definite matrix-pattern. The figure in the carpet is then expected to stabilize at later textual junctures when the gaps are at least partly closed; the closure of the gaps is expected to select a single pattern from a number of latent ones between which we hesitate in the absence of clinching clues.

Thus, a touch of indeterminacy is perceived as an informational gap only when the reader expects the content of the missing information to be of some consequence. For instance, in Dickens's *Hard Times*, we are never told exactly how Sissy's father dies after he runs away from the circus, and yet we are well aware of what the sad end of the indigent old alcoholic would be like; we also feel that the novelist appeals to this awareness. The concrete details of old Jupe's death have no further influence on the characters, the themes, or the action of the novel; nor does this blank turn into a gap in retrospect, as so often happens with inoffensive-looking blanks in detective novels. By contrast, when in Conrad's *Nostromo* we are informed of the death of Martin Decoud, the manner and the cause of this death are perceived as centrally important. We expect to be given information about them, not so much because this information can have any bearing on further plot developments, but because it is necessary for our comprehension of the psychological patterns that the novel explores. Decoud's death, moreover, is rather unexpected: according to the basic law of information theory, the amount of information carried by a message (and hence its importance) increases in inverse proportion to the probability of the production of that message—narrative fiction bears this out.

While reading detective novels we try to guess "who dunnit" and then wait to see whether our conjectures prove right. In other words, the "who dunnit" is perceived as a gap because we stake our belief in our own sagacity or in the wit of the author on the correctness or incorrectness of our hypothesis. By analogy, a blank turns into an informational gap if we are not sure that our way of filling it in is correct and if the correctness of our surmise seems to be of issue. The surmise usually concerns the information that is to come later, though in the process of reading we usually perceive it as information about what already exists but is hidden from our view. (Unless one keeps critical theory fatally in mind, in individual reading experience the "story" is perceived as preexisting its narration.) This is particularly true of narratives that withhold information: their *sjuzhet* has the effect of a curtain that must be drawn, or canceled, so that we can get to the picture that it is believed to veil. In eloquently reticent novels there are moments when, as in the Greek parable of painters, the curtain turns out, dramatically, to *be* the picture. Such moments of reorientation often have an ethical significance, but their specific effects vary in individual texts.

As noted above, narrative gaps are associated with, or produced by, our estimation of the completeness or incompleteness of the *fabula* information at our disposal at any given moment of the reading. Estimation is a mental act symptomatic of an attitude; hence it is the correctness of our attitudes that gaps seem to test. At the same time, however, our estimations are formed under the influence of a complex of rhetorical devices in the text. The process is dialogical: features *a*, *b*, and *c* of the text influence the audience to treat feature *d* as an informational gap; yet they do so by taking advantage of the attitudes, often unconscious, that the audience brings along to its encounter with the text. Our response to the gap is a conjecture and a set of expectations that are either fulfilled or thwarted by subsequent portions of the text. The thwarting is usually a more interesting phenomenon, not only because, like everything unexpected, it carries more information, but also because it can alert us to subjective reasons for our mistakes. Then our own attitudes, formerly unconscious or taken for granted, become the object of our attention.

Thus, gaps in the make-believe information concerning the world of the characters can lead to unexpected insights into the attitudes and mental habits that have made these gaps, or their effects, possible. This is the case with most of the seven novels discussed below. In a way the self-reflexive insight produces what it reflects: the novel elicits certain potential features of the reading process and turns them into a virtual object of the reader's perception. The process of reading creates mock circumstances that can reveal real toads in imaginary gardens; it becomes a play dialogue in which the text and the audience read one another.

The discussion of the seven novels along these lines proceeds from three principal assumptions concerning (a) the value of multiple readings, (b) the ideal of careful reading, and (c) the selectiveness of the reader's attention.

Reading and Rereading

The interaction of the text and the reader unfolds in time: it is a process during which the audience's response to and perspective on the text undergo changes. The syntagmatic experience of these changes is no less meaningful than the paradigm of the novel's motifs.

In his *Expositional Modes and Temporal Ordering in Fiction*, which deals extensively with the withholding of information (limiting its inquiry to expositional material), Meir Sternberg notes that "the meaning of a literary work, on all its levels, is not confined to the fully warrantable conclusions we reach at the terminus, but is made up of the sum total of expectations and effects, trial and error included, produced throughout the eventful, tortuous journey."[19] It must be emphasized that the "eventful, tortuous journey" is a double one. Any good novel should, of course, be read at least twice; a great novel invites us back again and again. But the difference between a second reading and the subsequent readings is usually quantitative: one sees and understands "more" rather than "in a different way." On the other hand, the difference between the first and the repeated readings is qualitative: on the first reading certain attitudes are elicited and processed; on a rereading, these attitudes are rejected or modified. Our response becomes a complex of error, anagnorisis, and reorientation.

In the case of "reticent" novels the main difference between the first and the repeated readings is that at the outset of the latter we possess the information that was withheld from us for some time during the former. Hence, the structure of our expectations on a repeated reading is radically different and cannot be accounted for merely by the absence of the "what-happens-next" sort of suspense. This is where I disagree with Michael Rifaterre, who, in his otherwise wonderful analysis of Baudelaire's "Les Chats," neglects this difference. The "superreader" postulated by Rifaterre[20] reads the text over and over again and adopts the insights of previous readers, yet the response attributed to this ideal audience is of a kind possible only on an extremely perceptive first reading. Rifaterre notes, for instance, that the contrast which the components of poetic structure create "is what forces them on the reader's attention; these contrasts result from their unpredictability within the context. This unpredictability is made possible by the fact that at every point in a sentence the grammatical restrictions limiting the choice of the next word permit a certain degree of predictability. Predictability increases as the number of levels involved and the number of restrictions increase, which happens with any kind of recurrence, like parallelism in general and meter in particular—and where predictability increases, so does the effect of an unpredictable element." [21] Yet the unpredictability is largely reduced on a rereading, though the contrasts remain in force: we cannot help knowing what comes next unless we have forgotten the text so completely that it is no longer perceived as familiar. The effect of unpredictability yields to that of irony: if on a first reading a unit arouses expectations that are later frustrated, on a rereading this unit tends to be perceived as ironic. For instance, Rifaterre's observation that the definite article and the plural in the title of "Les Chats" "lead us to expect a precise and concrete description" and that "against such a backdrop the spiritualization of the cats will be more arresting," [22] applies strictly to the first reading. Then, indeed, one is affected by the unexpectedness of the poem's treatment of its subject. On a rereading the emotional neutrality of the title, instead of creating the same expectations as before, strikes us as contrasting ironically with the disquieting image that, as we already know, is forthcoming. As Wolfgang Iser suggests, a rereading is characterized by a kind of "advance retrospection." [23]

The multiple ironies produced on a rereading activate the intellectual constituent of audience response, often at the expense of the emotional involvement with the characters and their predicament. To some extent a rereading is a reenactment of the movement toward maturity: wisdom (or its model approximation) tempers impulses and desires, and attention is at any moment divided among a greater number of irritants than in one's more intense early day. Such a development of response leads to changes in attitude, though not necessarily in interpretation: interpretation is a somewhat reductive intellectual *post rem* processing of attitude, usually more inert than the attitude itself.

The intellectual component of audience response, intensified on a rereading, often has an anaesthetic effect, which facilitates rereadings of "tear-jerking" novels. In this respect, as in many others, the difference between our response to the text on the first and on repeated readings leads to prolonging the perception commanded by a work of art.[24]

The Careful Reading

Rifaterre advises repeated readings for the wrong purpose—to "guard against physical interference with contact, such as the reader's fatigue or the evolving of the language since the time the poem was encoded."[25] The absence of environmental uncertainties (otherwise called "noises") of this kind ought to be postulated as a condition for an experimentally ideal first reading. Other noises that we would like to avoid in practice and must discount in theory are long or frequent interruptions of the reading process, the absence of pages in one's volume, hunger, headaches, private worries, and the like. The first chapter of Italo Calvino's *If On a Winter's Night a Traveller* advises the "Reader" to find a comfortable posture, make sure the light is sufficient, and so on: it thus actually describes the elimination of noises. Eventually, however, the various noises with which the Reader (the protagonist of this novel) is struggling turn out to be life itself, the text-without-a-text to which any worthwhile metafiction ultimately refers. A careful reading is an interlude, a temporary opting out of the extratextual world, yet, as another novelist has put it, when one so much as turns a page, the world will "avidly, like a playful dog waiting for that moment, [dart] up to [one] with a bright bound."[26] The crude materiality of pagination, alien markings in library books, discomforts of pocket-size paperbacks (that vastly prefer the closed to the open state) are also noises that fragment attention and interfere with the accuracy of individual response.

An ideal purity of a laboratory experiment presupposes not only the "noiselessness" of the reading situation but also the careful and qualified reader. The major requirements that such a reader must satisfy are listed in an early article of Stanley Fish. Fish's "informed reader" is "neither an abstraction, nor an actual living reader, but a hybrid—a real reader (me) who does everything within his power to make himself informed. That is, I can with some justification project my responses into those of 'the' reader because they have been modified by the constraints placed on me by the assumptions and operations of the method: (1) the conscious attempt to become an informed reader by making my mind a repository of (potential) responses a given text might call out and (2) the attendant suppressing, in so far as that is possible, of what is personal and idiosyncratic and 1970ish in my response. . . . Each of us, if we are sufficiently responsible and self-conscious, can . . . become the informed reader and therefore be a more reliable reporter of his experience."[27]

The competence required of the "informed reader" is linguistic (he must understand the language of the text), semantic, and literary. Approximately the same demands are made of his "model reader" by Umberto Eco, who, however, modifies the concept by observing that "a well-organized text on the one hand presupposes a model of competence coming, so to speak, from outside the text, but on the other hand it works to build up, by merely textual means, such a competence."[28] Eco's "model reader" thus stands midway between the "informed reader," who is a precondition for a proper response, and the "implied reader" of Booth.[29] The "implied reader" is, in fact, a personification of a complex of attitudes produced by the rhetoric of the novel. A full description of such a complex is a goal that recedes on approach: any "reading" of the novel—in Todorov's sense of the word "reading"[30]—is equivalent to a model approximation that always remains incomplete.

For the model approximation based on response to informational gaps on the first and then on repeated readings it is essential that the reader should not be familiar with the plot of the novel in advance. Unfortunately, this condition is seldom observed in the days of blurbs and indiscreet reviews or introductions—it is not for nothing that Scott Fitzgerald insisted that there should be no blurb on the covers of *The Great Gatsby*.[31] In professional literary circles one is apt to know "everything" about a novel before so much as glancing at its first page. Neither was the danger fully avoided in the good old days of illustrated editions: the effect of Dickens's *Bleak House*, for instance, is impaired if, prior to reading the corresponding episode, one chances to open the Chapman and Hall edition at the illustration in which Lady Dedlock is making her confession to Esther Summerson. Ideally, the first reading of a novel should be unadulterated by a foreknowledge of the plot, except, perhaps, a foreknowledge that stems from general competence and allows one to predict, for instance, that a Jane Austen novel is bound to end in a reasonably happy marriage.

Selectiveness of Attention

As Stanley Fish has argued in "Affective Stylistics," units of the text are events that happen to the reader; they *do* rather than *mean* things, and their significance consists not in the statements that they make but in the effects that they produce.[32] Taking a less radical position, let us say that the significance of textual units is composed both of their mock-informational content and of their rhetorical effect.

The rhetorical effects studied in this book are products of an uneven distribution of *fabula* information, that is, of the text's reticences, gaps, vague anticipations, delays. These effects are canceled on a rereading (when, as mentioned above, we are in possession of all the *fabula* information), yet the textual information-withholding devices that produced them remain in place and form the basis for a new set of effects. These secondary effects are, indeed, new—because now they combine in new ways with material whose relevance was less appreciable on the first reading. The study of the audience response is the study of techniques that provide stimuli and conditions for the response of a careful reader; it neglects the extratextual noises and individual idiosyncrasies that may modify or neutralize such stimuli and conditions. In this sense, one can say that the audience response is "encoded" in the text.

"Encoded," or perhaps "foreseen," though not quite in the terms of Jorge Luis Borges's "Theme of the Traitor and the Hero": when the Irish historian Ryan, the protagonist of this Borgesian allegory on reading, solves a riddle in his country's past, he feels that his solution was "foreseen" by the people who had enacted the charade. Eventually, he decides against making his discoveries public: "this too, perhaps, was foreseen."[33] Like a reader of a detective novel, Ryan starts by estimating the information at his disposal as incomplete. The effect of this estimation is the pressure of unfinished business: he *must* hunt out answers to the questions that arise in his mind. In the end Ryan comes to believe that the information reconstructed by him is less important than the moral issues related to it. Ryan's version of ethical truth thus comes into conflict with his commitment to factual truth—and takes the upper hand. His estimation of the importance of the suppressed information thus changes in the course of his intellectual adventure.

Ryan, however, overcomes the pressure of unfinished business because for himself, at least, he obtains, or perhaps creates, the information whose absence has troubled him: Borgesian characters tend to remain content with private undivulgeable knowledge. Such a satisfaction is denied the protagonist of Henry James's "The Aspern Papers." This story contains an apt parable of one of the patterns of audience response to be traced below: the protagonist's wish to gain specific information is so intense that, without becoming aware of the moral significance of his attitudes, he slips into a disrespect for the dignity of the people who bar his way to the desired documents. From the beginning to the end of the story the protagonist shows no interest in the personalities of these people for their own sake: their images in his eyes are always influenced by his estimation of how strong an obstacle or how convenient a tool they present for his avid gap-filling research.

Such a detachment from the emotions of the characters who function as sources of information is legitimized in many detective stories, whatever lip service they may pay to sympathy and considerate conduct. The detective genre owes at least part of its popularity to precisely this convention: the sleuth and the reader are absolved, *in advance*, from paying attention to the characters for their own sake rather than for their role in suppressing or revealing information. Murder mysteries, in particular, tend to be games with convenient rules; their appeal is due not to the audience's insecurities or grisly interest in bloodshed but to the fact that the imperative of discovering the killer is unquestionable: all but the most blatantly cruel means of retrieving information are justified by this goal.

Yet a truly artistic "reticent" novel—and that includes the best of detective fiction—does not simplify its game with the reader, even though on the first reading our interest in what we estimate as suppressed clues tends to be the most intense element of response to the ludic flow of information. In other words, our interest tends to be most powerfully attracted to what Roland Barthes calls the hermeneutic code: "all the units whose function is to articulate in various ways a question, its response, and the variety of chance events which can either formulate the question or delay its answer; or even to constitute an enigma and lead to its solution."[34] In a work of art, none of Barthes's five codes, the semic, the symbolic, the proairetic, the cultural, and the hermeneutic,[35] is supposed to take precedence over any other so far as narrative choices are concerned, especially since Barthes's analysis is a matter of rereadings. It seems, however, that on the first reading the hermeneutic code—the withholding and monitoring of information—

does take precedence in audience response: it has the power to dull our response to the symbolic and semic codes and thus to divert our attention, temporarily, from details or whole layers of meaning that could, in principle, be perceived on the first reading.[36] This does not mean that a response dominated by the hermeneutic code on the first reading amounts to a "bad reading"—our mistakes are legitimate and usually "foreseen."[37] Moreover, a strong hermeneutic code is only one of the techniques that rely on our estimation of the relative importance of different narrative strands in order to first divert our attention from certain areas of meaning and then to bring about a reorientation whose significance we are invited to probe.

As John Gardner has remarked, "an important work of art is at least some of the following: (1) aesthetically interesting, (2) technically accomplished, and (3) intellectually massive."[38] The novels studied in this book satisfy all the three requirements—but so do scores of other literary works. The seven novels analyzed below have been chosen as "aesthetically interesting" in a specific way: more or less centrally important for the rhetorical effects are their techniques of withholding information within the framework either of what is known as "omniscient" narrative or of multiple perspective. The common denominator of their point of view is best defined with the help of Gérard Genette's distinction between "voice" and "focus."[39] These narratives combine the voice of a third-person narrator (at least in some stretches, as in Dickens's *Bleak House* and Faulkner's *The Sound and the Fury* and *Absalom, Absalom!*) with zero or variable focalization. In the case of zero focalization, for example, in Fielding's *Tom Jones* (as in most "omniscient" novels—the stance that Wayne Booth has, in *The Rhetoric of Fiction*, successfully defended from post-Jamesian censure) the narrator's cognitive privilege does not depend on the amount of information available to the characters. Variable focalization means that two or more characters are used (one at a time) to function as focalizers, whether first- or third-person.

The study does not examine narratives where the voice is, throughout, that of a dramatized first-person narrator (like Pip in Dickens's *Great Expectations*) because their gap-forming techniques tend to be more straightforward: information is usually withheld under the pretext that it was inaccessible to the narrator at the time of the story-events (the represented time)—or even, as in episotolary novels or in Nabokov's *Despair*, at the time of the telling (the representational time).[40] The same narrative convention extends to the monitoring of information in most third-person center-of-consciousness narratives, where the voice is that of a third-person narrator but focalization is internal and fixed, that is, attributed to a single personage, as in Henry James's *The Ambassadors*. Even if the focalization is variable but the narration is conducted only by personages in the first person (as in Faulkner's *As I Lay Dying*), the convention is still at work: the characters are not responsible for what they cannot know, and there is no third-person narrating voice that can be expected to synthethize or supplement information. Where such a voice is present and focalization or cognitive privilege are not limited to those of one character, the withholding of information is motivated not realistically but rather in terms of its interaction with the novel's aesthetic stance or metaphysical and moral problematics.

The ways in which information is withheld can be classified according to the structure of the suspended material.

Chronological displacement. A considerable portion of the *fabula* is first suppressed and then revealed in long narrative blocks. This technique will not be examined here because it has been discussed by Sternberg in relation to Faulkner's *Light in August*.[41] The informational delay involved is actually perceived as such mainly in novels that otherwise tend to proceed chronologically rather than in jigsaw-puzzle texts like Huxley's *Eyeless in Gaza*.

Diffusion of information. A great number of separate pieces of information are suppressed, thus creating numerous small gaps. The two novels discussed in part 1, Faulkner's *The Sound and the Fury* and Conrad's *Nostromo*, exemplify this technique.

Temporary suspension of information. A crucially important separate piece of information is first suppressed and later analeptically[42] revealed. The delayed information consists not in a portion of the story but in a fact that gives the story its shape. A novel may contain more than one gap of this kind but our attention is usually held by one gap at a time. The variants of this technique in Dickens's *Bleak House*, Jane Austen's *Emma*, and Fielding's *Tom Jones* are analyzed in part 2.

Permanent suspension of information. What seems to be a crucially important separate piece of information is suppressed and never revealed. Such permanent gaps underlie the structure of E.M. Forster's *A Passage to India* and Faulkner's *Absalom, Absalom!*, analyzed in part 3.

There is no consistent correlation between a certain information-handling technique and a set of rhetorical effect.[43] The technique can create conditions for a type of effects, but their exact quality depends also on previous textual devices in combination with the thematic concerns and emotional coloration of the narrative. I shall attempt to trace the dynamics of audience response and relate it to the rhetorical devices that condition it as well as to the thematic structures with which it interacts in each novel, bearing in mind that a comprehensive paradigm of the dependence of effects on techniques is impossible and unnecessary. Nevertheless, some limited regularities may emerge—and the much studied canonical novels are the best material for pointing them out.

I.A. Richards believed that great art educates by eliciting and refining complex attitudes that have the power to irradiate on one's personality even away from the sphere of aesthetic perception.[44] This belief is sometimes borne out by evidence of striking persuasiveness.[45] The mechanics of the process often involves eliciting attitudes that eventually prove to be wrong: in a number of the novels discussed below such attitudes are promoted, intensified, and eventually rejected after being brought to the self-critical attention of the audience. This quasicathartic pattern is more central in some novels and less in others. In the latter, the game of provision and suppression of *fabula* details is associated with the distribution of emphasis between various aspects of the theme.

In all cases, however, the uneven pulse of the stream of information constitutes an aesthetic game, analogous to the play of light and shade or curve and color in visual arts. Therefore, despite its ethically oriented conclusions, the study of information-withholding techniques always remains an inquiry into the features of aesthetic experience provided by individual texts.

PART ONE

The Diffusion
of Information

CHAPTER TWO

The Sound and the Fury
The Milk and the Dew

A time to get, and a time to lose; a time
to keep, and a time to cast away;
A time to rend, and a time to sew; a time
to keep silence, and a time to speak
Ecclesiastes, 3:6-7

By giving the floor to a mentally retarded person, William Faulkner's *The Sound and the Fury* realizes the metaphor to which it alludes in the title: life "is a tale / told by an idiot, full of sound and fury, / signifying nothing." This speech of Macbeth is a misreading of the Solomonic belief that all is vanity: an individual's life, even his own, matters ("signifies") little for a king. Most characters in *The Sound and the Fury* show little concern for the inarticulate rage of the so-called "idiot," yet the reader's quest for meaning can offset the aridity of the novel's moral landscape.

The text of *The Sound and the Fury* is at first difficult to follow. The diffusive presentation of material impedes the imaginative construction of the scenes: words fail to come alive in a dramatic illusion. And since the initial mist is at its densest in section 1 ("told by an idiot"), it seems to be a side effect of Faulkner's experiment with the point of view. Actually, however, the diffusion of information is, *its own right,* a rhetorical procedure that monitors the reader's emotional and interpretive response.

The diffusion of information in *The Sound and the Fury* is the effect of numerous minor informational gaps that delay pattern recognition. Some of these gaps are *motivated realistically,*[1] while others are *rhetorically oriented.*

Realistically motivated gaps are those called for by the point of view. The first three of the novel's four sections are written "from the point of view" of Benjy, Quentin, and Jason Compson, respectively; the last section is presented by a nondramatized third-person narrator. The three brothers are, strictly speaking, "focal characters" rather than "narrators"—they cannot perform the acts of narration allotted to their sections: Benjy is mute; Quentin is on the verge of suicide; and Jason is too stubbornly self-righteous to have an urge for an *apologia*.[2] Hence the "voice" that we hear throughout the novel is that of the third-person narrator who can be identified with "the implied author": in the first three sections the "Faulkner" of *The Sound and the Fury* imitates the thought processes or the idiom of the focal characters[3]—speaking *with* the three brothers. The grammatical first person of sections 1 through 3 is a sign of the imitation. In the third-person section 4 the focus is also attached first to one then to another character yet without concentrated attempts to convey their styles of thought.

This interpretation of the novel's structure is supported by the novelist's on-record remarks[4] as well as by the narrative convention according to which the co-presence of the undramatized third-person narrative and of first-person narratives in the same work is perceived as the "insertion" of the latter into the former, as if the third-person narrator had access to the minds or the written or oral narratives of the characters. In the first-person stretches, however, the cognitive privilege of this authorial narrator is limited to the information available to the focalizers. Therefore, in the first three sections of *The Sound and the Fury*, the features and predicaments of the focalizers lead to the opening of realistically motivated gaps that account, to a large extent, for diffusion of information.

The numerous time-shifts of *The Sound and the Fury* are unaccompanied by clear chronological references that could help us piece together scattered bits of information on the first reading. The novel contains only four explicit chronological reference-points—the four dates that serve as titles of the four sections. The absence of additional explicit guidelines is a consequence of focalization: if time-shifts are supposed to imitate the spontaneous associative backward and forward movement of the focalizers' minds, they cannot have date tags. For Benjy even notions like "before/after" and "past/present" do not exist; and Quentin keeps his mind away from concepts related to time. One of the reasons why confusion is reduced in section 3 is that Jason does not block time references from his consciousness.

It therefore takes us a long time to classify separate flashes of scenes around such events as the grandmother's funeral, Caddy's affair with Dalton Ames, her wedding, Quentin's suicide, Benjy's castration, the arrival of Caddy's newborn daughter (the female Quentin), the deaths of Mr. Compson and of Roskus Gibson.[5] The sequence of some minor occurrences remains unclear to the end.

Imitation of the characters' "stream of consciousness" involves a delay of expositional material. Our filling in of the "who's who" is slow because the main characters, with the exception of "Father," "Mother," and Uncle Maury, are referred to only by their names and because for a long time we are not informed about their appearance, family status, place in society, or antecedents. Allusions are made to facts with which we are not familiar. For instance, when Jason says to his mother, "Father and Quentin cant hurt you" (12)[6] we cannot possibly infer that she is going to visit the graves of the father and the eldest son of the family: the only Quentin mentioned so far is the little girl playing in the yard with Luster. Nor is it possible to understand that Mrs. Compson's carriage has stopped by Jason's store. On the first reading veiled references of this kind make most of the conversations in section 1 sound like indistinct background noise.[7]

Veiled references are associated with the focal characters' failure to conceptualize, their short-cut thinking, or their too profound familiarity with their environment. In section 1, for instance, Luster's personality takes several pages to materialize from a collection of nagging remarks and mischievous actions[8] because Benjy has no reason to think of him as a fourteen-year-old Negro or Dilsey's grandson. In section 3 some confusion results from the abuse of the pronoun "she" which Jason applies to all the women who encumber his existence: "I opened her letter and took the check out. Just like a woman. Six days late. . . . And like as not, when they sent the bank statement out, she would like to know why I never deposited my salary until the sixth" (236). Even if we guess that the check is from Caddy, on the first reading we can hardly realize that the exophoric "she" of the last sentence refers to Mrs. Compson. We cannot, therefore, understand that Jason deposits Caddy's checks in his mother's account, pretending they are the salary that he actually hoards in his room or speculates with on the cotton market. Jason does not dwell on these machinations because for him they are a matter of routine.

The use of a retarded person as the focalizer of the first section motivates elisions of whatever is not directly perceptible. Benjy cannot use inference or memory to supply the missing elements in the flux of perception; we have to do it for him. In the following passage, for instance, the rapidity of movement prevents Benjy from getting a clear view of what is taking place: "[the flag] was red, flapping on the pasture. Then there was a bird slanting and tilting on it. Luster threw. The flag flapped on the bright grass and the trees" (2).

Benjy has not had time to identify the object thrown by Luster. Our reading pace slackens as we translate "Luster threw" into "Luster threw something at the bird." We must also fill in the fact that "the bird flew away": the repeated statement that the flag "flapped on the bright grass and the trees" implies that the bird is no longer perched on the flag—it has been frightened off by Luster. The metonymic nature of the repetition suggests that the concepts of "cause," "presence," and "absence," are beyond Benjy's comprehension. So while elision is necessitated by the point of view, it is also a means of character portrayal. Moreover, it prolongs our attention to the image of the red flag flapping against the green pasture and prepares us for Benjy's tenacious attachment to the few "bright shapes" of his world.

Similar effects are produced by such cases of propositional metonymy as "the room came back" (53) used in lieu of "Dilsey switched on the light." Here the local rhetorical effect of the substitution is emphasis on "going away" and "coming back" as one of the main reference points in Benjy's experience, a pair of notions that replaces the "presence/absence" pair. Each metonymic proposition, as well as each case of veiled reference or elision, has such a specific local effect; cumulatively these defamiliarizing devices diffuse *fabula* information and slow the pace of reading.

This cumulative effect is not a mere by-product of the point of view:[9] it is enhanced by gaps that are not demanded by focalization, that is, by *rhetorically oriented* gaps.

The text, indeed, frequently elides things of which the focal characters are well aware.[10] Section 1, for instance, suppresses references to Benjy's minor wishes. We learn that Benjy wants a particular object from other characters' remarks—such as "He wants your lightning bugs, T.P." (43), or "Give him a flower to hold. . . . That what he wanting" (10). The narrative omits mention of the object on which the focalizer's attention is riveted; instead it records conversations ("the sound") that are of no interest to him. This selection of material conflicts with psychological accuracy, yet it emphasizes Benjy's lack of self-awareness and thus functions as part of the code that renders the world view of a retarded person.[11] For a brief moment the "inside view" of the focalizer is discontinued and replaced by a diagnostic suggestion without letting us register the jolt.

Section 2 excludes references to Quentin's conscious intentions. In particular, we are not explicitly informed that Quentin has decided to commit suicide at the end of the day. The same principle extends to the purposes of his seemingly humdrum activities: for a long time we cannot understand that many of them are a suicide's last tasks, especially since section 1 has not made it clear that Que in has killed himself. His intention is gradually revealed by the recurrence of the images related to death by water, by his fatigue and morbidity, his packing up, writing notes, mailing letters, and buying flatirons. The motif of suicide grows, passing from our subliminal awareness to conscious certainty. We are thus led through a process parallel to the gradual crystalization of the thought of suicide in Quentin's own mind in the preceding year.

Another detail that the narrative neglects to mention explicitly is Quentin's experiment with time, his attempt to *deny time instead of renouncing life*.[12] This rhetorically oriented elision leads to a new set of puzzles. For instance, when we read that "Spoade had a shirt on; then it must be" (118), we wonder what the fatal "it" that "must be" is. Actually the sentence means "it must be about noon," but we can understand this only on a rereading, when familiarity with Quentin's attitude to time permits us to connect the aposiopesis with the remarks made about Spoade at the beginning of the section—only around noon would that gentleman appear in full attire (see 96–97). On the first reading it takes us a long time to understand that Quentin is dodging all sense perceptions that signal the hour of the day, yet we can hardly fail to notice the energy with which he deliberately fragments his thought process. This energy meaningfully conflicts with the death-wish languor and suicidal impulses recurrent in Quentin's section.

The absence of reference to Quentin's intentions is an appropriate form of rendering his attitude to death and time. For Quentin, suicide is an intimate act, the privacy of which he guards even at the cost of repulsing his roommate Shreve's solicitude. It is his strongest argument against his father's quasi-Solomonic suggestion that love and grief pass like everything else.[13] His conflict with time is a straw at which he clutches like a drowning man whose body does not yet wish to die. Both the misguided self-sacrifice and the unwillingness to commit it are screened from the strangers' eyes. On the first reading the omniscient narrator protects Quentin's privacy from the reader just as Quentin himself protects it from the people who crowd his world.

In section 3 the intentions of the focalizer likewise never make their way into the text. This concerns not only Jason's habitual activities (where the withholding of information may be explained by his taking his course of action for granted) but also his specific decisions at landmark points of his life.

One of these landmarks is the day of his father's funeral. As the narrative records the subterfuges that Jason uses in order to let Caddy see her baby in secret from Mrs. Compson, we are never warned of his malicious attribution of the strictly literal meaning to the word "see." Only when shown how he lets Caddy catch a glimpse of Quentin and run after the carriage that is taking the baby away do we realize what Jason has been planning all along. We find ourselves unprepared for Jason's cheating Quentin out of her mother's money order or for his burning the passes to the show instead of giving them to Luster. Section 3 contains a series of such surprises: we know that Jason is an unprepossessing person, yet we repeatedly find out, as Caddy does in her turn, that we have underestimated his meanness. Surprise, indeed, is Jason's own favorite tactic in personal relationships: "Always keep them guessing. If you cant think of any other way to surprise them, give them a bust in the jaw" (240). Thus, while the first-person narration yields insights into the focal character's mentality, rhetorically oriented gaps suggest what it would be like to have to deal with him. They supplement the imitation of his mental processes with a distancing external view.

Whatever the local effects of rhetorically oriented gaps, cumulatively they contribute to our confusion on the first reading of the novel. Faulkner seems to have fully appreciated and explored the aesthetic potentialities of this initial confusion.

On the first reading the initial confusion provides a contrast for a few clear scenes, thus bringing them into high relief. These are the scenes that present Benjy's relationship with his sister Caddy. They stand out against the unlocated images and incomprehensible utterances of the rest of the section because they describe self-explanatory action: Caddy understands her little brother's wishes and "translates" his conduct for us. For instance, we do not know why Benjy insists on going out to the cold gate until Caddy fills in the gap: "Hello, Benjy. . . . Did you come to meet me?" (5). When Caddy is absent it often remains unclear why other characters have to hush Benjy; when she is present, the cause of his tears is usually revealed by her removing it. In most cases his tears are associated with the thought of her going or having gone away:

"I'll run away and never come back," Caddy said. I began to cry. Caddy
turned around and said "Hush." So I hushed. Then they played in the
branch. . . . Caddy was all wet and muddy behind, and I started to cry
and she came and squatted in the water.
    "Hush now." she said. "I'm not going to run away." So I hushed.
Caddy smelled like trees in the rain. [21-22]

Because of our clear understanding of this one relationship set
against a background of unassimilated information, our response to
section 1 is parallel to an important aspect of Benjy's own experience.
For Benjy the world is divided into a foreground and a background; in
the foreground are Caddy (later the old slipper, her vestige) and the
smooth bright shapes that he enjoys watching—in the fire, in the
mirror, in the jewel box, from a rolling carriage, or else in his dreams.
As he holds Caddy's slipper during a meal, he recollects the days when
she fed him and remains undisturbed by the conflict between Caddy's
daughter and Jason. This indifference is reenacted by the reader: on the
first reading of section 1 young Quentin does not evoke sympathy
because we do not know who she is and only remember that she has
been unkind to Benjy; moreover, the scene is so chopped up that its
dramatic tension is lost even on a repeated reading. The violent confrontation seems to be taking place in the background while the foreground is occupied by the gradual improvement of Benjy's state of
mind.
    The lucid parts of section 1 carry the major theme of the novel—the
frustration of a fundamental human need, the need for love.[14] Very
early in the novel, in what we can identify as Benjy's memories of his
childhood, it is made clear that the egocentric Mrs. Compson does not
satisfy her children's need for affection. Even her distress on account of
Benjy takes the perfunctory form that does not deceive the sensitive
though uncomprehending child:

"Come here and kiss Mother, Benjamin."
    Caddy took me to Mother's chair and Mother took my face in
her hands and then she held me against her.
    "My poor baby." she said. She let me go. "You and Versh
take good care of him, honey." [8]

Significantly, Mrs. Compson delegates her responsibility for Benjy to
Caddy; as it soon becomes obvious, Caddy fills the void that her
coldness leaves in Benjy's life. It is on Caddy, a substitute mother, that

his well-being depends: "You're not a poor baby. Are you. You've got your Caddy. Haven't you got your Caddy" (8). Such a distribution of roles explains Benjy's misery in the fictional present: Caddy has gone away.

We then wonder why Caddy has left home and whether her absence is permanent. For Benjy's sake we hope, as we might do in more conventional novels, that she will eventually return. The abruptness with which her absence is suddenly explained parallels the brutality of the blow that it inflicts on Benjy:

> You cant do no good looking through the gate, T.P. said. Miss Caddy done gone long ways away. Done got married and left you. You cant do no good, holding to the gate and crying. She cant hear you.
> What is it he wants, T.P. Mother said. Cant you play with him and keep him quiet.
> He want to go down yonder and look through the gate, T.P. said.
> Well, he cannot do it, Mother said. It's raining. You will just have to play with him and keep him quiet. You, Benjamin.
> Ain't nothing going to quiet him, T.P. said. He think if he down to the gate, Miss Caddy come back.
> Nonsense, Mother said. [62-63]

The callousness of the conversation casts a shadow on Caddy's image (even though a young woman's getting married is not an unnatural development): did she leave Benjy with the same coldheartedness that rings in Mrs. Compson's reference to her absence? Caddy can now remain "beautiful" and "moving"[15] only if she is shown to be contrite and unhappy. This demand, strangely different from the conventional concern for a heroine's happiness, is, to some extent, satisfied in the scene where Caddy is crying in Benjy's lap: "*I could hear the clock, and I could hear Caddy standing behind me, and I could hear the roof. It's still raining, Caddy said. I hate rain. I hate everything. And then her head came into my lap and she was crying, holding me, and I began to cry. Then I looked at the fire again and the bright, smooth shapes went on again. I could hear the clock and the roof and Caddy*" (69). Caddy has, evidently, no one to turn to except the partly responsive Benjy. She is now the one whose need for love and understanding is frustrated. The intimation of adolescent despair ("*I hate rain. I hate everything.*") is later modified by Quentin's complaint about entrapment: "*I wish it wouldn't rain. . . . You cant do anything*" (81). Caddy, the narrative suggests, is trapped.

Her conduct in further episodes gradually becomes less self-explanatory. In the following scene it is positively opaque: "Her hand was against her mouth and I saw her eyes and I cried. We went up the stairs. She stopped again, against the wall, looking at me and she cried and she went on and I came on, crying, and she shrank against the wall, looking at me. She opened the door to her room, but I pulled at her dress and we went to the bathroom and she stood against the door, looking at me. Then she put her arm against her face and I pushed at her, crying" (84-85).

Our former uneasiness about Caddy's conduct is now revived—not because of the hint at her loss of virginity but because of her unusual reluctance to do something that would soothe her brother. Taking advantage of focalization, the novelist makes it difficult for us to understand that Benjy is pushing Caddy to the bathroom, as if to make her wash and regain her smell of trees. Therefore, on the first reading we do not know that her lack of responsiveness stems from her sense of futility: water can no longer help.[16]

Since the beauty of Caddy's image depends on her ability to love, we expect the narrative to provide not merely details of her marriage but also a possibility to justify her defection or at least to reconcile it with the sympathy that she has evoked on the opening pages of the novel. Benjy's section does not meet this expectation. The tranquilizing effect of its ending is produced by a sequence of pleasant memories that come to Benjy after supper and while falling asleep. Here Caddy is again the tender little girl who smells of trees. The past and the present mingle in the darkness that begins "to go in smooth, bright shapes, like it always does, even when Caddy says that I have been asleep" (92). Yet these bright shapes are a tenuous oneiric comfort. We still wonder about Caddy's betrayal as we proceed to section 2.

Though references to objects and people mentioned in section 1 are by now more or less intelligible, Quentin's section presents us with new difficulties. There is not even a pretense of showing us the way through the focalizer's mind. Fragments belonging to different events are massed together; italics mark off not time-layers but themes and motifs; and syntax appears to have a new set of rules. Eventually, Quentin's section becomes easier to follow because narrative stretches belonging to the same time-layer are longer than in section 1.

Absence of reference to Quentin's intentions often impedes our understanding of his experience in the fictional present. Other gaps make us lose track of his movements: when the narrative shifts to his thoughts and then returns to the account of the outer scene, some part of the story time elapses unrecorded and our hold on the fictional present becomes as uncertain as Quentin's grasp on reality. Therefore, in the bulk of the section the confusing account of Quentin's thoughts comes into contrast not with the fictional present but with two relatively clear flashbacks—his memories of Caddy's marriage and of her affair with Dalton Ames.

These two episodes gain prominence for a number of reasons: their length favors sustained attention; they are typographically distinct (scenes that pertain to the latter event have no punctuation at all, whereas those pertaining to the former are printed in italics); the sequence of their parts is not distorted; and the context makes it clear "who says what." Moreover, the information contained in these episodes is precisely what we have been expecting since the middle of section 1: it sheds light on the events that drove Caddy away from home.

Thus, as in Benjy's section, the alternation of clarity and confusion enhances the impact of the episodes that involve Caddy and develop the theme of the need for love. Quentin's affections, like Benjy's, are entirely concentrated on his sister: he is conscious of Mrs. Compson's failure as a mother ("if I'd just had a mother so I could say Mother Mother," 213) and disgusted by her petit bourgeois pretensions, her Griselda pose, and her part in arranging Caddy's marriage. He expects Caddy rather than his mother to be the pride of the dynasty (toward the end of section 2 the motif of a substitute is emphasized by the episode with the little Italian girl—another relatively clear stretch of the narrative). Yet this task, like that of being a mother-figure for Benjy, is too restrictive for Caddy. The two painful flashbacks present Quentin's and Caddy's inability to perform the parts that each assigns to the other. Quentin fails in the strength, courage, and confidence that fascinate Caddy in Dalton Ames; and Caddy cannot renounce the whole world for his sake, as he would have her do in his vision of platonic incest beyond the flames of a disinfected hell (144).

Unable to control his sister, Quentin wishes to hurt her—just as the reader wishes to see her suffer lest the beauty of her image be marred by a suggestion of callous egotism. This expectation, aroused in section 1, is largely satisfied in section 2. In Quentin's flashbacks we see Caddy trapped, frightened by her own initiation, "sick" (early stage of pregnancy combined with existential nausea), tormented by anxiety about Benjy and by guilt for having stimulated her father's alcoholism:

I'm just sick I can't ask anybody yet promise you will [138]

There was something terrible in me sometimes at night I could see it grinning at me I could see it through them grinning at me through their faces it's gone now and I'm sick [138]

it'll be all right it wont matter dont let them send him to Jackson promise [139]

I've got to marry somebody [143]

can you think of Benjy and Father and do it not of me [153]

Father will be dead in a year they say if he doesnt stop drinking and he wont stop he cant stop since I since last summer and then they'll send Benjy to Jackson I cant cry I cant even cry [154]

The end of section 2 thus creates a faint sense of completion. Caddy's suffering cancels the suggestion of cold betrayal; its pathos restores the appeal of her image and makes the frantic young woman as "moving" as the headstrong little girl of the novel's early pages. The second half of *The Sound and the Fury* is, therefore, somewhat anti-climactic: it never reaches the pathetic pitch of the first two sections.

Confusion is not intense in section 3, yet some episodes are more difficult to understand than others. In keeping with the demands of focalization, all the references to Jason's salary, Caddy's money, blank checks, investments, and cotton market gambling remain unintelligible for a long time. By contrast, the episodes involving Caddy's daughter, Quentin (whom we finally identify as such), stand out much more clearly against this background. Their action is self-explanatory; their obscure references are few. Thus the foiling effect of the confusion of sections 1 and 2 is reproduced, in a fainter form, in section 3.

In the more comprehensible parts of Jason's section, it is now the turn of young Quentin to be the bearer of the theme of lovelessness. Like Benjy, Quentin is denied her mother's love. Though vulgar and ill-tempered, she becomes pathetic when she cries, "Dilsey, I want my mother" (230). Her subsequent rudeness to kind-hearted Dilsey is symptomatic: the exhausted old housekeeper is a poor replacement for Caddy.[17] Unlike Benjy, young Quentin has never enjoyed the tenderness of even a substitute mother. Our uneasiness about Caddy is revived again: here it is associated with her having left her child in the household that has grow even gloomier than in her own day. Though there is aesthetic appropriateness in this girl replacing both her mother and her namesake uncle in the Compson house, it now seems possible that Caddy has not escaped the contagion of Mrs. Compson's callousness. This suspicion is eventually allayed by Jason's memories of Caddy's persistent attempts to visit little Quentin.

Thus the audience response undergoes a development analogous to that of the first half of the novel, only here it is compressed into one half of a section. As in section 1, a shadow is cast over Caddy's image, and then, as in section 2, the shadow is removed when Caddy is presented as trapped by a new set of bans.[18]

Caddy still embodies the capacity for love that has not completely vanished from the novel's world though thwarted by the jealousy of the Compson brothers, the weakness of the father, and the egocentric affectations of the mother. In section 3 these qualities—with the addition of sadism—combine in Jason Compson. Jason was harshly condemned in early critical discussions of *The Sound and the Fury*. Yet the view of him as an unmitigated villain, a Snopes among the Compsons, a traitor to the values of the aristocratic South is a somewhat simplified absolutization of the response elicited by section 3 on the first reading.

This response is largely caused by a touch of resentful impatience. The narrative of section 3 is tantalizing: its comparative clarity promises further elucidation of Caddy's fate, yet, much as we would like to see Caddy again, she appears only in the scarcely recognizable shape of Jason's subdued antagonist. Jason's cherished memories are not of Caddy's personality or fate but of the revenge that he took on her for having unintentionally deprived him of a job in a bank. By the middle of section 3 Caddy's image recedes from the narrative as the account of Jason's affairs becomes progressively more intelligible. Jason's meanness and self-defeating impulses gradually capture our reluctant attention, and we let Caddy's story fade out, leaving the foreplane for precisely that part of the fictional world which was formerly perceived as the hazy background of Benjy's section.

In section 4 the alternation of confusion and clarity is further compressed into a still shorter stretch of the narrative—the account of Parson Shegog's Easter sermon. The bulk of the section is not confusing, even though the absence of explanatory comments and the selectiveness of the camera eye often delay our understanding of the characters' movements. The only really incoherent part of the discourse is Parson Shegog's Application, during which he slips into the Negro accent and starts bombarding the congregation with incomplete, disconnected, allusive, emotionally charged phrases: "'When de long, cold—Oh, I tells you, breddren, when de long, cold—I sees de light en I sees de word, po sinner! Dey passed away in Egypt, de swingin chariots; de generations passed away. Wus a rich man: whar he now, O breddren? Wus a po man: whar he now, O sistuhn? Oh I tells you, ef you aint got *de milk en de dew of de old salvation* when de long, cold years rolls away!' " (368-69; my italics).

This poetic confusion serves as a foil for an unexpectedly clear image that the preacher evokes at the end of the sermon. He presents the Passion in terms of the thwarted feelings of Mary, who emerges, in an apocryphal scene, as an ordinary loving "mammy" helpless in the face of a hostile power: " 'Breddren! Look at dem little chillen settin dar. Jesus wus like dat once. He mammy suffered de glory en de pangs. Sometime maybe she helt him at de nightfall, whilst de angels singin him to sleep; maybe she look out de do' en see de Roman po-lice passin. . . . Listen, breddren! I sees de day. Ma'y settin in de do' wid Jesus on her lap, de little Jesus. . . . I hears de angels singin de peaceful songs en de glory; I sees de closin eyes; sees Mary jump up, sees de sojer face: We gwine to kill! We gwine to kill! We gwine to kill yo little Jesus! I hears de weepin en de lamentation of de po mammy widout de salvation en de word of God!' " (369). The emphasis given to the clear and pathetic image by surrounding it with a farrago of fragmented motifs reproduces the novel's central rhetorical effect. As in the preceding sections, the image brought into relief by the contrast of confusion and clarity embodies the theme of love, yet Caddy and her kin are no longer the exponents of this theme. Their function is transferred to the Eternal Motherly. By comparing Jesus to the children in the church choir, the preacher emphasizes the universal human significance of Mary's image and underplays its supernatural connotations. A miniature model of the novel's rhetoric, the sermon evokes in Dilsey a response analogous to our own experience on the first reading of *The Sound and the Fury:* it directs her attention to the essence rather than to the details of the Compson tragedy.

When young Quentin's room is found empty in the morning and Jason calls the police, Dilsey seems curiously unconcerned about the girl's whereabouts. Her energies are directed to preserving a semblance of peace in the house, and, having done her utmost to calm Mrs. Compson, she sets out for church, as planned, as if nothing were wrong. The seeming callousness of her conduct is the result of efforts to persevere despite nervous exhaustion ("I done stood all I kin," 357). To stave off a breakdown and cope with her duties, she defers her understanding of the new catastrophe.

Parson Shegog's sermon releases Dilsey's grip on the immediate situation. She stops hushing Benjy and cries unashamedly, ignoring the people around her. The sermon sanctions the luxury of emotional release and allows her to attain an overview ("I seed de beginnin, en now I sees de endin," 371) of the fall of a family that could not endure in the face of social change because its roots were cut by lovelessness. In this context, Parson Shegog's old salvation, "de milk en de dew of the old salvation," is love rather than faith: the "milk" is the mother's sustaining care for the infant; the "dew" is the regeneration to be achieved through love. The "dew" is also the weeping, the uninhibited response to grief, not easily available to the Compson children.

Dilsey's cathartic weeping aroused by pity for the unloved and for those whose love is subjected to torture renews her power of endurance; she can again "lif up [her] tree en walk" (370). The use of the word "tree" rather than "cross" plays a double role: in addition to forming an important recurrence (compare the tree that Caddy climbs in section 1), it activates the connotation of endurance rather than that of martyrdom.

Dilsey's repeated cryptic remark, "I seed de first en de last" (375), puts an end to our expectations that section 4, which is directly presented by the omniscient narrator, will give us concrete information about the fate of the main characters. Despite the open ending, the story is completed: like Dilsey, we have "seen the last." The lives of the Compson children have been wasted, no matter what shapes their fate may now take. Society is moving forward, the slaves, according to Parson Shegog's allusion, have come out of Egypt, and the "swinging chariots," the generations of the Southern upper classes, cannot rally as long as among them love is withheld, banished, crushed. The recurrent Faulknerian themes of inner conflict, social mobility, and psychic inertia gain prominence on repeated readings; on the first reading, however, it is the theme of the frustrated need for love, the *differentia specifica* of *The Sound and the Fury*, that is made most prominent by the interplay of clarity and confusion.

The Sound and the Fury contains a built-in demand for a repeated reading and not only because all great books must be reread. Its last section, which purports to be the clearest, fails to elucidate a great number of points. At the same time, since many of our early questions ("Who is the female Quentin?" "Why does Caddy not return home?") have been answered and since we now possess the facts to which the veiled references and allusions of the first two sections pertain, we expect a rereading to yield a clearer view of story events. The portrait sketches of Dilsey, Benjy, and Jason provided in section 4 likewise contribute to our wish to return to the novel's early scenes and reconstruct them with a new precision in visual detail. The transition to a rereading is facilitated by the open ending, by the absence of a formal introduction or exposition in section 1, and by the fact that the fictional present of section 1 refers to the day immediately preceding the one described in section 4—in effect, section 1 reads as if it were section 5.

A repeated reading, however, both frustrates and exceeds our expectations. We find that a full explication, an unambiguous imaginative construction of the characters' actions and thoughts, remains unavailable. To give but one example, we do not know what passes in Quentin's mind when Shreve urges him to hurry to chapel:

> He looked at his watch. "Bell in two minutes."
> "I didn't know it was that late." He was still looking at his watch, his mouth shaping. "I'll have to hustle. I cant stand another cut. The dean told me last week—" He put his watch back into his pocket. Then I quit talking. [95]

Quentin's reply may be one of the last sallies of his smouldering vitality—he "quits talking" when he remembers that he is going to die that night, so he need not worry about the dean. Or else it may be a sham: he starts talking in order to prevent Shreve from naming the exact hour and stops as soon as Shreve gives up this intention. If we resolve the ambiguity by saying that Quentin's wish to ignore time is a remnant of his vitality, we pass from explicating to interpreting the text.

Section 1 never makes it clear how much Benjy's intuitive understanding exceeds or falls short of the material presented in his section. In section 2 the status of the narrative blocks remains vague to the end—we cannot establish, for instance, whether Quentin recollects the end of the Dalton Ames affair *while* or *after* he is beaten by Gerald Bland, whether he actually relives the past or has it flash through his mind in an instant, whether the textual space devoted to his memories is supposed to approximate the duration of the Bland picnic. Section 3 never explains Jason's feelings: his cruelty to young Quentin may be an expression of sadistic vengefulness or of incestuous attraction; his "feeling funny," that is, crying after his father's funeral, may be caused by genuine grief or by a childish resentment at being left alone in the rain. Section 4 gives no specific insights into Dilsey's or Luster's mind.

Thus the inner worlds of the characters resist penetration. After any number of readings, *The Sound and the Fury* still gives us the impression of overhearing people who have been close to one another and need not explain the things to which they refer. In time, we begin to grasp the meaning of their allusions, yet, not having shared their common experience, we remain excluded from their mutual understanding. This effect sharply contrasts with audience response to traditional novels: on rereading *War and Peace*, for instance, we feel that we know the characters better than they know themselves.

We are thus given some taste of the sense of exclusion that falls to the lot of the Compson children, though here the difference between audience response and the experience of the characters is more important than the analogy, since for the Compson children exclusion is a kind of emotional deprivation that takes the surface shape of being barred from knowledge. This is one of the motifs symbolically expressed by Caddy's climbing the tree to look in through the parlor window when the children are excluded from mourning (though their mental health requires participation in the ritual). The reader's reenactment of the characters' sense of exclusion is a kind of a compensation for the insufficiency of sympathetic identification or "vicarious experience": on a rereading this emotive element of response is sabotaged by essentially the same techniques that account for the confusion on the first reading.

Indeed, whereas in personal relationships a deeper understanding usually promotes sympathy, this does not always happen in the reading of fiction. In *The Sound and the Fury* the opposite is true: the more subtle and precise our imaginative reconstruction of the characters' predicament, the greater our detachment from them, the stronger the "anaesthetic" element of the aesthetic distance.

During a rereading, our increased familiarity with the fictional world and our success in piecing together disparate strands of information are sources of pleasure in themselves, largely divorced from vicarious experience. For instance, in Benjy's first drive to the cemetery with Mrs. Compson we are pleased to recognize the precedent of his habitual Sunday drives. It is delightful to be able to connect the flower that he likes to hold during such drives with the plant that Dilsey detaches from Mrs. Compson's bouquet on the first occasion. If we remember the broken narcissus that Benjy is holding during his drive in the last scene of the novel, it is with a touch of jouissance that we read the account of its precedent as a symbol in the making. The joy of difficulty overcome screens the emotional reality of the scenes.

On the first reading our emotional response was promoted by the prominence of the episodes that emphasize the poignancy of the need for love; it was also largely limited to those episodes. The scenes in question attract less attention on a repeated reading because our new competence neutralizes the device that made them prominent, that is, the interplay of clarity and confusion. For instance, on the first reading, Benjy's hope that Caddy will come home if he waits for her near the gate at the end of schooltime is especially moving because among the little that we have so far understood there is the scene of his meeting Caddy by the cold gate at Christmastime. On a rereading the connection between the two episodes is diluted by the multitude of details presented in between. Whereas on the first reading most of these details merged into the vague background complex, now, being much more intelligible, they acquire an interest of their own and so reduce the impact of the Benjy-Caddy plot line.

Though even on a first reading the intellectual challenge presented by the diffusion of information in the text may channel part of our attention away from the self-explanatory drama of thwarted feelings, it is mainly on a rereading that we are constantly diverted from the pathos of the scenes to the configuration of clues and other features of the narrative and of the reading process.[19] For instance, though we may have grown accustomed to the special code used in Benjy's section and can automatically "translate" a metonymic proposition like "the bowl went away" (30) into "Versh took the bowl away," there still remain stretches of narrative that are less easily "translated" into conventional notions. One of these is the description of the carriage stopping in the street: "I could hear Queenie's feet and the bright shapes went smooth and steady on both sides, the shadows of them flowing across Queenie's back. They went on like the bright tops of wheels. Then those on one side stopped at the tall white post where the soldier was. But on the other side they went on smooth and steady, but a little slower" (11-12). On the first reading it is practically impossible to understand that the shapes that cease moving are houses on Benjy's side of the street (the carriage has stopped), and the shapes that go on moving on the other side are vehicles on the roadway. And it certainly takes a rereading of the novel to achieve a full imaginative reconstruction of the scene because we must know the significance of smooth bright shapes in Benjy's life in order to visualize him sitting in placid contentment during Mrs. Compson's nervous dialogue with Jason. On a rereading we construct both the outside scene and the way in which it is reflected in the character's consciousness. Such dramatic irony increases our detachment from the character and weakens the impulse of sympathetic identification.

Another reason for the weakening of the emotional response to the main characters on a rereading is a reassessment of their conduct and its significance.

Our newly improved comprehension of *fabula* details casts a less indulgent light on Benjy and Quentin. On the first reading of the following episode, for instance, we are inclined to understand Benjy's assault on a schoolgirl in the street in the literal terms of his section's discourse: abandoned by the only person who understood his unarticulated meanings, Benjy seems to be making a pathetic attempt to overcome his muteness in order to talk to the schoolgirl about Caddy: "I was trying to say, and I caught her, trying to say, and she screamed and I was trying to say and trying and the bright shapes began to stop and I tried to get out. I tried to get it off of my face, but the bright shapes were going again. They were going up the hill to where it fell away and I tried to cry. But when I breathed in, I couldn't breath out again to cry, and I tried to keep from falling off the hill and I fell off the hill into the bright, whirling shapes" (64).

On a rereading we know that Benjy is castrated because of this incident. His assault on the schoolgirl must have looked like a sexual assault; perhaps this is, indeed, how it should be understood since, in any case, Benjy could not know or convey the difference between sexual advances and regular communication. Such a possibility calls our attention to the metaphorical meaning of the word "say" (compare the eighteenth-century euphemism "conversation"): both talking and sex are means of communication, of overcoming exclusion from the life of another, of a fulfillment in union; both can signify love. On the first reading both the literal and the symbolic significance of the episode are eclipsed by the pathos of Benjy's frustrated search for his sister, a more powerful but less versatile expression of the theme of the need for love. Moreover, on the first reading it is difficult to understand that what Benjy recollects in the next narrative block is his being etherized for castration. His horror is conveyed by style but the reason for it is obfuscated by the incompleteness of reference on the first reading, and on a repeated reading our attention is divided between the contents of the passage and the need to decipher it, between the object and the medium of presentation.

If Benjy's assault on the schoolgirl is sexual without his knowing it, then, by extrapolation, his love of Caddy may contain an element of incestuousness. This is suggested by the scenes pertaining to the time of puberty when Caddy and Benjy stop sharing a bed; it is also indirectly borne out by Quentin's explicitly incestuous fantasies with which we are now familiar. Benjy is no longer perceived as merely a defenseless innocent, a victim of cosmic injustice; he also emerges as the most complete embodiment of the Compson brothers' childlike possessive egotism. A rereading likewise brings out Quentin's morbid and somewhat brutal self-centeredness, which has been screened by the diffusion of information and eclipsed by pathos on the first reading.

By contrast, our attitude to Jason is now mollified. His character holds no more unpleasant surprises—we have already seen him at his worst. A better understanding of the details of section 1 offers insights into Jason's motivation. On the first reading of the scenes pertaining to Grandmother's funeral Jason seemed to be a mean boy suffering from middle-child syndrome. On a rereading the emotional vacuum in which Jason finds himself very early in his life is more obvious:

> After a while even Jason was through eating, and he began to cry.
> "Now you got to tune up." Dilsey said.
> "He does it every night since Damuddy was sick and he cant sleep with her." Caddy said. "Cry baby." [31]

Since this scene is placed *before* the references to Benjy's trauma at growing up and being put to bed without Caddy, on the first reading it is difficult to understand that Damuddy plays the role of a substitute mother for Jason, as Caddy does for Benjy. The possibility of perceiving the analogy between Benjy's and Jason's emotional destitution is thus delayed until a repeated reading. While on the first reading the most prominent feature of the adult Jason's character is a craving for re-venge, a rereading shows that his main obsession is with getting back what he has lost: "I dont want to make a killing; save that to suck in the smart gamblers with. I just want an even chance to get my money back. And once I've done that they can bring all Beale Street and all bedlam in here and two of them can sleep in my bed and another one can have my place at the table too" (329).

Jason does not know that what he really wants—the affection lost too long ago to be remembered—cannot be replaced by a fetish. Nor does he realize that his losses of the promised bank job, of the family property squandered on others, or of Caddy's money carried away by the eloping Quentin, are only emblems of his major loss. He eventually seems to understand that the symbolic weight of these losses does not measure up to the real value of endurance and survival. Jason's fight with an old man in the show caravan is followed by a relief that places things into perspective: nothing could have been as bad as senseless death; having escaped that, he can endure the rest, "lift up his tree and walk."

The adult Jason's compensation for being emotionally orphaned is his role as head of the family, symbolized by his place at the table. This explains his insistence on going home for dinner despite the protests of his boss. It is not so much for Dilsey's cooking that Jason comes home: he needs the presence of his mother and niece at the table so that he might enjoy his precedence and his role as the provider.

The reduction of the reader's sympathy for Benjy and Quentin and the growing understanding of Jason on a repeated reading is the justice (the "even chance") that Jason receives from the reader. The novel, which condemns maternal coldness and parental favoritism,[20] first leads us through an analogous favoritism and then demands a rectification of this attitude. This is one example of the quasicathartic reorientation that is part of audience response to most of Faulkner's novels, a reorientation that provides, as it were, a critical comment on the moral impasse from which his central characters cannot break away.

Our movement toward a moral/intellectual stance unavailable to the Compson children also involves a passage from the orientational (explicative) to interpretive activity. On a repeated reading each of the sections reveals layers of significance[21] that have been veiled by the diffusion of information on the first reading. The delay in our response to these layers of meaning is associated with the hierarchy of the novel's values.

On the first reading of section 1, diffusion of information obstructs our understanding of the symbolic connotations inherent in the novel's central image, Caddy's climbing the forbidden tree in pursuit of the mystery of death. This image, surrounded by such details as the snake that crawls from under the house, the timid brothers who condone the action against their better judgment, the muddy drawers, and Dilsey's exasperated "You, Satan" (54), strongly suggest the story of the Original Sin, yet on the first reading we practically ignore these hints. Unaware of the compositional centrality of the episode, we concentrate on its literal meaning.

As soon as Caddy settles down between the branches of the tree, the narrative moves to Benjy's memories of her drifting away from him and his temporary success in arresting her. These scenes form a clear pattern of their own, and we do not expect the narrative to return to the tree-climbing episode. Our memory of the image of the snake is further dulled by a sudden increase of confusion: it is in this part of the section that the alternation of Roman type and italics to indicate time shifts is often neglected. When the tree-climbing episode resumes, the snake seems to be just one of the pretexts for the children's bickering. *The Sound and the Fury* camouflages its allegorical element on the first reading.[22]

On a rereading the symbolic meanings are activated. What had seemed to reflect the associative sequence of the focalizer's memories now emerges as careful architectonics. Thus, though Benjy's flashbacks are usually not arranged according to the sequence of the events to which they pertain, the account of the evening of the grandmother's funeral is always resumed precisely at the point where it was discontinued. Therefore this time-layer is singled out from Benjy's other memories and forms the second major line of action, intertwining with the fictional present. Whereas on the first reading the confused stretches of the narrative foiled the episodes presented with a degree of clarity, on repeated reading the distortions of chronology foil the two chronologically consistent accounts. Moreover, since now we know that the tree-climbing episode will be resumed, the narrative shift that occurs when Caddy is hidden among the branches freezes the scene into a tableau, and its memory lingers over the sequence of the scenes in which Benjy is shown losing his hold on Caddy.

Finally, the symbolic connotations of the tree-climbing image are enhanced by ingenious transitions between narrative blocks. The scene immediately following this image refers to Caddy's wedding:

[Versh] went and pushed Caddy up into the tree to the first limb. We watched the muddy bottom of her drawers. Then we couldn't see her. We could hear the tree thrashing.

. . . .

The tree quit thrashing. We looked up into the still branches.

"What you seeing." Frony whispered.

I saw them. Then I saw Caddy, with flowers in her hair, and a long veil like shining wind. Caddy Caddy

"Hush." T.P. said, "They going to hear you. Get down quick." He pulled me. Caddy. I clawed my hands against the wall Caddy. [47]

The transition is not effected through verbal association: in the wedding episode the word "see," which forms the link between the two narrative blocks, is never pronounced. In a way, however, the words "I saw them. Then I saw Caddy" are Benjy's mute answer to Frony's question "What you seeing" uttered in the tree-climbing scene.[23] Benjy tries to catch sight of Caddy in the tree but she is hidden from his view.

Instead, in his telescoped memories, he has a vision of her at her unhappy wedding. A connection is thus established between Caddy's pursuit of forbidden knowledge and the tragic outcome of her desire for romantic love.

If the symbolism of the Original Sin had been obvious on the first reading, we would have been inclined to connect it with Caddy's sexual promiscuity. On a repeated reading, however, under the influence of the earlier impression that the novel deals with a frustrated need for love,[24] we realize that the sin lies in the lack of love that excludes the children from the ritual and from their places in each other's lives—at a time when history forces them out of their hereditary place in society. The diffusion of information is, among other things, a means of controlling interpretation so that the heavy-duty scriptural symbolism should be read in accordance with the novel's scale of values.

Sections 2 and 3 provide a metaphysical, historical, and socioeconomic perspective on the story of the Compsons' decline and fall. In section 4, the scion of the aristocratic family turns into a tired inconspicuous man in a small car in the street. Even though Jason can still rally in an emergency, his history and emotions are incidental to the life of the community, in particular to the life of the black congregation at the Easter service.

If this impression of the family's and individual's diminishing importance had not been tempered by the strong emphasis on the need for love produced on the first reading, Parson Shegog's references to the passing of generations (his allusion to Ecclesiastes 1:4—"One generation passeth away, and another generation cometh: but the earth abideth for ever") would suggest that individual life, with its transient sounds and furies, signifies little. However, owing to the residual prominence of the novel's major theme, the main meaning of this allusion seems to be that basic principles and values remain unaffected by the passage of time.

Thus the diffusion of information in *The Sound and the Fury* channels our attention to the theme of the need for love and defers our understanding of the symbolic layers connotative to this theme so that they should modify, expand, but not block it. It encourages interpretive activity on a rereading by promoting a detached attitude, yet it also controls interpretation. It leads us through an experience parallel to the characters' attitudes yet eventually invites us to transcend it by cautious reassessment and a delayed move from explicative to interpretive attention.

As has often been noted, numerous images and motifs of *The Sound and the Fury* are reminiscent of T.S. Eliot's *The Waste Land*. Eliot's poem is based on massive allusions to the Holy Grail romances in which the waste land can be redeemed by the knight who asks the right question. No such knight is in evidence in the poem: his role is played by the reader who probes the meaning of the text. The reader of *The Sound and the Fury* is assigned a similar role—to integrate the Compson tragedy into a broader perspective, yet without losing the aftershine of the emotional response that it has elicited on the first reading.

CHAPTER THREE

Nostromo
"Shaded Expression"

when you look long into an abyss, the
abyss also looks into you.
—Nietzsche, *Beyond Good and Evil*

The fragmentariness and the baffling narrative shifts of Conrad's *Nostromo* are most often accounted for as a structural counterpart of the vision of the world "that lacks a moral center"[1] and is devoid of a stable system of norms. Similar observations about the fragmented narrative reflecting a disorganized world have, however, been made about the work of writers as different as T.S. Eliot, Joyce, Hemingway, and Poe—which, of course, does not mean that they are not correct. In what way, however, are they correct of *Nostromo*? In what way is the form of this novel linked to its ideological "repertoire"?[2]

I shall suggest that this link lies in audience response and discuss *Nostromo* as one of the novels in which elements of audience response are analogous to what takes place within the fictional world. In particular, on the first reading of *Nostromo* our nonvicarious information-processing experience is parallel to the dynamics of the moral and intellectual attitudes of the major characters.

The presence of the reader-character analogy is suggested by the novel's "mock reader,"[3] a nonindividualized "privileged passenger" (446)[4] entertained by Captain Mitchell, the local superintendent of the shipping company. In chapter 1, we "arrive" in the fictional country of Costaguana from the Placid Gulf, a fictional sleeve of the Pacific Ocean. When its remoter shores and its three islands called the Isabels have been pointed out to us, the camera eye moves to the port of Sulaco, as if tracing the course of the steamer that carries the "privileged" guest. In the harbor, we are, like this "bird of passage" (458; "Costaguana" literally means "the coast of bird droppings"), greeted by Captain Mitchell. The narrative of chapter 2, interspersed with quotations from Captain Mitchell's tourist-guiding monologues, floods us with references to people, places, events, and objects (Smith, Ribiera, Capataz de Cargadores, the Alameda, Socorro, a riot, a battle, the railway, the silver ingots, the *Minerva*, and so on) that we cannot connect. Like the "privileged" tourist, we feel "stunned and, as it were, annihilated mentally by a sudden surfeit of sights, sounds, names, facts, and complicated information imperfectly apprehended" (458). Unlike the tourist, however, we spend more than one "memorable day" (445) in Sulaco. We part company with the "privileged" guest when, by the end of chapter 2, the account of Captain Mitchell's harangues is discontinued and we face a different set of trials.

These trials are a form of tantalization, the opposite of "privilege." Part 1 of *Nostromo* is a sequence of narrative blocks devoted to separate episodes, scenes, characters, and historical retrospects; it is characterized by paucity though not total absence of references to spatial, temporal, or causal connections between these blocks. For a very long time we cannot organize the blocks of information into a pattern, and yet some tantalizing pattern seems to be there—just beyond our reach.

The characters of *Nostromo* are also tantalized. The legendary gringos are believed to have discovered the treasure of Azuera and to remain "rich and hungry and thirsty" (5); Nostromo steals another treasure but cannot use it and dies while trying to "grow rich very slowly" (473); Giselle Viola complains that her lover is to her what the treasure is to him—"it is there, but [she] can never get enough of it" (514). The love of other characters, Mrs. Gould, Dr. Monygham, and Linda Viola, is close yet unattainable; the riches of the treasure-laden Occidental Province trickle down but sparsely to its native population. Sotillo's desperate search for the treasure at the bottom of the Sulaco harbor ("it is there! I see it! I feel it!" 455) is a reductio ad absurdum of the same theme.

The reader's search for an informational pattern is a quest for an organized system of significances. It is an eventful quest, though, as in the case of Sotillo, its object is not where it is sought. *Nostromo* is a precursor of the modernist works where the burden of constructing significance is overtly transferred from the text to the reader.

The narrative shifts of *Nostromo* are effected in a way that causes a certain tardiness of our imagination and that directs our attention to matters that eventually turn out to be secondary in importance. Both these effects lead, in their turn, to a series of minor and major shocks of readjustment.

The central factor accountable for the tardiness in our imaginative construction of the *fabula* is the smoothness of associative transitions from one narrative block to another. For instance, Don Vincente Ribiera is linked to the railway workers in Casa Viola as the man who called their work "a progressive and patriotic undertaking" (33), and through him the transition is made from the setting of chapter 3 to the scene of the banquet on the *Juno*. The transition from the story of Mrs. Gould's early activities in Costaguana to the account of Holroyd's visit is made through a remark on the former subject that Mrs. Gould addresses to a visitor from abroad; the reference to the visitor is then used as a springboard for the account of the visit (64). Such associative links suggest the abundance of material and double as the narrator's alibi for not presenting this material in a systematic way.

As a result of the smoothness of transitions, which is not impaired even by chapter division, the borderlines between consecutive blocks are blurred: while our imagination is still involved with one episode or scene, the narrative has already passed on to another. For instance, the first sentence of chapter 3, "It might have been said that there he was only protecting his own" (16), is a commentary on the last sentence of chapter 2, "Nostromo, with his cargadores, was pressing [the rioters] too hard then" (15). The use of the personal pronoun suggests the continuity of the subject matter, thus "pressing" *us* on to the episode at Casa Viola "too hard" to allow us a pause for reorientation. Our attention thus lags behind the narrative shifts: we tend to miss the precise moment when a shift occurs. We register it in the midst of a new narrative block; and it is belatedly that we readjust our attention. The first reading of part 1 of *Nostromo* is thus characterized by the "missed-moment" pattern, even though, after a series of minor jolts, we learn to expect narrative shifts and become alert to the moments when they occur. This pattern is isomorphic with an important constituent of the novel's thematic structure.

Indeed, "missing the moment" is one of the main features of the experience of the characters of *Nostromo*, a motif that spills over to audience response. The main exponent of this motif is, paradoxically, Gian' Battista Fidanza, alias Nostromo, the title character famous for popping up in the right place at the right time. Wary, quick-witted, and judicious, Nostromo reveals a deficiency of moral alertness when he fails to recognize, at the right moment, the major test of his life.

During a revolution Nostromo is called upon by the rulers of Sulaco to spirit Martin Decoud and a big load of silver out of the harbor. He expects this to be his most desperate and glorious adventure, yet he has to delay it by a few hours in order to fetch a doctor for Teresa Viola. Then, however, Teresa asks him to bring her a priest. He refuses, stifling the momentary oppression of his heart: " 'Padrona . . . , you have been like this before, and got better after a few days. I have given you already the very last moments I can spare.' " Priests he regards as useless—his employers are waiting for him; Decoud's life is at stake; and further delay would jeopardize his mission. For a moment he thinks about "what absolution would mean to her if she believed in it only ever so little," but then decides, "No matter . . . he had given her already the very last moment he could spare." Too intent on silencing his conscience, Nostromo misses the moment for generosity, for what he can give Teresa—his sympathy, his pledge of commitment, perhaps humility. Instead he angrily rejects the interference of female whims with "the most desperate affair" of his life. It is at this moment that he fails his "supreme test" (240).

Teresa likewise misses a crucial moment. Being denied absolution troubles her as a symptom of Nostromo's disloyalty rather than as a threat to her eternal soul. "Then God, perhaps, will have mercy upon me" (241) she says to Nostromo, before warning him, in accents that he mistakes for those of a malediction, against his ending in "poverty, misery, starvation" (242). She is too mortified to make her most important request—that he should protect her daughters. It is much later, when he is gone, that she shouts, "The children, Gian' Battista! Save the children!" (320). Nostromo never understands that this, above everything else, is a belated expression of her dying wish.

Charles and Emilia Gould fail to notice that they have started drifting apart. It is not clear at which point their love could still have been saved: early in his career, after the millionaire Holroyd's visit to Costaguana, Charles already feels remorseful for an emotional infidelity to his wife. Though they still have their moments of intimacy, though "the best of [his] feelings" are still in her keeping (69), he knows that the mine has "decoyed him further than he meant to go" (81).[5] His conversation with Emilia is already evasive, and their relationship moves toward what Borges calls "one of those close (the adjective is excessive) English friendships that begin by excluding confidences and very soon dispense with dialogue."[6] Their "confidential intercourse" begins to fall "not in moments of privacy, but precisely in public, when the quick meeting of their glances would comment upon some fresh turn of events" (156).

In private, Charles has no psychic energy to spare for his wife's anxieties, and Emilia learns to conceal them. Ostensibly so different from the ladies of patriarchal families, she is too timid to make a timely claim on Charles's "best feelings." Or perhaps, in a "woman's love of excitement" (140), she misses the right time.

The right moment might, it seems, have been during her conversation with Charles on the morning of Holroyd's departure. This is the last episode in which the Goulds are shown engaged in a frank and significant private interview. The description of the morning (65-66) starts as a characteristic household scene—the novel, indeed, abounds in "iterative"[7] scenes, such as, for instance, the account of how old Giorgio Viola would choke over his frying pan and curse Cavour as the author of his misfortunes. The iterative scenes are part of the expositional material—part of the setting even, if the concept of the setting is extended to the deployment of forces on the fictional battleground. They are usually marked by the modal "would"; for example, "Don José Avellanos would mutter 'Imperium in imperio, Emilia, my soul'" (106). Yet we often miss the moment when such scenes slip into accounts of "historical occasions." In the morning scenes at Casa Gould it is not clear where the shift takes place—especially since in a sentence like "Then the old porter would hobble in, sweeping the flagstones, and the house was ready for the day" (65-66) the word "would" may have either a modal iterative meaning or the meaning of the anticipated future (future in the past). How, indeed, can one tell a regular morning from the morning of a crucial day? On the other hand, while reading about the first silver escort from the mine to the city, we suddenly notice that the narrative has come to dwell on a regular procedure that takes place several times a year (107-8).

Our tendency to overlook the borderlines between scenes that further the plot and scenes that merge with the setting is a separate case of the tardiness of imagination. If parallel experience is turned into an interpretive strategy, this might call our attention to Charles Gould's tendency to confuse active moral choice with its circumstances. While fighting local corruption and political instability with their own weapons, Charles Gould becomes increasingly involved in both. Decoud, Dr. Monygham, Father Corbelán, and Antonia Avellanos display a similar lack of self-reflective moral alertness. As in Jane Austen's novels, value is a matter of measure, yet in Conrad's work the awareness of both the need for and the dangers of compromise is closer to the tragic.

The pattern of tardiness, of "missed moments" suggests that there *are* moments to be caught or missed. Its significance comes into conflict with the suggestions of a *refus de commencement* that presents any action as inevitable. Nostromo's decision to appropriate the treasure, for instance, displays an almost Schopenhauerian determinism: being what he is, he apparently could not have acted otherwise. The tauntings of the greedy Morenita, the reproaches of Teresa, the chief engineer's irresponsible remarks while loading the silver into the lighter, Dr. Monygham's disrespect for the mission, and the narrator's comments on the spell of any treasure form what Ford Madox Ford called the *progression d'effet*[8] leading up to the fatal development. Nostromo's sense of being betrayed by his employers and the disappearance of the four ingots for which he would not be able to account are immediate factors in his decision.[9] Yet insistent references to Teresa Viola trace the cause of his fall further back—to his refusal to fetch a priest for her. The main motive for this refusal is his vanity—which can, in its turn, be traced to his past experience as an abused orphan. Yet Conrad does not resign his character to a chain of motivations: somewhere along the lines the right moment has been missed; the wrong choice has been made. The words "supreme test" in the scene at Teresa's deathbed locate the crucial moment, though they leave it undetermined whether the "test" implies a revelation of what cannot be changed or a moment for a decisive act of free will.

But to return to the texture of the narrative and its effect on audience response: because of the smoothness of the transitions, each narrative block first continues the *couleur locale* of the previous block but then moves to a different part of the spectrum. The monotony-breaking game of contrast between cultures, classes, activities, and ways of life is the main principle that underlies the sequence of narrative blocks—the associative links are its rhetorically oriented mask. The aesthetic effect of this game is indirectly described in the iconic passage where the chief engineer of the railway contemplates "the changing hues on the enormous side of the mountain, thinking that in this sight, as in a piece of inspired music, there could be found together the utmost delicacy of shaded expression and a stupendous magnificence of effect" (38-39).

The changing hues of consecutive narrative blocks do indeed create a "stupendous" ("mentally annihilating"?) magnificence of a panoramic canvas, while individual narrative blocks contain delicate "shaded expression," where "shaded" means (a) penciled in so as to produce the illusion of depth and (b) "veiled." The narrative of *Nostromo* is "shaded" in both senses: it produces the illusion of the yet unprobed depth or thickness of the setting and "veils" its subliminal rhetorical effects by salient conscious impressions.

These salient impressions make us turn upon our own performance as readers. Belated readjustment to narrative shifts calls our attentiveness into question. Allusions to Bolivar and Garibaldi and occasional information concerning the age of the characters or the length of time between events suggests the presence of chronological guidelines that *we* fail to organize. The narrative's tendency to ruffle our confidence is laid bare by the end of part 1. When after a long interruption the account of the banquet on the *Juno* is resumed, we recollect that Mrs. Gould was talking to the chairman of the railway. Suddenly, however, we are startled by the following: " 'You were good enough to say that you intended to ask me for something,' he reminded her gallantly. 'What is it? Be assured that any request from you would be considered in the light of a favour to myself' " (115). The word "reminded" suffices to make us wonder when it was that Mrs. Gould intended to ask Sir John for a favor, but straining our memory is of no avail. In fact, the request has not been recorded in the text. The narrative only tricks us into believing that we have forgotten something previously mentioned. Since Conrad usually sought synonyms for the conventional tags "she said"/"he said," the word "reminded" may be regarded as a technical flaw, an unnecessary synonym of "said." However, in *Nostromo* Conrad turned quite a number of his potential weaknesses to artistic advantage, having, like Nostromo, "the gift of evolving safety out of the very danger" (497). In this particular instance he elicits a readiness for self-criticism in audience response.

Until halfway through the first reading we are repeatedly forced to pause, look up from the text, and register a need for a belated readjustment. Yet the ostensible failures of our attention to spatial and temporal links are in fact a "shading," a metonymy for our failure to dwell on (or rather for our having been diverted from) the submerged moral and psychological complexities of character portrayal.

In the experience of the characters the theme of "shaded expression" likewise takes the form of metonymy: goals are screened by means, and symptoms are taken for causes. Patriotic propaganda, political ambitions, managerial enthusiasms, and even philanthropy are shaded expressions of greed, love, power struggle, vanity, or guilt.

Even Nostromo is not spontaneous in his munificence: his courage and efficiency are real but his generosity is a pose calculated to keep him "well spoken of" (232). After stealing the silver, his conduct, outwardly unchanged, becomes the sham that, to some extent, it has always been.

Nostromo's consciousness works through metonymy. The need to replace the obscure by the manifest is an important factor in his decision to steal the silver. His mind is not equipped for dealing with vague self-reproach: unable to rationalize his feelings of guilt about Teresa, he externalizes them by an unambiguous betrayal of trust. Teresa herself "shades" her deep feelings for Nostromo by ill-tempered railing, while both Dr. Monygham and the narrator refuse to probe the nature of these feelings.

In Emilia Gould's case metonymy takes the shape of a confusion of effect and cause. After the Sulaco revolution she feels remorse for having withheld crucial information from her husband when the fatal load of silver could have been prevented from coming down the mountain. And yet, by the end of the novel, she refuses to learn the hiding place of this treasure, even though its bulk could still be restored to Gould. It is as if subliminally, and belatedly, she understands that her having kept a secret from Charles was but a symptom of their estrangement and that the responsibility for this estrangement was at least partly her own.

Emilia is presented as "highly gifted in the art of human intercourse, which consists in delicate shades of self-forgetfulness and in the suggestion of universal comprehension" (45)—the words "delicate shades" echo "the utmost delicacy of shaded expression." The suggestion of "universal comprehension" is a screen for failure of intimate understanding; "self-forgetfulness" turns into an inability for timely self-assertion. The Victorian "art of human intercourse" cannot replace cultivation of genuine intimacy. The ostensible compliment that the narrative pays Emilia is a piece of "shaded" criticism: her "gift" is also her flaw.

The major effect of the gradually changing hues of the narrative blocks is diversionary. The narrative shifts of *Nostromo* take the shape of "digression,"[10] yet after a short while the subject matter of a new block temporarily dispels the images created by previous blocks. For instance, the story of Hernandez is introduced by Don Pepe's remark about the first silver ingot from the mine (102), yet the eventful biography of Costaguana's Robin Hood relegates the frame dialogue into the background; eventually we are surprised to be brought back to the dialogue and hear Mrs. Gould's reply (104) to a remark made two pages

earlier. On the first reading the "digression" does not freeze the interrupted dialogue into a tableau: it moves into the foreplane and pushes
the frame out of our scope of vision. We are not allowed to synchronize
different spaces of the novel's world.

Most odysseys of the narrative in part 1 fail to return to their
starting points: primary digressions develop into new digressions,
with "footnotes" explaining "footnotes" and new loops commenting
on comments. Thus the reference to the railway evokes the scene of the
banquet celebrating the inauguration of the railway. During the banquet Mrs. Gould talks to Sir John, and the narrative slips to a flashback
account of Sir John's journey through the mountains with the assistance of Nostromo. Once Nostromo is mentioned, the narrative
passes to the account of his character, about which only Dr. Monygham
is sceptical. Then it must be explained who Dr. Monygham is, and,
since he frequently visits the Goulds, we are told about the Gould
family, their house, and their other vistors, such as Don José Avellanos, whose remarks are explained by a long account of the Goulds'
family history. This account is taken as far as the inauguration banquet,
and the dialogue between Sir John and Mrs. Gould is then resumed.
On her way home from the banquet Mrs. Gould stops at Casa Viola in
order to give old Giorgio a piece of good news; the old man is congratu-
lated by Nostromo. The narrative then winds to Nostromo's carnivalis-
tic amours, and the chain ends with a return to Captain Mitchell's
remarks about this mysterious hero.

This spiral contains a number of frames-within-frames, such as the
scenes in Casa Viola and at Mrs. Gould's tea table, but the chronology
of events referred to in these frame passages does not correspond to
their sequence in the text. The first scene in Casa Viola, (part 1, chapter
3) refers to the day of the riot and takes place eighteen months after the
second scene (part 1, chapter 8), which refers to the day of the inauguration banquet. The third scene in the sequence (part 2, chapter 4)
is analogous to the second—Mrs. Gould's carriage stops near Old
Giorgio's house on the way home from the harbor—only this event
takes place a day or two before the first (part 1, chapter 3). We understand this sequence of events only while reading Decoud's letter, that
is, after the third scene at Old Giorgio's is left far behind. As a result,
while reading the third episode, we do not attach sufficient importance
to Old Giorgio's remark that his wife is ill and cannot come out to meet
Mrs. Gould. Nor do we realize that in the scene of the riot Teresa is not
just ill-tempered but also very ill, that on hearing the banging on the
shutters she shrieks not out of female nervousness but with the phys-

ical pain of a heart seizure. The flashes of the iterative scenes of the past that follow this episode show Teresa active and scolding Old Giorgio— we therefore do not realize that she never rallies after the day of the riot and that the agony in which Decoud and Nostromo find her on the night of their adventure is a development of the cardiac condition that has lasted ever since the embarkation of Barrios. This is one of the reasons why we almost share Nostromo's impatience when Teresa interferes with his plans. Moreover, we have been led to this episode by sympathetically following Decoud (through the departure of Barrios, the soirée at the Goulds, and the first day of the riots as described in the letter); we are intrigued by his schemes and by the expedition upon which he entices Nostromo. This expedition and Decoud's success now form the main line of interest; the episode at Casa Viola comes as interruption of it. Thus if part 1 has kept our attention lagging behind narrative shifts, part 2 forces us to overlook Teresa's suffering and the callousness of Nostromo.

The failure of imaginative commitment to other human beings is most prominent in the experience of Decoud, who commits suicide because his distorted literalization of subjective idealism leads him to madness.[11] Decoud cannot imagine the reality of the other people beyond the data provided by his senses. Prolonged solitude and silence on the island, with no external movement to fill the hollow of his dilettantic mind, make him doubt not merely the prospect of being rescued by Nostromo but even the very existence of Nostromo—or of his own subjective self, the last vestiges of which he decides to destroy. The thought of Antonia does not sustain him: unable to evoke her image otherwise than in a grotesque hallucination, he arbitrarily decides that she must be dead. Decoud's imaginative failure is of the kind that in Conrad's early novels is associated with primitive mentality:[12] the oversophisticated consciousness makes a full circle to barbarism. The failure of imaginative commitment to other people is tantamount to betrayal: by using four silver ingots to help him drown, Decoud exposes Nostromo to suspicions of murder and theft.

Various degrees of solipsism are also evident in a number of other characters: Old Giorgio prefers to live enveloped in his memories, fails to see that Nostromo loves Giselle rather than Linda, and ends up shooting Nostromo, mistaking him for Ramirez; Charles Gould placidly ignores the unhappiness of his wife; and Dr. Monygham is driven to denounce his friends under torture in Guzman Bento's prison (where he may have missed his moment for committing suicide[13]). By the end of the novel, while going to Old Giorgio and Linda with the expected news of Nostromo's death, Dr. Monygham tries "to imagine Linda and her father, and discover[s] a strange reluctance within himself" (529). There is more pain than pleasure in one's imaginative commitment to the reality of other people—by eschewing this commitment through diversionary strategies, Conrad's characters seek to reverse the proportion.[14]

Even Emilia Gould yields to the temptation of solipsism. The idealized struggle for "material interests" diverts her attention from the need to cultivate genuine family feelings. During their courtship, Charles's moodily spiritualizing attitude "towards the world of material things" is a "pinnacle" from which "her delight in him, lingering with half-open wings like those birds that cannot rise easily from a flat level" can "soar up in the skies" (57). The sky is the limit; the promise of excitement in supporting him is immensely appealing to a young girl who lives in almost monastic austerity with her impoverished widowed aunt in a dilapidated palazzo. The metaphoric style of this passage (a case of "shaded expression"?) blocks its vague reminiscence of George Eliot's Dorothea Brooke.

The fulfillment of the promise temporarily blinds Emilia to the loss of her husband's "best feelings." Her concern for the poor, the miserable, the homesick, her promotion of the philanthropic side of the "material interests," tends to divert the audience from her part in the conjugal estrangement. Moreover, though Emilia attempts not to lose sight of human realities, she almost willfully ignores the dangers run by Nostromo, Decoud, and Dr. Monygham in their missions during the Sulaco revolution. At crucial moments she has no energy to spend on sympathetic imagination.

The general development of Mrs. Gould's experience is analogous to the dynamics of audience response. She is an intelligent and committed newcomer in Sulaco, which is what the reader is invited to be. Like the reader, she is placed in the position of an auditor—of Gould's apologiae, Don José's doctrines, Don Pepe's ethnographical sketches, Giorgio Viola's anxieties, young Scarfe's tactless outpourings, Decoud's schemes, Captain Mitchell's raptures, and the checked confidences of Nostromo. The beginning of her involvement in the affairs of Costaguana is marked by the same kind of diffuse interests in the conditions of human life. She is the "Never-tired Señora" (85) whom practical activity diverts from the emotional plane of her life.

In audience response, the "cowboy-Machiavelli" type of entertainment likewise takes precedence over psychological complexities. This is a matter not of a reader's priorities but, as in *The Sound and the Fury*, of the relationship between clear and entangled narrative blocks. The length and relative clarity of the account of the revolution on the one hand and the chopped up nonchronological story of Teresa's illness on the other cannot but tip our interest in the direction of the former in the first half of the novel.

As suggested above, the spiral-like structure of part 1 baffles our attempts to find a foothold in the *fabula*. Even the story of Ribiera's escape in chapter 2 reads not as one of the central events of the plot but as part of the setting, an illustration of the generalized description of the political instability of Costaguana: "The fugitive patriots of the defeated party had the knack of turning up again on the coast with half a steamer's load of small arms and ammunition. Such resourcefulness Captain Mitchell considered as perfectly wonderful in view of their utter destitution at the time of flight. . . . And he could speak with knowledge; for on a memorable occasion he had been called to save the life of a dictator, together with the lives of a few Sulaco officials" (11).

The expression "had a knack of" refers to the return of the fugitives, yet on the first reading it seems to extend to the "memorable occasion," which thus seems to be a typical occurrence. Even the subsequent scene in Casa Viola, a crucial part of the plot, reads rather like an ethnographical sketch showing how the riot might affect an Italian family. Chameleonic play of the plot with the setting, of the action with the dramatized expositional material, keeps us wondering what the novel can be about.

Indeed, no sooner has the Viola family enlisted our sympathies than the narrative moves away to a succession of other people, culminating in the lengthy account of the Goulds. From then on the novel seems to be a leisurely tale of Charles Gould's struggle to revive the silver mine and of his belief in "material interests" as the way toward a general well-being. Nostromo does not yet seem to be the protagonist.[15] He keeps reappearing—picturesque, efficient, reliable, impecunious, vain, larger than life—yet his portrayal in part 1 is mostly external. So far he is an image rather than a human being; a symbol, perhaps, of something patently ubiquitous and vague.

Part 1 closes with a reference to a "misfortune" in which Nostromo was involved: "he has never been the same man since," comments Captain Mitchell (124). Yet as part 2 begins, the foreshadowing of Nostromo's downfall fades from our memory—not least owing to our impatience with Captain Mitchell. The story of the political changes and their effect on the Gould concession is resumed with but a few explanatory digressions (for instance, when we meet Martin Decoud at the scene of the embarkation of the Sulaco garrison, his antecedents are presented as accounting for his Parisian air; the scene of the embarkation is then resumed precisely where it was interrupted). The narrative of part 2 unfolds in a roughly chronological order, covering a couple of days. It is not yet clear whether this is another longish narrative block haunted by the threat of interruption or whether the main line of the plot has finally emerged. We do not yet understand, for instance, that the riot mentioned in part 1 breaks out within forty hours of the embarkation of the troops.

The connection between the two events is established in approximately the middle of the novel—by Decoud's letter to his sister. The main pieces of the puzzle suddenly fall into place.

Having painstakingly arrived at a sort of clarity, we allow ourselves to relax. The reading no longer strains our attention. Our former patience is, we believe, finally rewarded: the narrative seems to be straightforward, touched with suspense, and almost as undemanding as popular fiction; the novel seems to be the tale of the Sulaco revolution, the struggle for progress, the confrontation between the enlightened supporters of material interests and the primevally ferocious plundering chieftains. This is a misleading and trivializing attitude to the novel, not unlike Mrs. Gould's relatively carefree (if not complacent) attitude to her and her husband's achievements during the seemingly peaceful rule of the enlightened president-dictator Ribiera.

This political stability is short lived, and Mrs. Gould, like most people around her, is shocked out of her sense of security by the Monterist coup. Audience response undergoes a similar jolt in a later part of the novel (preserving the pattern of retardation). Just as the adventures of the characters in their fight against the coup promise to reach the peak of excitement, the notorious "split"[16] of *Nostromo* shakes us out of self-forgetful absorption in the text. Chapter 10 of part 3 begins with the words "The next day," as though the account of the adventures were to continue. When Captain Mitchell is mentioned in the second sentence, we expect to learn about his activities on the day in question. His first direct-speech remark (445) seems to satisfy this expectation. Suddenly, however, we are shocked into the discovery (which, as usual, lags behind the narrative shift by a few lines) that here begins another of the old seaman's tourist-guiding speeches, of which we have already had two or three samples. With the reversed-telescope effect, the dramatic events that loomed large only a few moments ago are now relegated to the fictional past. The shock is all the greater since by now, like the victims of Pedro Montero, we have been lulled "into a sense of security" (363).[17] We resent the intrusion almost as we would resent untimely promptings that destroy the suspense of a detective story. Yet the fact that the "historical moments" that we have expected to see in their full glory (Nostromo's dash to Barrios, Dr. Monygham's struggle with Sotillo, and Charles Gould's with Pedro Montero) are waived as unimportant, makes us realize that *Nostromo* is not, after all, an adventure story or a British version of a (Latin-)American dream.[18]

The novel's central concerns are forced on our attention by the double flashback that follows Captain Mitchell's monologue. Of the great number of events related to the Sulaco revolution, only two are singled out for a scenic presentation—the corruption of the incorruptible Nostromo and the suicide of the hopeful lover Decoud. The two episodes are given the optimal position in the narrative. Since shortly before the "split" we saw Decoud safe on the island and the silver carefully hidden away, Captain Mitchell's references to Decoud as dead and the silver as lost make us wonder what has reversed the auspicious circumstances. The flashback account of Nostromo's return to the island is an answer to this question, therefore our interest in it is particularly keen. In the middle of this episode the mystery deepens: together with Nostromo we wonder what has become of Decoud, who is not discovered on the island. By way of reply, in a flashback-within-a-flashback, we are offered the account of Decoud's suicide. The relative scarcity of outward action in both episodes promotes our concentration on their psychological and moral significance, thus bringing into high relief the themes of missed moment and metonymic "shading" that culminate in this island setting (as Conrad notes in *Victory*, an island is, in fact, the top of a mountain[19]). When the focus shifts back to Nostromo on the Great Isabel, it becomes clear that the narrative has been working up to his moral suicide rather than to the Sulaco revolution.

This major readjustment is parallel to Mrs. Gould's belated realization that a single-minded channeling of energies to the pursuit of idealized "material interests" is fatal to family life and that economic progress does not suffice to ensure lasting peace.

In the final chapters of *Nostromo*, as in the third and fourth sections of *The Sound and the Fury*, there is an additional cycle of audience response, a miniature reproduction of the preceding cycle. We are confronted with a new farrago of facts concerning the Sulaco revolution, yet we organize them fairly soon and shift our attention to Nostromo's relationship with the Viola sisters.

The dubious aesthetic quality of these love-story chapters is often related[20] to Conrad's generally ineffective treatment of romantic love. In *Nostromo*, however, this is another potential weakness used to a rhetorical advantage. The melodramatic atmosphere of the love scenes induces us to expect a traditional denouement. This expectation is enhanced in the deathbed episode by Doctor Monygham's curiosity about Nostromo's confession.

A melodrama would have Nostromo disclose the hiding place of the silver to Mrs. Gould so that the treasure might return to the rightful owner and, according to familiar formulae, the soul of the sinner might be relieved of its burden. As the "monastically hooded" (524) Emilia Gould grows "cold with apprehension" (525) at Nostromo's bedside, the disclosure seems to be slowly making its way into the dialogue— until, contrary to all conventional presentiments, she refuses to learn where the silver is hidden.

The unexpectedness of this development, contrasting with the traditional trappings of the situation, forcefully reminds us of Nostromo's treacherous refusal to bring a priest for the dying Teresa. Yet Emilia Gould is not a traitor: on the contrary, her refusal to hear Nostromo's confession is an expression of a staunch loyalty. It means that Nostromo's fame, the goal of a lifetime, will not be destroyed by posthumous disclosures.[21]

Thus, on the first reading of *Nostromo* our response moves from a diffuse wondering about the conditions of human existence to the story of political struggles and heroic adventures, then, with a shock of readjustment, to individual psychological experience, and, finally, at the end of the second cycle, to a particular aspect of this experience— personal loyalty. Our attention is thus steered away from external action to the inner conflicts that the characters have to resolve without the guidance of conventional codes, conflicts that arise from the temptation to follow "strange gods" at the expense of solidarity with fellow human beings. Conrad was well aware of the economics of psychic energy: he criticizes not the development of "material interests" per se but the imbalance in the energies devoted to Mammon and to God, where God stands for genuine respect and sympathy for one's neighbor, for family life, and for "a few very simple ideas" referred to in the "Familiar Preface" of his autobiography.[22] The temporary detour of our own interests testifies to the universality of the temptation.

Like the reader, and unlike the people around her, Emilia Gould eventually readjusts her moral attention. She is disappointed with utilitarian principles and has lost that "strongest of illusions" (71) or "the

supreme illusion" (178), which Conrad, like Schopenhauer and Kierkegaard, considers love to be. She is, nevertheless, sustained by her
sense of loyal responsibility to other people, by the thought that life
must still "contain the care of the past and of the future in every passing moment of the present." And though her belief is couched in words
reminiscent of a demagogue "shading" ("Our daily work must be
done to the glory of the dead, and for the good of those who come after,"
489), its sincerity is borne out by her conduct at Nostromo's deathbed.

"I know you will defend my memory," Doctor Monygham has said
to her before departing on a deadly mission (387). Eventually, it is
Nostromo whose memory Emilia undertakes to defend. Unlike Antonia, Mrs. Gould does not believe the legend; unlike Teresa, she does
not resent it. It is partly out of concern "for the good of those who come
after" that she decides to preserve "the glory of the dead."

Nostromo's fame must remain untainted, so that the very notion of
fidelity should not be undermined. The ending of the novel is analogous to the endings of Conrad's "Heart of Darkness" and Borges's
"Theme of the Traitor and the Hero," where legends of fidelity are
likewise preserved at the expense of truth. In *Nostromo*, however,
fidelity does, in fact, survive, though in a nonconventional way. Just as
it does not matter that Linda and not old Giorgio is the real keeper of the
symbol-making lighthouse, so it does not matter that the myth of the
Incorruptible is based not on the hero's integrity but on the "shaded
expression" of a woman's faithfulness. The fact that faithfulness exists
must be conveyed to people in a form that they can understand, and
the illustrious Capataz provides the most apt material for a legend.[23]
And the legend is, perhaps, morally true, even though, as in Borges's
"Emma Zunz," some of the circumstances are false, "the time, and one
or two proper names."[24]

The attitude assumed by Emilia Gould by the end of the novel is
equivalent to our response on the repeated reading, when we rectify
the former insufficiency of our attention to the psychological dimension of the narrative. The novel discourages our attempts to dwell on
its mise en scène: a careful sorting out of chronological reference, for
instance, will reveal fatal self-contradictions. According to one calculation, the Sulaco revolution takes place twenty-two years after Guzman
Bento's death, according to another—less than eight.[25] With a novelist
like Nabokov this would be a deliberate device; in Conrad it is, probably, another flaw in the "stupendous" canvas. In any case, however,
the chronological inconsistency may remind us that the political farce
of Costaguana is a dispensable stage setting and that the main concern

of the novel is with the struggle for a moral foothold amid the instabilities of the modern world.

Conrad's novels create test situations in which the beliefs and the secret liabilities of the characters become tragic. Thus Decoud's belief that "every conviction, as soon as it be[comes] effective, [turns] into that form of dementia the gods send upon those they wish to destroy" (188) leads to his own dementia and death when circumstances are created for it to become effective. None of the moral values in Conrad's worlds are successfully maintained without being occasionally abandoned:[26] the hypertrophy of the Augustan belief in the importance of reputation destroys Nostromo even as it defeats the moral skepticism of Dr. Monygham; while the obsessive Victorian belief in vigorous activity and "unselfish ambitions" destroys the human qualities of Charles Gould. By contrast, Emilia Gould remains faithful to humanistic ideals at the price of a temporary breach of loyalty to her husband—by denying him, for instance, the chance to recover the long-lost load of silver. Conrad's heroes must occasionally relinquish their "few simple ideas" in order to sustain them.

While the plot of *Nostromo* draws out the hidden flaws of the characters, its rhetoric draws out the equivalent intellectual liabilities of the reading process. The audience of *Nostromo* is made fully conscious of the need for a readjustment of its attention. Few individual readers, however, become aware of the multiple analogies between their responses and reorientations and those of the characters. Yet when such analogies *are* drawn and probed for meaning, they highlight the ideas that may otherwise remain insufficiently prominent, such as the possibility of choice and self-assertion as opposed to fatalistic determinism and the existence of the shaded fidelity that has resigned recognition. If parallel experience becomes an interpretive strategy, it may also support the reading of *Nostromo* as a philosophical novel, a battlefield where a Schopenhauerian pessimism is pitted against a Nietzchean concern for the future, where the moral improvisation of superheroes is balanced by a weary return to a few "simple ideas," and where determinist moods clash with an existentialist belief in free will.

PART TWO

The Temporary Suspension of Information

CHAPTER FOUR

Bleak House

"Not Quite So Straight, but Nearly"

> The first object of a novelist is to interest
> the reader; the next object is the quality
> of the interest. Interest in his story is
> essential, or he will not be read; but if the
> quality of the interest be not high, he will
> not be read a second time.
> —Bulwer-Lytton, "On Certain Princi-
> ples of Art in Works of Imagination"

Like most mid-nineteenth-century English novelists, Dickens believed
that the aim of his art was to negotiate social change and foster his
audience's capacity for sympathy. Though an individual writer's success in such endeavors cannot be measured in terms of actual improve-
ments in the civilization that he addresses, a large readership is usually
a prerequisite and a sign of influence. It was not merely for pecuniary
reasons that Dickens always kept an anxious watch over the numbers
of copies that his works sold. An advocate of public entertainment, he
felt an ideological commitment to providing its aesthetic equivalent in
literature. This commitment legitimized his use of such popular narrative conventions as obscure births, mysteries, recognitions, coincidences, tear-jerking deathbed scenes, and before-the-curtain happy
marriages. As is well known, however, he seldom failed to breathe
new life into conventions by endowing them with a specific thematic
significance.[1]

The entertainment value of *Bleak House* depends on its splendid
character types, on its fulfillment-cum-surprise approach to a series of
conventional expectations, yet also to a considerable extent on its
detective plot, a set of new narrative procedures that Dickens, a
contemporary of Edgar Allan Poe, can largely be credited with inventing. *Bleak House* is the precursor of modern detective fiction, yet it
differs from its later-day popular spin-offs in its subtle blending of

realistic, moral, aesthetic, and detective facets. Its detective interest is not given the pride of place, nor does it match the intellectual intricacy of Poe's Auguste Dupin stories, if only because it does not praise the power of human reason but reveals the powerlessness of reason when divorced from sympathy and will. More important still is that the detective interest of this novel is a means to an ethically oriented end.

In post-modernist novels of quest, for example, Nabokov's *The Real Life of Sebastian Knight* or Pynchon's *The Crying of Lot 49*, the process of detection tends to lead to an almost entropic fragmentation of the image of the object sought. Classical detective novels, still abundantly written and read these days, are characterized by the opposite movement, that of a progressive focusing on a one-line solution. *Bleak House* differs from both primarily in that the detective interest is limited to a relatively small portion (less than half) of its material. Within those limits it is a classical detective story, characterized by a process of convergence rather than fragmentation. And yet the one-line solution to which the detective plot line ultimately arrives is almost anticlimactic in comparison with the passions and errors involved in the process of detection.

The effects of the detective plot line in *Bleak House* are not confined to the material that belongs to it directly; rather, they irradiate, unevenly perhaps, upon the narrative as a whole. These effects may be considered both paradigmatically and syntagmatically. In paradigmatic terms, the process of detection constitutes a movement toward a comprehensive revelation of concealed coherences that demonstrate the interconnectedness of all the members of the troubled and divided society.[2] This, however, does not account for the specific aesthetic achievement of *Bleak House*, since there are few detective novels of minimal quality about which the same statement cannot be made. The uniqueness of—and the potentialities suggested by—the "hermeneutic code"[3] of this novel lie in its cathartic syntagmatic effect. In the bulk of the first reading, detective suspense partly eclipses the other spheres of interest and contributes to the formation of erroneous attitudes; by the end of the novel the audience has to readjust its view.[4] The errors that we are then forced to admit are a matter of an almost inevitable response to the entrapment of suspense-creating devices of the text rather than a matter of a "bad reading"; nevertheless, they display a meaningful similarity to the errors committed within the fictional world. On repeated readings our attention is distributed in a different way and, in quality, brought closer to the attitudes that the novel suggests as constructive alternatives to the moral misprisions that it explores.

Dickens does not resort to crude mystification. His chapters and monthly installments do not end arbitrarily ("in the most interesting place") with the villain raising his gun to shoot the hero or the jury foreman rising to announce the verdict. Nor does he use equivalents of such modern cinematographic techniques as keeping the camera away from the message that spurs the hero into action or from the scene that frightens the ingenue.[5] In *Bleak House* the balance between the information withheld and the information provided is maintained through cognitive principles that limit the privilege of the narrators.

A conventional restriction on how much the narrator can tell is observed in portions of the novel narrated "in the first person" by Esther Summerson: here the novel takes advantage of the first-person narrator's prerogative not to divulge more information than she herself possesses at a given moment in the represented time. In other words, the delay in revealing the secrets of, for instance, Esther's birth or Krook's weird sense of power is sanctioned by focalization.

By contrast, the cognitive principle of the third-person narrator is tailor-made for *Bleak House*. This narrator seems relatively ubiquitous but not literally "omniscient":[6] he avoids detailed inside views, frequently refers to characters as sources of his information, "writes entirely in the present tense, as if the action were just unfolding before his eyes," and on many occasions "describes actions and persons in terms of their appearance or their effect on others"—Tulkinghorn's murder is, for instance, "described as a shot which disturbs a few passers by."[7] Given this quasijournalistic cognitive principle, the narrative erases the distinction between the delay of information and the delay of action: secrets are kept by the novel's reticent characters and their revelation is made dependent on the timing of these characters' narrative acts.

The location of the disclosures in the narrative is, of course, influenced not only by plot events but also by the multiplot structure of the novel. Narrative shifts from one plot line or micro-setting to another are often perceived as retarding devices that prolong the movement toward disclosures. The shifts usually occur between chapters, and, while they seem to delay revelations, they often, paradoxically, foreshadow them.

The first abrupt shift takes place between chapters 1 and 2, in the transition from the world of Chancery to the world of fashion, which, the narrator says, "is not so unlike the Court of Chancery, but that we may pass from the one scene to the other, as the crow flies" (10).[8] The latter idiom, meaning "in a straight line," "in the shortest way," suggests a connection between the two settings. Presently, indeed, the crow flies out of the dead metaphor and appears on stage in the person of the "bird of ill omen," Mr. Tulkinghorn, the lawyer who reports on the development of the Chancery suit to Sir Leicester and Lady Dedlock.

Some time later, a nonmetaphorical crow flies "across Chancery Lane and Lincoln's Inn Garden, into Lincoln's Inn Fields" (119), leading the camera eye from Mr. Snagsby's shop to the residence of Mr. Tulkinghorn (other cases of the realization of metaphors, that is, of turning metaphors into literal events, are Krook's spontaneous combustion and Esther's becoming physically "marked" or "scarred" after her illness[9]). A page later, "Mr. Tulkinghorn goes, as the crow came—not quite so straight, but nearly" (120) to Mr. Snagsby's. The new simile refers to Mr. Tulkinghorn's subterfuge. At the same time it self-reflexively refers to the devious course that, as if in imitation of Tulkinghorn, is occasionally taken by the narrative itself. The narrative is "not quite so straight" with the reader when the camera eye half overlooks the things that take place on the periphery of the scenes. However, the parallel between the conduct of the fictional characters and a technique of the authorial narrator is here much vaguer than analogous cautionary parallels (discussed in the following two chapters) in Austen's *Emma* and Fielding's *Tom Jones*.

This technique of *implied simultaneity* is based on the virtual rather than the actual omnipresence of the third-person narrator. Though the narrator seems to be granted the power of changing his location in the fictional world, within the chapters, at any given moment, the scope of his camera eye is denied spherical comprehensiveness and made subject to common human limitations. While the camera eye follows the movements of some of the characters on the stage of the action, the simultaneous movements of other characters remain outside—but only just—its field of vision: the camera closes up on only one segment of space at a time, often being impelled to follow a more salient movement. For instance, while Krook diverts Tulkinghorn from the late Nemo's portmanteau, Tulkinghorn diverts the camera eye from the exact movements of Krook:

> "Call out for Flite, will you?" says Krook, with his lean hands spread out above the body like a vampire's wings.

Mr. Tulkinghorn hurries to the landing, and calls, "Miss Flite! Flite! Make haste, here, whoever you are! Flite!" Krook follows him with his eyes, and, while he is calling, finds opportunity to steal to the old portmanteau, and steal back again. [125]

The narrator's repeated use of the word "steal" in the meaning of "move on the sly" suggests that Krook may have realized another metaphor by actually stealing something from the portmanteau. The camera eye fails to register the details, yet the ensuing four references to the portmanteau as the object of Mr. Tulkinghorn's particular attention (126, 127, and 129), prevent us from forgetting the presence of a gap.

The technique of implied simultaneity provides a kind of alibi for the third-person narrator—"not quite so straight, but nearly." It also points to informational gaps. In the episode that lays the groundwork for the novel's first major enigma, Lady Dedlock becomes strangely agitated while Mr. Tulkinghorn is making his routine report on the Jarndyce and Jarndyce case:

My Lady, changing her position, sees the papers on the table—looks at them nearer—looks at them nearer still—asks impulsively:
"Who copied that?"
Mr Tulkinghorn stops short, surprised by my Lady's animation and her unusual tone. [16]

The words "impulsively," "surprised," "animation," "unusual tone" contrast with the motif of boredom that has so far accompanied Lady Dedlock. The repetition of the words "looks at them nearer" produces the impression of the camera eye closing in upon the document on the table. The asyndetic construction reenacts the withholding of information about the cause of Lady Dedlock's sudden interest. The sense of an enigma is then promoted by the further development:

Mr Tulkinghorn reads again. The heat is greater, my Lady screens her face. Sir Leicester doses, starts up suddenly, and cries, "Eh? what do you say?"
"I say I am afraid," says Mr Tulkinghorn, who has risen hastily, that Lady Dedlock is ill." (16)

The phrase "the heat is greater" is equivocal: while accounting for Lady Dedlock's faintness it also suggests the growth of emotional tension. As the camera eye settles on Sir Leicester, it misses (implied simultaneity) Lady Dedlock's sinking and the lawyer's prompt reaction to it. Sir Leicester's utterance shows that Tulkinghorn has just said something that has not been recorded in the narrative. Even when Tulkinghorn repeats his remark, thereby supplying the omitted information, we feel that something has been concealed, though not, perhaps, in the account of the scene itself.

The technique of implied simultaneity, in which the camera eye focuses—"not quite so straight, but nearly"—on one line of movement and misses the ramifications of the simultaneous peripheral activities, is, in a sense, homomorphous with the experience of a number of characters in *Bleak House*. It is also a miniature model of audience response to the first reading of this novel: one tends to concentrate, not exclusively but to a large extent, on a salient movement of the plot, the movement toward the solution of the enigmas. This automatic privileging of the detective interest is what will create the need for a readjustment.

The narrative of *Bleak House* contains a number of gaps that are eventually filled. When the presence of these temporary gaps is conspicuous, they are perceived as enigmas (or, given an admixture of the Gothic flavor, as mysteries): why does Lady Dedlock overreact to the handwriting of a legal document and Mr. Guppy to her portrait? Who are Esther Summerson's parents? What is the nature of her relationship with Jarndyce? Why does the illiterate Krook boast of his familiarity with the spelling of Jarndyce's name? Who is Nemo? Who has killed Mr. Tulkinghorn? The enigmas underlie the novel's chain-like suspense: a new riddle emerges as soon as—or just before—the previous one has been solved.

The chain of enigmas usurps a greater part of our attention on the first reading, largely diverting us from the complexity of character portrayal and from the pervasive thematic analogies between separate plot lines and scenes. The resulting tendency to treat characters as stereotypes geared up to action, is, as I shall attempt to show, eventually brought to our attention and "purged" by the rhetoric of the novel. On the other hand, the postponement of the recognition of thematic patterns has no cathartic significance since comprehensive pattern recognition naturally depends on our being familiar with the text as a whole. Suspense even justifies the deferral of the audience's quest for meaning and provides welcome "rest areas"—it is seldom admitted that at times one has to work hard in order to follow Dickens's texts. Indeed, the famous first paragraphs of *Bleak House* are no light entertainment; a masterpiece of poetic prose and, like the overture of an opera, an intricate compendium of the novel's main motifs, they must be read slowly. The ensuing scene within the Court of Chancery plunges us into an almost Faulknerian confusion, as if the discourse were pervaded by the fog that it describes. On the first reading we cannot make sense of the lawyers' mumbling; it is not clear whether the chancellor must decide on the fate of a girl, or a boy, or both, whether the guardian to be appointed is the wards' cousin or uncle, and whether or in what way these people are related to the Mr. Jarndyce who has committed suicide. Since the following chapter moves into a totally different setting, it is not even clear whether the Jarndyce family, the mad little old woman, the man from Shropshire, or the sallow prisoner are active characters of the novel or mere exempla of legal abuse. The information concerning them is too diffuse for gaps to develop into enigmas or to exert an influence on the focusing of our attention.

Thus it is not at once that Dickens allows suspense to become coercive. As Fielding does at the beginning of *Tom Jones,* only less explicitly, he allows seekers of crude entertainment to take an early leave of the novel. The quality of the interest to which his work appeals is not entirely a matter of suspense-free rereadings: it is not before the end of chapter 2 that the first coercive enigma is formed as Lady Dedlock's reserve breaks down at the sight of a document copied in a familiar hand.

The chapter (which is approximately in the middle of the monthly installment) closes on this enigmatic note, and the narrative shifts away, intriguingly, from the Dedlock house to the story of Esther Summerson. We are now faced with another enigma, that of Esther's birth, but the new hermeneutic interest fades in proportion to Esther's progress toward a degree of contentment. Esther's own wish to know the identity of her mother loses its intensity as soon as she finds the affection that she was denied while living with her godmother. Hence her narrative arouses not suspense but a sympathetic wondering ("wonder" being one of the most frequently recurring words of chapter 3) about what fate has in store for her.[10] However, by placing her narrative immediately after the emergence of Lady's Dedlock's enigma (an "as the crow flies" transition, similar to the transition between chapters 1 and 2) Dickens makes us suspect, at least subliminally, a connection between the two women. Eventually, Esther's anticipatory remarks (for instance, about the handkerchief that she leaves in the brickmaker's cottage) as well as the recurrent motifs of absent, inefficient, bereaved, or wrongheaded mothers, suggest, with ever increasing force, that she must be Lady Dedlock's child.

This suggestion is reinforced by cases of uncanny anagnorisis: Mr. Guppy recognizes something in Lady Dedlock's portrait and Trooper George in Esther's face; the sight of Lady Dedlock arouses strange feelings in Esther; and Ada mistakes Lady Dedlock's voice for that of Esther. Meanwhile, other elements of the hermeneutic code punctuate the narrative: Mr. Tulkinghorn's suspicions, his sadistic game with Lady Dedlock, his discovery of Nemo, his interest in Nemo's portmanteau, Lady Dedlock's excitement and anxiety, the missing-person case (Captain Hawdon), a lady's visit to the slum graveyard where Nemo is buried, Hortense's passionate appeal to Esther for employment, Guppy's courtship of Esther and his interest in Krook's shop, his interview with Lady Dedlock, her ensuing lamentation, and so on.

We learn to expect such clues in most of the episodes. Accordingly, we tend to regard the episodes belonging to subplots as occasions for the planting of clues. For instance, the scenes of the Chadbands' visit to the Snagsbys or Trooper George's to the Smallweeds appear to acquire a significance beyond social satire only when Mrs. Chadband turns out to have been Esther's nurse, Mrs. Rachael, and when Trooper George turns out to have served Captain Hawdon, whom we begin to identify with Nemo. In the first reading one generally tends to be satisfied with the most obvious single raison d'être for the narrative details; and the detective interest provides this raison d'être. Secondary plot lines therefore tend to attract less attention for their own sake and to be perceived as retardatory. The delays that they create are often unwelcome on the first reading, especially since their comic element is rather sinister—as befits a prophetic adumbration of the power wielded by the lower middle-class characters who inhabit the novel's somber urban microcosms. Dickens was sometimes criticized for the so-called "episodic intensification";[11] such criticism is symptomatic of the audience's tendency to miss the thematic analogies of the subplots with the main lines of action on the first reading.

On the first reading suspense is largely responsible for deferring our awareness of the comprehensiveness and coherence with which the novel catalogues various forms of parasitism (the maggot or ghoullike existence of the lawyers, the abuses of the Chancery, sponging, usury, emotional exploitation, and so on)[12] and various forms of constructive "opting out"[13] from pseudosymbiosis. It must be noted, however, that the comic element of the novel produces a similar effect. It is not at once that we notice, for example, that the funnily boring Mrs.

Bayham Badger plays an important role in the novel's thematic structure: all three of her husbands, Captain Swosser, Professor Dingo, and Dr. Badger, are self-made men with shipshape professional careers; their comic names (in Dickens's novels successful citizens can afford to let us laugh at them) suggest the absence of high connections that could have smoothed their way. The entertainment value and the retardatory effect of the episodes involving Mrs. Badger deflect our attention from the light that they shed on Richard's prospects: inauspicious beginnings need not prevent a person from professional achievement, from rising to a position that commands respect. For Mrs. Badger ethics matters more than income: it is she who suggests that Richard, a negligent apprentice, should discontinue his studies of medicine. Yet it is only on a rereading that we appreciate the contrast between this lady's brand of professionalism and that of the novel's bureaucratic institutions, whose main business is to make business for themselves.

In their inexperience and impatience Esther, Richard, and Ada ignore the significance of the examples set by Mrs. Badger's husbands. "I get too much of Mrs. Bayham Badger's first and second," says Richard to Ada, and her reply is "I am sure *that's* very natural. . . . The very thing we both said yesterday, Esther!" (208). Their response to her garrulousness is thus, to some extent, parallel to the audience's wish to get on with the plot and postpone the recognition of the patterns of significance. Yet deferral of thematic analogies characterizes the reading of most "thick" novels, exceptions being the novels which, like Solzhenitsyn's *Cancer Ward*, pointedly use thematic analogies and contrasts as the basis for the sequence of the episodes. The crucial transformation of audience response in *Bleak House* lies, rather, in the interaction of suspense with character portrayal.

On the first reading of the novel there is an obvious parallel between our detective watchfulness and the obsessive watchfulness of a number of characters. At one point or another most of the characters come to feel that something is being withheld from them.[14] The effects of the resulting agitation go beyond the moments of the characters' perplexity that makes the audience aware of gaps. Not only Tulkinghorn and Bucket, but also Mrs. Snagsby, Guppy, Hortense, and Grandfather Smallweed undertake detective investigations. On the other hand, the watchfulness of Lady Dedlock, Jo, Snagsby, and Richard Carstone develops into panic, disorientation, or paranoia.

Excessive and selective watchfulness is a symptom of suspense. In life, as in the reading of fiction, suspense is a state of uncertainty combined with an anxiousness to pursue one single path of interest. It is accompanied by an impatience with distraction, deviation, or delay. Like obsession, suspense impairs the clarity of one's vision and leads to psychological traps. The characters of Bleak House tend to become spellbound and insensible to everything except one fear or one hope.[15] Suspense blinds Tulkinghorn to the violent hatred of Hortense, Hortense to expediency and caution, and Lady Dedlock to the genuine quality of her husband's love.

Under the influence of suspense the audience is likewise led into mistakes of judgment. As noted above, very early in the novel we begin to suspect that Lady Dedlock is Esther Summerson's mother. From then on, no episodes grip our attention as forcefully as those that promote this surmise or promise its confirmation. When the confirmation arrives, we congratulate ourselves on a perspicacious guess and feel encouraged to make another one as soon as Tulkinghorn's murder creates a new enigma (an analogous effect is produced by the Elton affair in Austen's Emma). The juxtaposition of events and the evidence that Bucket seems to have accumulated point to Lady Dedlock as Tulkinghorn's murderer. Now the detective clues hold our attention more strongly than the memories of Lady Dedlock's self-denying kindness to Rosa and the notes of pain and remorse in her confession to Esther. In the episode of her interview with Guppy, the influence of the hermeneutic code is reinforced by the fleeting allusion to medieval power games: "Young man of the name of Guppy! There have been times, when ladies lived in strongholds, and had unscrupulous attendants within call, when that poor life of yours would not have been worth a minute's purchase, with those beautiful eyes looking at you as they look at this moment" (361). The passage appeals to stock expectations that archetypal mistresses of "strongholds" could secretly go any length to avoid disgrace—especially if they have married for social position and are passionate, proud, and disdainful. Bucket's apparent suspicion of Lady Dedlock eventually "infects" the audience—"contagion," in both the literal and figurative senses, is an important motif of the novel, first introduced in "a general infection of ill-temper" in the second paragraph (5).[16] Whether or not we fully believe that Lady Dedlock is capable of murder (the doubt is significant), while Bucket is making his lengthy account of the detective investigation to Sir Leicester (636-46) we fully expect him to name her as the guilty party. We have, moreover, been maneuvered to trust his professional prowess—the truth of his disclosures is not, it seems, to be questioned. Therefore, when Bucket announces that the murderer is Hortense

(647-48 ff), we are relieved and disconcerted at the same time: relieved because we have all along been unwilling to suspect Esther's mother, and disconcerted because we have nevertheless done so when the hermeneutic clues blocked the conflicting suggestions of the semic code.

Soon after the disclosure, we are presented with Lady Dedlock's letter, which explains her conduct by her wish for a *coup de grâce* (666-67) and by her sense of guilt: a complex character is now allowed to emerge forcefully from behind a stereotypical façade. The precise information about Lady Dedlock's choice of death over indignity (a stance reminiscent of Hardy's heroines and symptomatic of a cultural impasse—Dickens seems to be critical of it even while he admires it) comes at the right time to promote a new kind of suspense—the suspense of the rescue operation.

It may be argued that up to the moment of Bucket's disclosures Lady Dedlock's character has been presented in stereotypic terms and that the detective suspense did not reduce the force of clues to the depth of her character because such clues were insufficient in the first place. A rereading of the first half of the novel, however, clearly indicates that Dickens's satire on the upper classes is discontinued as soon as the camera eye closes in on Lady Dedlock, that she displays not only a passionate nature but also an emotional delicacy concealed by the mask of supercilious boredom. On the first reading the audience is definitely maneuvered into forming a reductive attitude. The means of entrapment are mainly the hermeneutic clues (circumstantial evidence and Bucket's conduct) whose force is bolstered by flattery, by appeal to the archetype of the ruthless aristocratic lady, and by a complex of red-herring foreshadowings with a logic of their own.[17] The chain of Gothic motifs in *Bleak House*—the legend of "The Ghost's Walk," the foreshortened allegory on Tulkinghorn's ceiling pointing through the window at a woman on her way to the graveyard, the ominous allusions in the Guppy interview, "the dark road" that Lady Dedlock mentions in her confessions to Esther, the precarious self-control that she displays in her interviews with the sadistic Tulkinghorn—is felt to move, inexorably, to its culmination in a fatal act to be committed by Lady Dedlock. Yet we are too ready to infer that this act would be aggressive. In fact, violence does not participate in the composition of Lady Dedlock's character. Even the commentary that intrudes into the account of her interview with Guppy is ambiguous: when in the apostrophe to Guppy the narrator affects to warn him that in olden times "that poor life of [his] would not have been worth a minute's purchase, with those beautiful eyes looking at [him] as they look at this moment" (361), it is not entirely clear whether Lady Dedlock's eyes are, indeed, looking "at" Guppy or "at the moment," whether, that is, the latter clause is a modifier of time or a prepositional object. The former meaning suggests itself on the first reading of the novel; the latter is rather more acceptable on the rereading, when we know that Lady Dedlock is trying to face the long-delayed moment of truth, much as she may despise Guppy as its catalyst. The syntactic ambiguity here is Dickens's prophylaxis against the charge of a blatant misleading.

The violence necessary for the act of murder is channeled to the character of the maid Hortense. It must be admitted that Dickens's handling of this detective entanglement and its "the-butler-did-it" type of solution is not unproblematic. Though Hortense has good reason to hate Tulkinghorn, her motivation is not sufficiently elaborated. Her violence is foreshadowed earlier in the novel (143), which, however, is likewise a somewhat trivial kind of prophylaxis. There are, however, two narrative features that redeem the detective solution of *Bleak House*.

One of them is a sort of oneiric logic—the good-looking yet somewhat ferocious servant, whose name begins with the same two letters as the name Honoria and whose height and figure reproduce those of Lady Dedlock, turns into a dark projection of her mistress: the Roman allegory on Tulkinghorn's ceiling points not only at Honoria Dedlock on her way to the graveyard but also at Hortense's clothes, which she is wearing for disguise. The next time Lady Dedlock goes the same way, she will wear the clothes of her other avatar, the brickmaker's wife, "the mother of the dead child" (713).

The other feature that makes the casting of Hortense in the role of the murderess acceptable is the thematic significance of such a development. In *Bleak House* the conventions of mysterious parentage and of the eventual convergence of different plot lines emphasize the idea of the connection between people in different walks of life as well as the idea of their shared lack of immunity to whatever is rotten in their state. The role of Hortense is part of the pattern that includes the convergence of the Snagsbys, the Smallweeds, and the Chadbands in the Dedlock house on the day of the crisis, the mysterious influence of Krook, the bungling fussiness of Guppy, the menacing forefinger of Bucket, and the humorless steadiness of Necket. The seemingly marginal lower middle classes (the small weeds and the insignificant guppies whose full force is to be appreciated only when they form the extreme right movements in the twentieth century) are gaining as deadly a power over the upper classes as they do over laborers like

Guster or Charley. The Dedlocks and the Jarndyces are oblivious to the rise of the sinister force; and this oblivion is enacted by the audience when, on the first reading, it perceives the episodes devoted to the Smallweeds, the Chadbands, and their likes as occasions for detective clues and retardatory exercises in grotesque comedy.

Thus the solution of the detective mystery highlights two errors of attitude into which the audience has been led by the automatic selectiveness of its interest and attention: insufficient attention to the comic monsters and injustice to the tragic heroine. The former reenacts the collective Rip Van Winkle lethargy of the upper and upper-middle classes of the novel; the latter is analogous to individual errors of judgment—Jarndyce's treatment of Skimpole as an archetypal Peter Pan; Richard's treatment of Jarndyce as an archetypal litigant; Sir Leicester's treatment of Tulkinghorn and Bucket as archetypal retainers and of Mr. Rouncewell as a Watt Tyler; and the Ironmaster's indiscriminate retaliatory resentments. Lady Dedlock commits a similar error when she fails to see that her husband's love for her does not depend entirely on the splendid image that she is determined to project; and Sir Leicester cannot escape it when for a moment he is misled by Bucket's red-herring suggestion of Lady Dedlock's guilt in the Tulkinghorn case. Most of these individual errors of judgment are symptomatic either of excessive class consciousness or of a cultural encapsulation from which the main characters of the novel attempt to break out. The reader's reorientation after the disclosures (and, in particular, on a rereading) is parallel to these attempts.

On the first reading, our reorientation includes change of attitude to Sir Leicester. Behind the stiffness and intellectual mediocrity of this absurd old gentleman, we find genuine love and generosity. Our surprise is qualified because the newly discovered features do not conflict with what we have seen of Sir Leicester so far, but our sympathy for him rests not only on his irreproachable conduct upon Bucket's disclosure. It is significantly promoted by the fact that we have been misled and then disabused by Bucket's discourse simultaneously with Sir Leicester; our suspense, our fear that Lady Dedlock will be charged with murder, our surprise and relief are *isochronic* with his experience (his prompt forgiveness of her past may to some extent be dictated by remorse for having for a moment admitted the thought that she might have killed the lawyer). In the bulk of later-day detective fiction isochronic parallel response is an almost automatic result of the presence of observer-narrators (like Dr. Watson) who tell the reader all they are supposed to have known at any given moment of the represented time.

Such fictions can delegate the construction of the mystified "confidants" to the sympathetic audience while the authors' creative energy is reserved for their impenetrable main heroes (Sherlock Holmes, Auguste Dupin, or Hercule Poirot).[18] In *Bleak House*, however, the parallel experience of suspense and its effects is usually not isochronic. The reader makes a mistake about Lady Dedlock under the influence of suspense, whereas Richard Carstone, likewise under the influence of suspense, makes an analogous mistake about Mr. Jarndyce—yet Richard's paranoia is presented in a totally different part of the novel.

The common denominator in the experience of the character and the reader is thus not merely an automatic by-product of suspense. The space covered in the first two chapters narrows down from the vast foggy haunts to the metaphorical fog of Chancery, to the mud and mire of Jarndyce and Jarndyce, and to the door through which the Chancellor exits in order to interview the still innocent Adam and Eve; it narrows from the world of fashion down to the Dedlock family, to their overheated parlor, and further down to a piece of paper on the table and the door from which Lady Dedlock is carried out of the room. This spacial focusing may suggest that the general realizes itself in the particular and is ultimately traceable to it. Social evils grow—"not quite so straight but nearly"—out of such imperfections in personal relationships as lack of sympathy, failure to discriminate between an individual and his predicament, the treatment of individuals—contrary to the ethical imperative—as means rather than as ends.[19] Almost every character of *Bleak House* turns out to be marked by these errors of attitude, which then spill over onto audience response.

Paradoxically, the abstraction of a moral conclusion about errors of attitude may further promote the tendency of identifying characters with their predicaments and treating them as functions, as means to didactic aims: intellectual activity is a well-known enemy of sympathetic response. Lest this should happen, the narrative creates new conditions for isochronic experience, so as to rekindle, for instance, our sympathy for Richard. When a conclusive will is discovered among Krook's belongings, we begin to share, in a microscopic way, Richard's hopes of a speedy termination of the Chancery suit—against our own and Mr. Jarndyce's better judgment. These hopes are duly thwarted, and we admit that they should never have been entertained. At about the same time Richard is shown finally accepting the validity of Jarndyce's uncompromising rejection of Chancery, its promises, delays, and suspense. It is partly due to the element of isochronic experience that when Richard, developing the metaphor that has accompanied him throughout the novel, finally "begin[s] the world" (763), he makes us pity him as a victim rather than judge him as a moral agent. This is also one of the ways in which the periodical thickening of chain-like suspense defers thematic analysis, while the periodical relaxation of the grip of suspense promotes melodramatic heightening and its appeal to sympathetic response.

Parallel features of audience response and the experience of the characters not merely highlight the similarity in the errors of attitude that underlie the corruption within the world of *Bleak House* but also suggest the virtual universality of these errors. The reading turns into a game in which the audience displays germs of tendencies that may become disastrous if developed outside the playground. Whether or not individual readers become conscious of the parallel between their own responses and those of the characters, they cannot escape a cathartic recognition of having had wrong impressions or expectations. A repeated reading is to some extent stimulated by the conscious need for a change of previous attitude and for a redistribution of attention between the different strands of the text.

On a repeated reading mystification creates a new dimension of interest: as in *The Sound and the Fury* and *Emma*, we enjoy being able to understand the details that formerly escaped our notice. For instance, we discover not only that Esther passes by the door of her father while he may still be alive (54-55) but also that her father may have copied the letters from Kenge and Carboy's that she used to get at Reading.[20] However, this line of interest (faintly analogous to the discovery of the secondary plot axis in *Emma*), extends to a very limited number of episodes.

The specific problem associated with the hermeneutic clues in *Bleak House* is that the suspense-creating devices that are so entertaining on the first reading may become transparent and may be perceived as arbitrary on a rereading. In particular, the hermeneutic code threatens the realism of character portrayal when the creation of gaps is delegated to the characters. Information is repeatedly delayed because the characters who possess it, Tulkinghorn, Bucket, and Jarndyce, do not hasten to divulge their secrets. Their reticence is, of course, a patent suspense-creating device. One may wonder, however, whether it is psychologically motivated, whether these characters profit or expect to profit by keeping the others in suspense, whether the behavior that involves the withholding of information is not gratuitous. I believe that the general impression is that the motivation of the characters is sufficient, though its exact nature may remain beneath the threshold of an individual reader's consciousness. I shall now draw together and process the results of various scholars' sporadic attempts to carry the psychology of the reticent characters over to this side of the threshold.

In *Bleak House* the motives for the characters' reticence are always grounded in specific features of their personalities. These features are integrated not only into the characters' psychological makeup but also into the novel's broader patterns of motifs. As the reticence of Tulking-horn, Bucket, and Jarndyce enters into conflict with other aspects of their identities, this conflict adds depth to their portraits and to the moral/psychological issues raised by the text. If the characters' reticence was initially devised as a means of prolonging suspense, Dickens did not leave it unexplored on the thematic plane.

Indeed, though Tulkinghorn's selective reticence and protracted cat-and-mouse game with Lady Dedlock seems uncharacteristic and unprofessional, it is clearly motivated by misogyny and class-conscious vindictiveness concealed beneath his dry manner.[21] Information is the content of Tulkinghorn's treasure chest and arsenal, and, where Lady Dedlock is concerned, he expends it in such a way as to inflict the greatest possible pain. Symptomatically, Tulkinghorn's favorite method of torture ("rack," as Lady Dedlock calls it, 666) is delay. He makes her wait for him, then makes her wait for him to act on his information—as if in imitation of the adjournments, vacations, and further adjournments in the Court of Chancery. Tulkinghorn's delay of information enters the pattern of variations on the motif of postpone-ments and delays that characterize the legal practice represented in the novel.

The secretiveness of the detective Bucket has an analogous motiva-tion and an analogous significance. Bucket's occasional surface kind-liness may at first seem to conflict with the brutality with which he denies information to people who are racked by suspense. Sadistically enjoying his power over a person of a higher social standing (whom he keeps pointedly addressing with his full title, "Sir Leicester Dedlock, Baronet"), Bucket drives Sir Leicester to a stroke by arbitrarily with-holding the name of the murderer in the disclosure episode (636-54), pretending to implicate Lady Dedlock ("What I have got to say, is about her Ladyship. She is the pivot it all turns on," 638), thus creating unbearable suspense.[22] The type of public disclosure where the ac-count of the detection flaunts the perspicacity of the sleuth, withholds the name of the culprit until the last moment, and ultimately turns the criminal into a victim is to be found in a multitude of later-day detective stories. An efficient means of prolonging suspense, it is also a way of self-assertion for a Hercule Poirot or an Ellery Queen.

Detective Bucket is not as much on the side of the angels as his later-day offspring. He may postpone George Rowncewell's arrest until after his friends' party (and thus, among other things, allow Dickens an opportunity to describe it) or attempt to divert Esther from her anxiety during the search for Lady Dedlock by criticizing Skimpole (and thus allow Dickens to protract the account of the search without making it tedious). Yet he remains unperturbed by having to arrest George on a false murder charge in order to trap the real murderer, nor will he say anything to allay the innocent man's anxieties. Even more callous is his treatment of Esther: he absolutely refuses to explain to her his surmises during their nocturnal search for Lady Dedlock, when Esther cannot understand why the direction of the search is suddenly changed. Esther thinks that with every minute she is leaving her mother further behind, yet Bucket answers her desperate appeals with his overbearing and self-congratulatory "you know me, don't you" (690), which promotes the curiosity of the reader but fails to reassure the heroine. Esther reaches such a stage of physical and mental exhaustion that when she mistakes Lady Dedlock for the brickmaker's wife, "the mother of the dead child" (713), the dead child of the brickmaker becomes, in more ways than one, a metaphor for herself. The delay of information about the course taken by Lady Dedlock is thus conducive not only to suspense but also to a complex epiphany. Yet whatever rhetorical feats are achieved through it, this delay is an act of cruelty on Bucket's part. And such cruelty is in tune with his conduct on other occasions: Bucket subdues Sir Leicester by leading him to falsely suspect his wife of murder, enjoys the feeling of superiority over the credulous Jarndyce who has failed to gauge Skimpole, is vengefully brutal to George Rowncewell and coldly brutal to the sick crossing-sweeper Jo, whose only crime is to have been on the spot where, realizing another metaphor, other people's paths repeatedly cross. Bucket is the forefather of the sagacious logical detectives as well as of the dark-clad indefatigable and ubiquitous sleuths who soak in the rain and cut through the winds in a multitude of paperbacks and movies, but he is also the ancestor of Porphiry Petrovich in *Crime and Punishment* and Mikulin in *Under Western Eyes*, characters who represent an impersonal Kafkaesque bureaucratic force yet enter into an oppressively personal, slightly sadistic and slightly amorous relationships with their victims.

Even the kindly Jarndyce inflicts pain by delaying information. At the end of the novel his task is to arrange for the survivors of the plot to live more or less happily ever after. For this purpose he must renounce his love for Esther and allow her to marry Allan Woodcourt. The slightly artificial sweet-and-sour ending based on Jarndyce's inexhaustible generosity is partly salvaged by a surprise gap: as Jarndyce takes Esther on a tour of the miniature Bleak House that he has prepared for Woodcourt far away from his own residence, he delays telling her that he intends to set her free from her engagement to himself so that she could marry Woodcourt. Jarndyce has always fled from the gratitude to which he was entitled, and this final piece of mystification allows him to revel in his generosity without eliciting any embarrassing expressions of that sentiment from Esther. Yet while his mystification is in progress, it subjects Esther to all the mental torment of renouncing love.[23] She cries on the night before the visit to the house and cannot persuade herself that she is crying with pleasure at her guardian's generosity ("I hope it was with pleasure, though I am not quite sure it was with pleasure," 750). Unconsciously Jarndyce seems to be taking his little revenge on Esther by making her undergo the painful experience that has fallen to his own lot. The somewhat cruel delay makes the ending of the novel more acceptable not only because the surprise diverts the reader from the patness of its poetic justice but also because the touch of sublimated resentment on the part of Jarndyce judiciously qualifies his otherwise incredible absolute goodness.[24] Jarndyce's withholding of information is, moreover, in keeping with a delay of which he has been guilty previously: the delay of Ada's and Richard's marriage. Jarndyce adheres to the conventional practice of postponing marriages until the prospective husbands have made their fortunes or careers and have ready-made comfortable homes for their wives. It is therefore natural for him not to let Esther know that she is to marry Woodcourt before she has seen the prospects of their well-being. Richard's earlier resentment of Jarndyce is hence not completely unjustified: unlike Ada, Jarndyce does not see the cruelty of leaving Richard to struggle on his own. Jarndyce has not, it seems, completely escaped the taint of the Chancery suit.[25] He is not free from the tendency to reduce human situations to social or economic categories and to ignore the extent of the individual anguish behind conventional social roles.

Delay, whether of action or of information, is thus invariably associated with the motif of cruelty, personal or institutionalized. It is due to a series of delays caused by personal sadism that Lady Dedlock's death is not averted: Sir Leicester suffers a stroke as a result of Bucket's maliciousness and therefore fails to prevent his wife's flight; the brick-maker's wife is too terrified of her husband's brutality to tell Esther the true destination of Lady Dedlock; and Guster cannot give Esther and Bucket directions with sufficient promptness because she has been driven into a fit by Mrs. Snagsby's blows. When Esther finds her mother, she seems to have come just a moment too late.

On the other hand, the delays responsible for the ruin of Richard Carstone stem from the impersonal cruelty of social institutions, from their traditional inefficiency and procrastination, from the inexorable vacations of the Court of Chancery and its interminable adjournments of the lucrative case. The common denominator of these two kinds of cruelty is the emotional or financial preying on a captive victim, a variety of the parasitism that reduces its human victims from ends in themselves to means for other ends. Delays, and the cruelty that causes them, form one of the motifs that cluster around the novel's central theme of parasitic exploitation much like ramifications of meaning cluster around the central symbol in a poetic work.

Whereas during the first reading, under the influence of suspense-generating delays of information, we reenact the mistakes of the characters, on a rereading our response is most closely parallel to that of the character who epitomizes the novel's system of positive values. This character is, of course, Esther Summerson, the keeper of Bleak House.

The structure of *Bleak House* is iconically reproduced in the following description of the eponymous building: "It was one of those delightfully irregular houses where you go up and down steps out of one room into another, and where you come upon more rooms when you think you have seen all there are, and where there is a bountiful provision of little halls and passages, and where you find still older cottage-rooms in unexpected places, with lattice windows and green growth pressing through them. Mine, which we entered first, was of this kind, with an up-and-down roof, that had more corners in it than I ever counted afterwards, and a chimney . . . paved all round with pure white tiles, in every one of which a bright miniature of the fire was blazing" (62).

What with its miniatures of the fire blazing in white tiles, Jarn-dyce's house is a case of *mise en abîme*, a miniature structure within a structure.[26] The novel itself is "delightfully irregular": we go "up and down" the social ladder from episode to episode and come upon more characters and human situations when we think we have "seen all there are." Esther's room, or life, with its uneven, up-and-down ceiling of expectations, has indeed "more corners" than can be counted: critical inquiry continually discovers new patterns of significance, psychological motivations, and uncanny impulses in her portrait.[27] The numerous little halls, doorways, and passages where "you might, if you came out at another door (every room had at least two doors), go straight down to the hall again by half-a-dozen steps and a low archway, wondering how you got back there, or had ever got out of it" (63) are appropriate symbols of detective clues.

The novel is permeated with imagery related to houses, building, architecture, closed spaces, and so on. Richard Carstone uses an image of an unfinished house to explain his predicament to Esther: "If you lived in an unfinished house, you couldn't settle down in it" (288); Skimpole uses the rhyme about "The house that Jack built" to explain his betrayal of Jo (728). The working class is represented, appropriately, by the brickmakers. The novel's catalogue of dwellings, philanthropic housecalls, and different modes of housekeeping includes, for instance, Woodcourt's exploration of the sanitary conditions of slum districts, the "telescopic philanthropy" (34) that creates a havock in Mrs. Jellyby's home, the irresponsibility that moves the mortgaged furniture in and out of Skimpole's lodgings, the accumulation of trash and treasure in Krook's rag-and-bottle shop, the money boxes of Grandfather Smallweed, and the document cases of Chancery lawyers.[28]

The motifs of the ordering of space, arranging and controlling one's environment, form a pattern that is homomorphic with the delay and disclosure of information in *Bleak House.* Just as every room in Bleak House has at least two doors, so each separate episode of the novel has at least two functions, a detective and a thematic one. In the first reading, under the influence of suspense, we neglect to open many of the doors: the emerging informational gaps lure us to the dark passageways where what we meet is poorly perceived.

On a rereading our attention is no longer subverted by the hermeneutic code. It is much more carefully distributed between the details of the novel's world, creating it, as it were, from the inside. This experience is comparable to that of Bachelard's housewife, who, by polishing objects, revives them, illuminates them by her attention, thus creating the house from within.[29]

Esther Summerson, with her housekeeping keys and her homely nicknames, is an archetypal mistress of the house. The house is metaphoric as well as literal. At first glance it may appear that the predominance of the motif of houses and housekeeping that accompany Esther's image are symptomatic of the cultural limitations that Dickens may have shared with his patriarchal Victorian society. The case, however, is more complex. Like Charlotte Brontë and George Eliot, Dickens sketches the social confines in which women are placed; yet these writers also show the ways in which the heroines explore their limited possibilities, actively seeking available channels of self-actualization. Jane Eyre's search of her desk drawers lest she leave anything behind in Lowood is symbolic of this exploration. Yet an even more important feature, which Dickens shares with George Eliot, is the implicit belief that the career, whether of a man or of a woman, should be a matter of a vocation rather than of a job. Throughout his novels Dickens contrasts a portrait gallery of characters who disconnect their professional or business lives from private lives and slip into various kinds of dehumanizing officialdom (from the comical Wemmick of *Great Expectations* to the sinister Vholes of *Bleak House*) with the portrait gallery of characters who, like the comic Bayham Badger, the idealistic Woodcourt, or the philanthropic Jarndyce, turn their professional or public activities into extensions of their genuine interests and domestic attitudes (though not always of domestic virtues). A vocation, it is implied, must stem from the same qualities of an individual's inner being that animate his or her home life—hopefully, from the care and sensitivity without which a house can really become bleak. Dickens relates social evils not just to flaws in personal relationships but aso to their derivative, that is, to the divorce of public functioning from private life.

Hence the centrality of Esther's character in *Bleak House*. Despite a touch of conciliatory neurosis stemming from her unhappy childhood, Esther is shown developing constructive attitudes that irradiate from the center of her being, through her private life, upon the community that forms her environment. What singles her out from other characters is her critical self-scrutiny. The power of keen observation, which qualifies Esther to be an engaging teller of her tale, is related to her attentiveness to detail, and her attentiveness is qualitatively different from the watchfulness of predators like Tulkinghorn or paranoids like Richard and Snagsby. Esther is critically watchful of herself. She has internalized the scriptural warning quoted by her dying godmother, "Watch ye therefore! lest coming suddenly he find you sleeping. And what I say unto you, I say unto all, Watch!" (21). In the context of *Bleak House* this warning is an injunction to watch one's conscience rather than the movements of an outside enemy or prey. Esther indeed, is constantly monitoring her interests and emotions so as not to fail in gratitude, claim more than her due, or neglect opportunities of active kindness.

Esther's attempts to suppress the feelings aroused in her by Allan Woodcourt or to discipline herself in her godmother's spirit may be morbid, yet they are not imprudent or inhibiting. Nor is Dickens unaware of the strain that they impose on her. She tries to convince herself that she has no autonomous private life, exerts her will power, and cheerfully goes about the household duties—in anticlimactic endings of emotionally charged scenes we find her literally and metaphorically jingling the housekeeping keys (215). Yet when her consciousness is blocked by the delirium of her fever, the keys are transformed into a string of burning beads (432): Esther feels that she is one of these beads and vainly begs to be released from the rest, groaning under the burden of responsibilities and connections. Upon her recovery, however, she reaffirms the responsibilities and connections, and blames herself when, torn between romantic love and affectionate gratitude, she fails to notice a similar plight in Ada.

It is, of course, Dickens's wish to surprise us with Ada's clandestine marriage to Richard that generates Esther's temporary ignorance of it: she would not have been justified in withholding this information if she had possessed it. Yet even here the novelist has made a virtue of necessity: the touch of egocentricity followed by remorse makes Esther's character more credible and appealing. Her self-criticism is, moreover, parallel to, though not isochronic with, the self-critical attitude that the novel demands of its audience.

A repeated reading reenacts Esther's opting out of suspense. Very early in her life Esther understands that her interest in her origins is a wish to break out from the emotional vacuum into which she has been placed by her godmother's rigor. With an effort of the will she gives up her search for her mother as soon as she is assured of Ada's and Jarndyce's affection. Just as Jarndyce refuses to be held in suspense by Chancery, Esther proclaims her freedom from the mystery of the past and her complete trust in him: "I am quite sure that if there were anything I ought to know, or had any need to know, I should not have to ask you tell it to me" (92), she says to him on an early occasion.

Esther's attention to her environment does not have the sifting quality that neglects lighted rooms for the sake of intriguing passageways. Nor does she use mystery to escape from the sight of misery: she joins Jarndyce in the investigation of those recesses of her environment where people's lots can be alleviated by concrete personal intervention. Like Richard, she lives in an unfinished house, an imperfect world, yet she spends her time trying to introduce some order into it. Whereas Jo, from whom she catches the fever and whose fate, but for the kindness of Jarndyce, she might have shared, sweeps a symbolic crossing in the street, Esther "sweep[s] the cobwebs" (90) in interior spaces, in the home lives of the people with whom she comes into contact. She cleans up the closets of Caddy Jellyby and helps her make a new home, accompanies Jarndyce on his visits to the Neckett children, brings a touch of human warmth to the house of the brickmakers and to the room of Miss Flite, comforts Ada and Richard in their lodgings during their brief and painful marriage. In one way or another all the people to whom she reaches out are centripetally drawn to her well-kept and no longer "Bleak" House, showing what kind of charity really begins at home.

On a rereading we are, like Esther, in a position to introduce order into the vast areas covered by the novel, probe more fully the meaning of human experience that it evokes, establish spatial links between characters and locations, structural links between motifs, thematic links between episodes. Repeated readings of *Bleak House*, readings during which the hermeneutic code no longer seduces our interest, clear the fog that reigns at the beginning of the novel, and effect a reorientation that goes a long way toward promoting the system of norms that Esther shares with her implied author. It was the historical author's hope that his readers would act on such a constructive system of values in their own lives, sallying forth, like Esther and Jarndyce, from the safety of their house to the haunts of misery that move into their ken. The house that serves as the novel's central symbol would then expand its sphere of influence beyond the channel of communication between the fictional world of the characters and the actual world of the reader.

CHAPTER FIVE

Emma
"Double Dealing" — Or Triple?

> I knew a councellor and secretary, that
> never came to Queen Elizabeth of Eng-
> land with bills to sign, but he would
> always first put her into some discourse
> of estate, that she mought the less mind
> the bills.
>
> —Francis Bacon, "On Cunning"

The plot of Jane Austen's *Emma* is constructed around a surprise gap: the fact there is a secret engagement between two of the novel's characters, Jane Fairfax and Frank Churchill, is withheld for a long time, yet on the first reading we are practically unaware of the omission until the suspended information is divulged. Then we realize that the texture of the preceding portion of the narrative is considerably richer than it has seemed to be. The disclosure is so well prepared that it seems to spell out what we should have known for a long while: we have been offered almost all the necessary *fabula* facts yet prevented from seeing their significance for nearly the whole duration of the first reading. And yet the recognition of the mistake and the delight with which we assemble the newly discovered layer of information is a hermeneutic decoy in its own right: it yields a clear and sympathetic view of the fictional world from "within" it, deferring our recognition of the criticism to which the value system of this world is subjected in the novel. The aesthetic game that competes for priority with the critical inquiry, from "without," into the culture of Jane Austen's world, is also a condition under which this inquiry is carried out.

In the course of the first reading we are presented with three successive romantic situations involving Emma, Harriet Smith, and an eligible gentleman; each time Harriet functions as Emma's blundering scout into the world of romance. In all the three cases we expect the gentleman to be a suitor of Emma herself, yet quite surprising variations occur in the second and the third triangles.

During the "Elton affair" we understand the situation fairly soon and do not share Emma's errors. The episode reveals all of her weaknesses and few of her redeeming qualities. She is obviously wrong in persuading Harriet to reject Robert Martin's proposal, and we agree with Mr. Knightley, who censures her. Mr. Knightley's character as Emma's reliable mentor is established early in the novel, and so far nothing has undermined his authority. Therefore, when he says that the young vicar "does not mean to throw himself away" (66)[1] on ʹHarriet, we take the warning with due seriousness. Emma, however, believes in romantic passions that surmount social barriers—at least for those who are not beyond the pale, like Martin—and concludes that Mr. Elton's feeling for Harriet must be very strong indeed if she herself "[comes] in for a pretty good share as a second" (49). But though her judgment is mistaken, her intuition is not entirely wrong:[2] despite Mr. Elton's gallantry she knows that he is not in love with her. Unwilling to attribute mercenary motives to a young man of her environment, she laughs at John Knightley's caution about Mr. Elton's attentions to her (112): if the vicar does not love her he cannot possibly be courting her. Her case is similar to that of numerous idealistic young people who tend to believe that comedies and novels have effectively done away with the kinds of conduct that they ridicule; eventually they are painfully astonished to find out that Vanity Fair is held not only in allegorical or satiric texts but also in "real life"—and in placid ignorance of its representations in literature. The audience, however, reads the case of Mr. Elton as an amusing variant of a transparent stock situation.

Emma's behavior becomes progressively quixotic. When Harriet falls ill and Mr. Elton fails to live up to Emma's views on what is expected of a distressed lover, she makes every effort to explain away his lack of concern for her friend. Her obstinacy is quite exasperating: we are not aware that very soon we too are going to "[take] up an idea" and make "every thing bend to it" (134).

When Mr. Elton starts making love to Emma openly, she is overcome with resentment, bitterness, humiliation, and remorse. We are sorry for her, yet flattered at finding our surmises fully corroborated. A touch of complacency now enters our attitude to the novel. "Conjecture—aye, sometimes one conjectures right, and sometimes one conjectures wrong" (242). The correct conjecture in Mr. Elton's case encourages extrapolations. Accordingly, when Emma fancies that

Frank Churchill is starting to take an interest in Harriet, we expect a recurrence of the familiar pattern: Emma is not in love with the young man; she is willing to pass him over to Harriet; Harriet seems ready to be guided; the young man is very attentive, though not to Harriet—of course Emma will once again turn out to be Harriet's reluctant rival. This time, however, information is withheld not only about the state of the gentleman's affections but also about Harriet. At first glance it seems likely that she should fall in love with Frank, who has rescued her from the gypsies; and so we share Emma's blindness to the fact that Harriet has set her heart on Mr. Knightley, who saved her from embarrassment at a party, another kind of rescue. Like Emma, we are led into a double error.

Now it is the turn of the audience to explain away all the evidence that conflicts with its expectations. The uncertainty of Frank's moods can be accounted for by the heat or by his aunt's demands; and he is certainly "too well bred" (193) to impose himself on Emma. There arises a difficulty when Mr. Knightley grows suspicious of Frank on detecting "symptoms of intelligence" (343) that pass between him and Jane Fairfax—here some readers do, indeed, begin to suspect a secret relationship; and yet these are not necessarily the most perceptive of readers. Indeed, the evidence is not conclusive: by now Mr. Knightley has been partly discredited because of his obvious prejudice against Frank. He may even be suspected of imagining a story about Frank, just as Emma imagines one about Jane Fairfax's attachment to Mr. Dixon. Emma supports this impression by drawing an implicit parallel between Mr. Knightley's letting his "imagination wonder" and her own past "essays" of this sort (350). This view is not totally unacceptable to the audience (especially since by now Emma has won our approval on a number of counts); nor is it unprepared for: we have already seen the admirable Mrs. Weston engaged in similar speculations about Mr. Knightley and Jane Fairfax (224). Mr. Knightley may also form wrong surmises about romatic possibilities—this seems to be quite a pastime in the novel's world.

If, however, we are not entirely convinced of the injustice of Emma's suspicions about Jane and Mr. Dixon, we may interpret the signs of the tacit communication between Jane and Frank as having a connection with the Dixon affair. Emma, for one, seems to believe so when she says to Mr. Knightley: "the appearances which have caught you, have arisen from some peculiar circumstances—feelings rather of a totally different nature:—it is impossible exactly to explain:—there is a good deal of nonsense about it—" (391).

"You take up an idea, Mrs. Watson, and run away with it," Emma has occasion to say to her friend (226). Miss Bates also makes a similar pronouncement: "One takes up a notion, and runs away with it" (176). The pronoun "one" may be taken to refer not only to the characters of the novel but also to the audience: our formed opinion heightens the threshold that Mr. Knightley's contradictory testimony must pass on its way to our consciousness and lowers the threshold for Frank's continuing attentions to Emma. Mr. Knightley, moreover, retreats from the foreground. Soon a new line of interest captures our attention: Emma has behaved unkindly to Miss Bates and must seek to make amends.

Then, after a short span of suspense occasioned by Mrs. Weston's worried summons of Emma (392-95), Frank's secret engagement to Jane Fairfax is revealed. This time our response is parallel and iso-chronic to that of the heroine: we are surprised not so much by the disclosure as by our failure to have foreseen it. As in *Bleak House*, the element of isochronic experience promotes sympathy for Emma: hav-ing reenacted her experience, we are more ready to forgive her past faults. This lenience is justified by Emma's immediate behavior:[3] she hastens to reassure Mrs. Weston that she is not in love with Frank. Her next concern is for Harriet, who seems to have been misled once again, but her greatest trial comes on learning that Harriet has been dreaming about Mr. Knightley rather than Frank. Emma is shocked into the realization that Mr. Knightley means much more to herself than she has ever thought and that now she may have turned Harriet into her rival. Her remorse is mixed with jealousy and resentment, yet also with humility, with a willingness to admit that she has been wrong in judgment and in deed.

The triangular pattern reappears. Again Emma believes Harriet to be the gentleman's object, only this time she herself is in love with him. Previously we were flattered into believing that we knew the truth about Frank and, as in *Bleak House*, found that a false surmise followed a correct one; now we make one more extrapolation—without the encouragement of previous success, yet assisted, this time, by the convention of a happy ending. To be taught a lesson, Austen's heroines are usually forced to lose all hope of happiness; they are ultimately rewarded if they bear the blow with penitence and fortitude.[4] Yet even if we are not sufficiently acquainted with the works of Austen to know that her novels end in happy marriages,[5] we cannot share Emma's illusions about Harriet or believe that Mr. Knightley can suddenly take a passionate interest in the very young woman whom he has deemed perhaps good enough—but only just—for his tenant. Therefore we apply the familiar pattern to the new triangle and expect that Emma will once more gain preference over Harriet. As this conjecture proves to be correct, part of our former complacency returns. The happy ending seems to restore the "natural" order of things.

Yet it is not for long that we are allowed to remain pleased by our sagacity. Our lack of perceptiveness in regard to the secret engagement is presently brought back to our attention by Frank's explanatory letter, which clearly shows how much has been really happening in front of our (and Emma's) eyes: Frank even suggests that he might have given himself away. Trying to justify his behavior on different occasions, he reveals links between apparent trivia and throws a new light over a number of incidents. "You can hardly be quite without suspicion," he had earlier said to Emma (260), and in his letter he flatters her once more: "I then fancied [Miss Woodhouse] was not without suspicion; but I have no doubt of her having since detected me, at least in some degree.—She may not have surmised the whole, but her quickness must have penetrated a part" (438).

Throughout Frank's letter, in addition to giving us a preview of the attractions awaiting us on a repeated reading, the novelist seems to be telling us that we were expected to guess at least part of the secret. In fact, very little information has been withheld: the secret engagement has not been mentioned, but all the signs of it were there to be perceived by a shrewd eye (like that of Mr. Knightley). We therefore sympathize more readily with the heroine whose disappointment in herself parallels our own response.

It has been noted that when Emma discards her fantasies and thinks that she has lost Mr. Knightley to Harriet, the reality that she braces herself to face is her last illusion.[6] The same is also true of our dissatisfaction with our performance as readers. Although in Frank's letter Jane Austen hints that evidence of the secret engagement lies plentifully scattered throughout the novel, she obfuscates the fact that she has taken pains to divert our attention from this evidence. We have, so far, been deluded twice: first into missing the clues and then into missing the fact that we have been tricked into this apparent obtuseness. Only on a rereading can we appreciate the stunning tour de force with which Austen has both provided and camouflaged a considerable amount of information.[7]

The camouflage techniques of *Emma* are an aesthetic "double dealing" (343): the narrative offers us a multitude of clues to the secret intrigue yet prevents us from seeing them. The analogy between audience response and the experience of the heroine is supplemented by (and based on) the analogy between narrative techniques and some aspects of conduct of the characters. As in *Bleak House*, the specific methods by which our attention is manipulated seem to be borrowed from the tactics of the characters within the fictional world.

One of the reasons for the tenacity of Emma's misprisions lies in her being constantly exposed to flattery. She is flattered by her father's reliance, by Mr. Elton's obsequiousness, by Harriet's submission, by the exaggerated gratitude of Miss Bates, and by the studied compliments of Frank Churchill. She is not susceptible to praise of her person or accomplishments—as Mr. Knightley observes, "her vanity lies another way" (39): compliments to her judgment and penetration strike home. Emma wishes to be the first lady of Highbury, and to maintain this position intelligence is as vital as gentility and fortune. In order to assert herself, she must have her taste and judgment universally acknowledged. Frank Churchill senses and exploits this successfully throughout their acquaintance, thus fostering one of the most dangerous tendencies in Emma's "disposition." Just as we are pleased with our sagacity concerning the Elton debacle, so Emma is proud of having made a correct prediction about Mr. Weston's marriage to Miss Taylor. Like the audience, she feels encouraged to extrapolate and is glad that Frank concurs in her suspicions of Jane's attachment to Mr. Dixon. Flattery is thus joined to self-congratulation; henceforth Emma relies on her own willful judgment more than on the testimony of facts. Even her failure in Mr. Elton's case does not curb her imagination.

The novelist explores the audience's susceptibility to flattery in the Elton episode. The nature of the technique becomes clear if one compares this episode with an analogous situation in George Eliot's *Middlemarch*. An eligible young neighbor is courting Dorothea Brooke while she believes him to be in love with her younger sister; Dorothea is surprised by the amount of attention he is paying her. In both cases the intellect of the suitors is greatly inferior to that of the heroines; the tiresome "Exactly" with which Sir James Chettam acquiesces in all Dorothea's opinions seems to be an echo of Mr. Elton's "Exactly so." Right from the start, however, the narrator of *Middlemarch* informs the reader of Sir James's precise motives in visiting the Brookes, while the narrator of *Emma* never explicitly states that Mr. Elton is trying to win Emma and not Harriet. Technically, this piece of information is withheld from us throughout the episode. And though "the truth" is easy to infer, the fact remains that we see it without being "told." This effect of disguised flattery is not sought in *Middlemarch*.

The narrative suggests, as it were, a convention according to which it must be read further: we are flattered into believing that "we see it all." The Elton episode thus conditions us for remaining unaware that the conduct and the psychology of characters, in particular Frank Churchill and Jane Fairfax, are more complex than they seem to us at first glance. The "flattery" of the audience increases the efficacy of camouflage devices like finesse and equivocation.

The word "finesse" is twice used by Mr. Knightley with reference to Frank Churchill. On the first occasion Frank is censured for neglect of duty toward Mr. and Mrs. Weston and for lack of manly firmness: "There is one thing, Emma, which a man can always do, if he chuses, and that is, his duty; not by manouevring and finessing, but by vigour and resolution" (146). On the second occasion, at the end of the novel, as Mr. Knightley reads Frank's letter and is inclined to forgive him, he still cannot forbear saying: "Mystery; Finesse—how they pervert the understanding!" (446).

Though the word "finesse" has a French sound, Austen's contemporaries would probably associate it not only with "fine skill" or French artfulness but also with a military stratagem or even with a card-game ruse.[8] At present "finesse" is a term used by bridge players, but it is also used in descriptions of whist,[9] a game played in *Emma*. "Finesse" is an attempt to evade or neutralize a high card, a king for instance, held by one's opponents and to take the trick with one's own high card in reserve. It usually involves a degree of risk.

Both as a term in card games and in military strategy,[10] "finesse" has the connotations of evasion: one does not confront the most dangerous issue but neutralizes it or passes it by. So, for instance, when Frank makes his blunder about Mr. Perry's plans for keeping a carriage, he has to evade the question about the source of his information. Instead of confronting the issue, he tries to divert everybody's attention from it by ascribing his knowledge of the episode to a dream and by launching a harangue about the wonder of dreaming.

Jane Fairfax likewise tries to divert her neighbors' attention to generalities when they attempt to dissuade her from walking to the post office every morning. She knows that she may be exposing herself to suspicions and, when pressed hard by Mrs. Elton, endeavors to change the subject by praising the efficiency of the post. Though John Knightley's kindly ironic remarks assist her, Jane's finesse, like that of

Frank Churchill, is not entirely successful: Emma realizes that Jane is involved in a secret correspondence though she does not correctly guess with whom.

Earlier in the novel Frank is more successful in finessing. Asked by Emma how well acquainted he is with Jane Fairfax, he tries to divert her attention by pointing to Ford's shop (199-200) until he can collect himself and produce a suitable answer.

Generally, however, this pattern of behavior is more marked in the other characters. It is part of filial duty in Highbury to divert older people's attention from matters that might discompose them. For instance, Miss Bates's desultory conversation keeps her mother from noticing Jane's lack of appetite ("I dare not let my mother know how little she eats—so I say one thing and then I say another, and it passes off," 237), and, as we find out at a later stage of reading, defuses other tensions in social intercouse.

Emma perfects the art of finesse. She often has to conceal minor matters from her father or "persuade away" (141) his anxieties. One of his distresses is Miss Taylor's marriage since, among other things, it entails the necessity for the Woodhouses to visit her frequently at Randalls. The prospect of the exertion for the groom and the horses weighs heavily on Mr. Woodhouse's mind, but Emma manages to direct his thoughts to a happier channel: James will only be too glad to go to Randalls where his daughter is a maid. The move is successful; the benign old gentleman is immediately made happy about James, about his own kindness in having procured the place for the girl, and about the merits of the girl herself, especially her never banging the door.

For the sake of his majesty's peace and her father's mental comfort Emma must be permanently on the alert during his conversations with John and Isabella Knightley. The gentle and silly Isabella is so much like her father that the two easily lapse into quarrels about their favorite physicians or ways of child care. Whenever Emma senses such a contingency, she interferes and changes the flow of conversation by bringing up matters close to their hearts—mild gossip and benevolent inquiries about old acquaintances. In chapter 12, for instance, she has to "finesse" several dangerous topics, so she reminds her sister to inquire about Mr. Perry, then about the Bateses. Yet it is easier to neutralize Isabella's absurdity than her husband's annoyance. When Isabella repeats her father's words of concern about John Knightley's health, the latter utters an abrupt and nervous remark that is actually pointed against Mr. Woodhouse: "My dear Isabella . . . pray do not concern yourself about my looks. Be satisfied with doctoring and coddling yourself and the children, and let me look as I chuse" (104). Emma succeeds in smoothing over this remark by apparently unconcerned chatter, yet presently John Knightley's irritation grows, and he vents it in an outburst ostensibly directed against Mr. Perry but actually against Mr. Woodhouse, who has been "attributing many of his own feelings and expressions" to the inoffensive apothecary. This time the embarrassment is grave; luckily, Mr. Knightley comes to the rescue and, after a perfunctory support of his brother's remark, changes the course of the conversation. Meanwhile, the "soothing attentions" of the ladies dispel the agitation of their father (106-107).

With her intellectual solitude and lack of assiduity in the kind of studies a young lady of her time could pursue, Emma's main exertion is, in fact, finessing her father's worries and complaints. From this duty, however, she has little respite. As a result, "manoeuvring and finessing" grow into a habit, and, never plaintive or disrespectful, she makes the best of it by learning to delight in these skills. The art of finessing, persuading, pretending to take the main issue of a contention for granted, diverting and directing attention, coaxing and subduing—the subtle art she learns in communicating with her father—she eventually practices on Harriet. When Emma wishes to dissuade Harriet from accepting Robert Martin's proposal, she must finesse against his merits yet avoid directly dictating to Harriet. First she disarms her by pretending to take a refusal for granted and think only about the wording of the reply. Having thus created an impression that there are strong reasons against the match, she announces that the decision is for Harriet to make. The confused girl starts deliberating aloud; Emma seizes upon the moment when she is weighing a refusal and pretends to take this for a decision. Unable to deny Robert Martin's virtues, she finesses against them by threatening Harriet with the loss of her friendship—the threat is carefully worded and sounds like a reference to what Harriet has avoided by declining the proposal. In the end, Harriet is won over by the timing rather than the strength of Emma's arguments.

The most disconcerting thing about the episode is Emma's obvious pleasure in the success of her strategy. In this respect she is a match for Frank Churchill, who comes to enjoy deception as a sport. Finessing is innocent at first; eventually it is abused. As is demonstrated so often in Austen's novels, ethical value is a matter of measure:[11] a little finesse may be unavoidable, but too much is wrong. The blame for the consequences must, of course, be partly borne by Emma's ineffectual exploiting father who is unequal even to the strain of self-composure and therefore unwittingly makes her learn to maneuver his states of mind. In a sense it is the culture of her society that puts Emma on slippery ground—Mr. Woodhouse is an instinctive arbiter elegantiarum in his social enclave despite, or perhaps because of, his own paradoxical departure from the golden mean, his excessive moderation of life-style.

The reader of *Emma* likewise falls a victim to finesse. This is a special kind of narrative entrapment: signs of Jane Fairfax's secret engagement are placed in immediate proximity to seemingly more important matters, so that the evidence is neutralized by the "high card" that follows. Important Highbury events are reserved for such moments when their occurrence ousts potentially queer impressions of Frank and Jane from the reader's memory.

For example, Frank's forthcoming visit is announced soon after Jane's appearance in Highbury. The reader must be prevented from paying attention to the coincidence; therefore it is at this juncture that Mr. Elton's marriage moves to the foreground. As J.F. Burrows has put it, the novelist "delays Frank Churchill's arrival only long enough to conceal his true object not only from the keen ears and idle minds of Highbury but also from the reader. . . . The chapters concerning Elton's engagement and the reappearance of Robert Martin are used to occupy—or, indeed, to create—this period of delay."[12]

Finesse involves the arrangement of *fabula* details into a pattern that suits the demands of the novel's rhetoric. Yet the arrangement never seems strained; all the *fabula* occurrences seem perfectly plausible so that the reader is almost never put on his guard. Whatever passes between Frank and Jane during his first stay in the neighborhood is blocked by Frank's courtship of Emma and by Emma's fantasies of Jane's attachment to Mr. Dixon: after all, it was not Frank but Mr. Dixon who saved Jane from falling into the water at Weymouth. For Emma a rescue is replete with romantic possibilities; as in the episode with the gypsies, it automatically triggers her imagination.[13]

Amid the excitement aroused by the adventure with the gypsies nobody pays attention to the fact that Frank was able to come to Harriet's assistance because, despite the haste of his departure, he had been calling on the Bateses: "happening to have borrowed a pair of scissars the night before of Miss Bates, and to have forgotten to restore them, he had been obliged to stop at her door, and to go in for a few minutes" (334). This dangerous moment is neutralized by another instance of narrative finesse: instead of remembering Jane, who lives at the Bateses', Emma at once sees Harriet as a possible object of Frank's attentions. Here the "high card" that neutralizes the possible suspicions of the audience is not the content of Emma's delusion but the very fact that she can still delude herself, even if she no longer attempts to actively promote the match made in her mind.

The technique of finesse is also employed in the account of the Coles' party. Very soon after Frank leaves Emma to talk to Jane, both Emma's and the reader's attention is engaged by Mrs. Weston's suggestion that Jane might marry Mr. Knightley (224). Again the real love affair is screened by an imaginary romance.

The novelist's finesse succeeds even when the character's finesse fails. It is in vain that Jane Fairfax endeavors to finesse when her walks to the post office become the subject of discussion. The reader, however, is prevented from connecting the new piece of information with what he knows about Frank Churchill, because the foreplane is ceded to Emma's automatic conclusion that Jane must be corresponding with Mr. Dixon. This time it is not so much our interest in the imaginary romance as Emma's suspiciousness that diverts us from the real cause of Jane's insistence on fetching her letters herself.

The effect of finesse is made possible by the same selectiveness of the audience's attention that leads to the prominence of the hermeneutic code in *Bleak House*. Though modern literature seeks to teach us better, we do not read a whole novel with the same degree of attention. Few novelists expect that we shall, and those who do—Joyce, for instance—confront us with an extremely difficult task. As a rule, our attention ebbs while we glide over catalysts and increases as we take in kernels.[14] In *Emma*, Austen has created conditions under which this common reading habit turns into a liability—not because there are no catalysts in her tales but because on the first reading we are made to expect them in the wrong places. As a result, we slip into what seems to be a negligent reading, which we eventually regret—an effect reminiscent of the major readjustment in *Nostromo*.[15]

Another camouflage technique is based on the impression of plausibility and involves only the narrative and not the "story." It will here be referred to as "equivocation," meaning not only verbal equivocation but also, and mainly, the different constructions that we put on certain episodes of the novel.

Emma's first recorded visit to Miss Bates looks like ordinary neighborly civility, while it is actually prompted by the necessity to provide a diversion for Harriet who is inclined to stay heartbroken after the Elton debacle. Thus the ostensible motive of Emma's action is different from the real one, and the visit has one significance for her and another for her friends. This kind of behavior sometimes turns into a subterfuge, as, for instance, when at the beginning of the novel Emma contrives to bring together Harriet and Mr. Elton. Likewise, though we are never told Mr. Knightley's real motive for sending Robert Martin to London while Harriet is staying there with the John Knightleys, we are at liberty to suspect him of his own little piece of double-purpose activity.

Such ruses are innocent so long as they help rather than hurt one's neighbors, but this is not the case when they become a source of enjoyment, as they do for Frank Churchill. On his arrival to the neighborhood Frank is obliged to lead a double life: "My heart was in Highbury," he will eventually write in his explanatory letter, "and my business was to get my body thither as often as might be, and with the least suspicion" (439). The predicament damages his character: Frank learns to derive pleasure not only from avoiding suspicion but from actually increasing the danger of the suspicion by a game of double entendre. He starts secretly making fun of the people he must endeavor to please. Emma is his immediate victim since she gives him a convenient clue, the imaginary Dixon affair. Because of Emma's fantasies, Frank can afford to pay much more attention to Jane in her presence. His words and actions acquire a different significance for each of the two girls: in the pianoforte episode, for instance, Emma thinks that he is flattering her and teasing Jane, while Jane is perfectly aware of the whole complex of his meaning.

The audience's response to a number of narrative details can be compared to the response of the two women in this episode. On the first reading, like Emma, we interpret the meaning and the function of these details according to our expectations; on a rereading, we know, as Jane does, that they have another meaning besides (though not in lieu of) the one that we attributed to it before.

For example, we do not wonder why it is significant that Frank and Jane become acquainted before they appear in Highbury because this acquaintance permits Emma to question Jane about Frank and Frank about Jane's relationship with Mr. Dixon. The real significance of Frank and Jane's having met at Weymouth lies, of course, in the timing of their secret engagement; ostensibly, however, it is presented as a plausible fact that serves to enrich the stock of Highbury conversation and provide Emma with food for fancy. The episode also contains an element of finesse: had the reader's attention not been diverted to Emma's fantasy, the reader might have taken greater notice of the previous connection between Frank and Jane.

The difference between equivocation and finesse involves the er-

rors into which they lead the audience. Finesse neutralizes the significance of a fact by eclipsing it with more conspicuous details: on a
rereading one perceives the meaning of such a fact as something that
has been overlooked. Equivocation does not belittle the importance of
an episode on the first reading but ensures an interpretation that does
not endanger the secret of the plot; although partial, this interpretation
is not wrong.

The discussion of Jane's walks to the post office is a case of structural equivocation. We seem to have already encountered a similar
episode earlier in the novel: when Emma's friends talk about her
portrait of Harriet, each utterance tells us more about the speaker than
about the matter under discussion. In addition to showing how Emma
distorts reality, the picture furnishes a pretext for comparative character portrayal. Jane's walks to the post office seem to perform the same
function. Like Emma's picture, they provide a theme for a general
conversation in which each character reveals himself. Besides, the
episode shows another case of Emma's tampering with reality. Thus an
ostensible raison d'être obscures the full significance of the episode.

The technique of equivocation in *Emma* is closely connected with
character portrayal. It is also a convenient neutralizer of evidence
flowing from a particularly voluble character, Miss Bates. "What is
before me, I see," says Miss Bates (176). "I do sometimes pop out a
thing before I am aware," she adds on another occasion. "I am a talker,
you know; I am rather a talker" (346). Miss Bates is, indeed, always on
the verge of revealing a secret that she herself does not know. It is to her
that we owe our knowledge about Frank offering to fix her mother's
spectacles (an occasion for a tête-à-tête with Jane), about his attentions
to Jane before, during, and after the ball; about Jane's having known of
Mr. Perry's plans to acquire a carriage; about Jane's ups and downs;
and, finally, about her decision to accept the post of governess immediately after the news of Frank's abrupt departure. Miss Bates is thus
one of the main channels through which the novelist smuggles in
information about the secret relationship. However, the ambivalent
treatment of this character blocks this information on the first reading.

Miss Bates is both an admirable embodiment of filial virtues and a
test for her friends' forbearance and generosity. Very early in the novel
her character is established as that of a kind but tiresome woman, and
her speeches, as the novel progresses, seem to do little else than bear
out the point. In defense of Walter Scott's opinion that characters who
are boring in life are also boring in fiction, it seems only fair to say that
on the first reading Miss Bates is actually made to sound as boring to

the reader as she is to Emma, especially since on her first appearance in the novel she talks at length about the Dixons and the Campbells *before* the audience has been properly acquainted with these names. Nothing has so far excited our curiosity about these unfamiliar people; nor can particular interest be excited when they are mentioned in the same breath with Miss Bates's "huswife" and what she said to her mother. As a result, Miss Bates's first speeches (156-62) with their mass of household details, gushing gratitude, and obscure references seem to be totally uninteresting. It is only in the following chapter, where the narrator tells us about Jane Fairfax and her relations with the Campbells and Dixons, that Miss Bates's words acquire relevance in retrospect; yet the damage has already been done. Miss Bates becomes an unconscious Cassandra to whom we do not listen because, like her neighbors, we have become used to being bored with whatever she says. Therefore, while Miss Bates supplies us (and Emma) with ample material for insight, one thinks that her monologues are only quoted to show to what trials the brilliant Emma and Jane are subjected. In structural terms, the handling of this character is equivocal: on the first reading the ostensible function of Miss Bates's *longeurs* is to enhance our sympathy for Emma and Jane and to further the plot by provoking Emma to a piece of rudeness that changes the whole flow of her emotional life.[16] On a rereading, however, Miss Bates is perceived both as a source of information about the hidden subplot and as a prism through which this information is amusingly refracted. She becomes one of the major exponents of the theme of selfishness and selflessness in interpersonal communication.[17] Our initial response to her character turns out to be reductive—though its basic validity is not denied.

Whereas the effect of finesse is based on the selectiveness of our attention, the effect of equivocation is made possible by our tendency to remain content with establishing a single plausible raison d'être for any narrative detail on the first reading—a similar tendency leads to our excessive preoccupation with the detective clues in *Bleak House*. Moreover, the effect of equivocation is often enhanced by our tendency to extrapolate. We expect a degree of predictability in the novel and, as in the case of the three love triangles, impose familiar patterns on situations that share familiar features.

Structural equivocation sometimes causes crucial changes in our view of the story; it can be responsible for a sudden surge of our sympathy toward a character whose experience is parallel and isochronic to ours. In Scott's *Waverley*, for instance, as in a number of more recent novels (Camus' *The Stranger* or Graham Greene's *The Confidential*

Agent) the unpleasant surprise that the reader shares with the protagonist is caused by the other characters' systematic misinterpretation
of the protagonist's actions and by the reader's underestimation of the
complex function of episodes. Thus the drunken debate in an inn near
Tully Veolan in *Waverley* seems to be just another touch of local color: it
displays the irrational conduct of the small gentry and the notion of
hospitality entertained by Baron Bradwardine. The episode does, indeed, perform these functions, yet, as it later becomes clear, they do not
exhaust its significance: when Edward Waverley is arrested, his behavior during the incident is one of the charges against him. The shock
that both Edward and the audience receive at such a turn of affairs
prepares the former for a change of political allegiance and the latter for
a more lenient attitude toward this breach of loyalty—isochronic parallel experience promotes our sympathy for the wavering protagonist.
Had any narrative commentary interrupted the Tully Veolan episode to
suggest the possibility of alternative interpretations of Edward's conduct on that occasion, our later attitude to his lack of firm principle
might have been more critical. Scott is unfair to himself—or perhaps
ironic—when he accounts for his withholdings of information as aim-
ing merely to excite the reader's curiosity, "according to the custom of
story-tellers."[18] The equivocation that produces the surprise gap in
Waverley leads to isochronic experience which, as in *Bleak House*, enhances the appeal of a character who has rather little to recommend
him. In life the charm of a human being is often quite divorced from his
or her moral merits; in fiction this charm is difficult to render discur-
sively. Isochronic parallel experience often goes a long way to compen-
sate for this limitation of the verbal medium.

Whereas the above techniques divert our attention from the clues to
the secret intrigue, the principle of narrative reserve involves a thor-
ough blocking of information. As in the case of flattery, finesse, and
equivocation, it also seems to be modeled on the conduct of the characters in the fictional world.

Jane Fairfax's "reserved" disposition is the ostensible reason for
Emma's dislike of her. Jane is, indeed, reluctant to communicate. She
never volunteers information and when asked direct questions returns
most general replies. Her face is often averted; at times she refuses to be
seen.

Jane has good reason to be reserved. The stock of Highbury conversation is poor, and any trifling detail that happens to enrich it is
given exaggerated attention. Having a secret to keep, attention is pre-

cisely what Jane wishes to avoid. After the disclosure, however, she becomes more natural and open: she does not seem to enjoy reserve— even in the first half of the novel she occasionally allows herself to admit her emotions to Emma.

When Frank Churchill first appears in Highbury, he also manifests considerable reserve with respect to Jane. But whether he thinks that this may endanger rather than protect his secret or whether such behavior is incompatible with his temperament, he soon sheds his reserve, and, seeing his secret still safe, grows less discreet, thus allowing the novelist to play her complex game with the reader.

Narrative reserve manifests itself in the degrees of the narrator's self-effacement, modeled, as it were, on the behavior of Jane Fairfax. For instance, wherever Frank is concerned, the narrator maintains strict neutrality, interfering neither to incriminate him nor to vindicate his eccentricities. If Frank chooses to explain his sudden trip to London by the need of a haircut, the narrator will not refute his excuse. Faithfully recording Frank's pretexts for visiting the Bateses, the narrator will not intimate that there is more to his civility than meets the eye. The same narrative neutrality is maintained when other characters misinterpret Frank's conduct. For instance, when Emma's suggestion that Jane is going to become governess makes Frank uneasy, Mrs. Weston, who is Emma's former governess, ascribes his confusion to his delicacy and respect for herself; it is never hinted that Frank may have different plans for Jane's future:

> "You know Miss Fairfax's situation in life, I conclude; what she is destined to be."
>
> "Yes—(rather hesitatingly)—I believe I do."
>
> "You get upon delicate subjects, Emma," said Mrs. Weston smiling, "remember that I am here.—Mr. Frank Churchill hardly knows what to say when you speak of Miss Fairfax's situation in life. I will move a little farther off."
>
> "I certainly forget to think of *her*," said Emma, "as having been anything but my friend and my dearest friend."
>
> He looked as if he fully understood and honoured such a sentiment. (201)

In Wayne Booth's terms, the incident is "shown" rather than "told about."[19] The element of "showing" is so strong that the manner in which Frank makes his utterance is presented in the form of a stage direction. The narrating voice is almost entirely eliminated. By using the phrase "he looked as if" the narrator escapes commitment: Emma's wrong impression on Frank's attitude is neither denied nor sanctioned. The technique is close to cases of equivocation and to the "half-truths" in *Tom Jones*.

Narrative reserve is sometimes achieved through the handling of focalization. For instance, the account of Jane's recent history is presented from the Campbells' viewpoint (164-66). This permits the narrator to withhold the fact that Jane has fallen in love with Frank Churchill—Colonel Campbell and his wife have not been taken into her confidence.[20] The ostensible reason for the shift of focus, however, lies in the need to explain why the Campbells do not oppose Jane's plan to become a governess: here structural equivocation extends to the choice of focus.

Another instance is the episode of Frank's first visit to Emma. Frank ignores his father's hint that he may stay on in Hartfield because he is impatient to see Jane, but we are told that he is "too well bred to hear the hint" (193). Had this observation followed a dramatically rendered scene, it would have been ascribed to the narrator who, in such a case, would have been totally misleading. However, in the preceding scene the element of "telling" is much stronger than that of "showing": parts of the conversation are curtailed, summarized, or rendered in represented speech, and, most important, commented on from Emma's point of view. Instead of giving us a clear image of Frank the episode conveys Emma's impression of him. Therefore the above-quoted phrase lends itself to being interpreted as Emma's assessment of Frank's conduct, even though the style of the passage does not corroborate this view of the episode in any significant way.[21]

The episode shows that at this point it is practically impossible for the audience to make a correct guess about Frank and Jane. Frank is, indeed, well bred, and his father's hint would not have made him stay at Hartfield too long, whether or not he had any other motive for leaving at the proper time. Thus far Frank is almost as reserved as Jane; and reserve seems to be not only the safest but also the most inoffensive way of protecting one's secret. This is true not only of the relationships between the characters but also of the narrator-reader relationship. Unlike finesse and equivocation, reserve does not involve the smuggling in of information. On the contrary, it consists in so handling focalization, "telling" and "showing," narrative commentary, and inside views[22] as to prevent the information from making its way into the text. Yet the use of reserve alone, without an interplay with other camouflage techniques, would have stripped *Emma* of its central rhetorical effect—the parallel and isochronic experience of self-reproach that enhances the reader's sympathy for the problematic heroine of the novel.

When we read *Emma* for a second time we are conscious of having missed a great number of things on the first reading. In a way, our self-critical attitude parallels that of Emma, who examines her past experience after emerging from solipsistic innocence. Emma comes to understand other people not as figures in her own world but as self-contained worlds in which she herself is but another figure, worlds in which her own actions can be misinterpreted and her motives perverted. In addition, we are now able to understand what Emma must have looked like to Frank and Jane. Yet the dramatic irony, which is thereby intensified, does not become "ponderous and schematic" as it might have been on a first reading in the hypothetical case of absence of mystification.[23] It is not schematic because its pattern changes: if in the Elton episode we were conscious only of Emma's misinterpretation of Mr. Elton's conduct, in the case of Frank and Jane we know not only that Emma is wrong about them but that they are mistaken about her. The presence of this double error, understood only after the display of Emma's best qualities at the end of the novel, precludes the monotony that could well have resulted from the recurrence of identical situations.

Moreover, on a rereading, dramatic irony escapes being "ponderous" for at least two reasons. First, Emma cannot appear absurd or ridiculous after we have seen how well she can cope with embarrassment and frustration. Second, our criticism of her is softened by the sympathy that has been promoted by parallel experience: we have erred together with her and have discovered that our selective attention, rigid forecasting, and extrapolation bear a pronounced affinity to her solipsism.

As the possible side effects of dramatic irony are neutralized by the impressions that we carry away from the first reading, its function as a comic device is considerably restricted. Instead, dramatic irony acquires thematic significance: it highlights the inadequacy of communication between people and the essentially alienated nature of the society where seldom "does complete truth belong to any human disclosure; seldom can it happen that something is not a little disguised or a little mistaken" (431). Insufficient receptiveness to information is an aspect of this inadequate communication, and on the first reading the audience shares it with the characters. On a rereading, therefore, we can recognize that the rhetoric, which, in a striking display of harmony between content and form, is modeled on the behavior of the characters, has not only induced us to reenact the temporary errors of the heroine but has also, as in *Bleak House*, proved that we are not immune from the tendencies that the novel diagnoses as universal.

Yet this is only part of the story. Austen's double dealing in *Emma* veils her detached criticism of the culture of the provincial gentry. On a rereading, the aftereffects of the surprise gap tend to divert the attention of the audience from this criticism. On the first reading of *Bleak House* our attention is largely seduced by detective clues; in *Emma* something similar happens on a *second* reading. Here, it is the newly discovered complex of dramatic irony and the related undercurrents of meaning that engross us: the delight of perceiving the previously unprobed plot dimension tends to blunt our interest in the more difficult issues raised by the novel.

A rereading of *Emma* most obviously instructs as well as delights. Its multiple dramatic ironies offer us a high degree of insight into the subtleties of interpersonal communication: we sharpen our sensitivity to the distinction between true and false manners, ostensible and hidden motives, correct and mistaken attitudes. These distinctions enhance a sympathetic view of Austen's culture *from within;* they show reasons and justifications of rules and customs, however oppressive. Yet the novel also contains material that may be understood to provide instruction of another kind, namely a view of the Highbury world *from without*. Like the narrators of Gaskell's *Cranford* and Thackeray's *Vanity Fair,* though less explicitly, Austen acknowledges her debt to this culture yet does not forgo her prerogative of viewing it from a critically detached position.[24] Her novel is a case of triple rather than double dealing: (1) the absurd aspects of the culture that she portrays strike us on our first approach to the novel; (2) we are then forced to change our attitude to a more complex and tolerant appreciation of the significance of restrictions, relationships, and manners on which this culture rests; (3) finally our initial reaction proves to have been essentially correct, even if lacking in subtlety and insight.

For instance, on the first reading Mr. Woodhouse's insistence that honoring a bride by a round of parties has nothing to do with encouraging matrimony seems absurd both to the audience and to Emma; on a repeated reading part of the irony is directed to Emma's flippancy as well as to her unwillingness to admit how strongly preoccupied she is with thoughts of marriage. Yet if we abandon the "from-within" perspective and concern for Emma's *Bildung*, Mr. Woodhouse will turn out to be right: the social functions are nothing but customary acts of the metatheatre of manners:[25] their purpose is to demonstrate the neighbors' civility rather than to display genuine kindness to the bride. The absurdity is there, but it belongs to the culture itself rather than to Mr. Woodhouse. Mrs. Elton makes the fatal mistake of taking the special treatment that she enjoys on her arrival to Highbury at face value. Emma, who thinks that the respects are paid to the position of the bride rather than to the person who fills this position, comes to conclusions that are little less mistaken than those of Mrs. Elton. And Mr. Woodhouse tells us the truth not because he shares Austen's detached vision but because his temperamental dislike of matrimony prevents him from lapsing into an error concerning the meaning of the customs that surround it, an error, or rather an illusion, common to healthier minds.

The case of Miss Bates is likewise complex. Though on a second reading she is no longer boring to us, it takes a further detachment to perceive that her participation in the author's "double dealing" is, in fact, a "cover story" that softens the feminist message of the novel.[26] Our very first view of Miss Bates is not wrong: Emma and Jane do have to curb their spirits in her company. The need to be cheerfully considerate to Miss Bates is, of course, a moral test for them—and yet Jane, the weaker of the two young women, develops headaches so bad that her physical and mental health are seriously endangered. Though the novelist's criticism is here leveled against Miss Bates as a character in her own right rather than an institution of the paternalistic society, society obviously makes use of her not only as an object of easy charities but also as a tool of oppression, of channeling the psychic energies of the intelligent young ladies to the laudable effort of self-restraint.[27]

Those of Austen's heroines who in one way or another revolt against their predicament eventually come to terms with it and find moral value both in the prescribed norms and in their own acceptance of them. Such is their process of maturing—which the audience re-enacts by learning to respond to a greater number of irritants at the same time. Yet the audience can also transcend the experience of the heroines in learning to appreciate the ambivalence of these irritants. While the maturing of the heroines entails an initial revolt against their cultural enclave and an ultimate constructive reintegration into it (only Fanny Price and Anne Elliot approach the position of viewing the social environment from the outside), the audience must learn to combine a tolerant understanding of that enclave's system of values with the consciousness of its limitations.

Austen is unique in her ability to suggest an outside view of her culture without including accounts of that amorphous "ground" that could, through contrast, give shape to the "figure" that she paints. She knows that each of her novels is a "little bit (two Inches wide) of Ivory," [28] and it is not only in order to maintain a modest lady's pose that she presents it in this light. Her affirmation that she writes only about what she can well understand must be taken seriously: it defines the kind of accepted restriction that can lead to most subtle aesthetic feats. The world of her novels is well grounded in the social history of England—the role of the influx of money from trade to the rural society, the hollowness of the class snobbery with which Emma tends to ignore the fact that her own capital came from trade a few generations ago (even the Knightleys were probably not "landed" until after the dissolution of the monasteries, when they could purchase Donwell Abbey), the Frankophobia[29] combined with attitudes that seem "to have the French Revolution in [their] bones," [30] the keen sense of the role of women and of the moral significance of manners[31] are accurate reflections of the structure of this microcosm. Yet the Napoleonic wars, the enclosures, the migration of agricultural laborers to the cities, the process of industrialization and the growth of city slums—all these have no place in Austen's novels. For her they are the kind of disorganization which in these days we call entropy; and she knows that her culture is powerless to encroach upon and assimilate those regions the way it can, expanding another frontier, absorb small farmers like Robert Martin. The shape and borderlines of her cultural "bits of ivory" are defined not by their contrast with such entropic "ground" but by shifts of perspective that accompany repeated examinations of these miniatures. We study her world from within and from without as we shuttle between the basically orthogonal lines of interest: on one axis lie distinctions between true and false manners, words and meanings, self-knowledge and self-deception, illusion and reality; on another axis, the anthropological significance of manners, the relativity of morals, and the gnomonic characters of the setting, implicitly defined by that which it excludes. While Austen distributes a great deal of material along the second axis, her delightful information-handling techniques lure the attention of the audience away from it—to the attitudes parallel to those required for the stability of her characters' world.

CHAPTER SIX

Tom Jones
"By Way of Chorus"

Some secrets deep in abstruse Darkness lye;
To search them, thou wilt need a piercing Eye.
Not rashly therefore to such things assent,
Which undeceiv'd, thou after may'st repent.
　　　　　—John Denham, "Of Prudence"

In a number of contexts the term "rhetoric" has negative connotations. Philosophical schools of ancient Greece disagreed about the aims and limits of rhetoric;[1] nowadays the word is frequently associated with demagoguery, cynicism, and opportunistic maneuvering. Stanley Fish opposes "rhetoric" to "dialectics": the former is flattering to the audience since it mirrors and presents for approval "the opinions its readers already hold," whereas the latter "is disturbing, for it requires of its readers a searching and rigorous scrutiny of everything they believe in and live by."[2] Every great work of fiction, however, combines both sides of this Gorgias-Socrates dichotomy, in different proportion. The eighteenth century was largely an age of rhetoric—its laurels were granted to "What oft was thought but ne'er so well expressed." Yet it was also an age whose best writers were determined not merely to divert the world but, as Swift might say, to vex it. Henry Fielding is one of these writers. The inquiry into morals and manners conducted in his novels upholds, perhaps, the basic beliefs of his society yet wipes them clear of cruder incrementa while also showing how difficult it may be to adhere to them.[3] If Fielding's audience does not emerge much sadder or wiser from his novels, it emerges less complacent, less confident that its moral and intellectual standards are easily available for either full understanding or implementation.

The playful reticence of Tom Jones contributes to this effect—within its limits. The details that constitute the hermeneutic code of this novel are not numerous; their role is restricted yet larger, in proportion, than the textual space that such details occupy. We are here confronted with a series of challenges to our sagacity and moral judgment.[4] The mystification is among the challenges: it tests our sagacity—but the test is "fixed," and we cannot help failing. We may well know that "to err is human," yet we learn it all over again through a personal, non-vicarious experience[5] in which vexation and its compensation can hardly be distinguished.

The eloquent reticence of *Tom Jones* bears affinities with the procedures used in both *Bleak House* and *Emma*. As in *Bleak House*, we are made aware of the existence of mystery; as in *Emma*, the mystery eventually transforms itself into a surprise gap to be closed toward the end of the novel. In the early chapters an enigma holds our attention, but its grip is loosened by the end of book 2.

The enigma appears at the dramatic discovery of an infant in the virtuous squire's bed. However, the comedy of the characters' reactions to the discovery partly diverts our attention from the question of the infant's origin; and in chapter 6 the puzzle seems to be solved with Jenny Jones's confession that she is the baby's mother. Jenny refuses to reveal the identity of the father, but this gap does not form a new enigma, mainly because there is no male character whose involvement would make a difference: Squire Allworthy is not suspect; Partridge, judging by the story given in book 2, is likewise innocent; and with the lads of Jenny's country entourage we are not acquainted. In general, the illegitimacy of a personage's birth does not automatically create a sense of enigma: in *Emma* the obscure birth of Harriet Smith is an element of character portrayal rather than of the hermeneutic code—it affects Harriet's social status and triggers Emma's romantic fantasies. In *Tom Jones*, moreover, the quasi-detective episodes of books 1 and 2 are structurally equivocal: the ostensible function of the official inquiry into the affairs of Jenny and Partridge is to show Allworthy's performance as a magistrate and to contrast it with the darker aspects of the "human nature" displayed by his neighbors. Later in the novel it becomes apparent that Allworthy's mistake in the case of Partridge prefigures the banishment of Tom. Yet only on a repeated reading do we perceive that the episodes have an additional dimension—the special role of Miss Bridget. On the first reading she ranks with the other comic secondary characters. Whereas in *Bleak House* the hermeneutic code diverts our attention from character psychology, here comic character portrayal "finesses" such hermeneutic clues as the inconsistencies in Miss Bridget's behavior and her unexpected lenience to Jenny Jones.[6] We note the promise of complexity of character portrayal, but the comic framework does not encourage us to interpret it as a hermeneutic clue.

As in *Emma*, the hermeneutic code is also camouflaged by structural equivocation. On the first reading we tend to see Tom's illegitimacy mainly as a cause of his social disadvantage and, perhaps, as a promise of a deus ex machina in the shape of a repentant father eventually salvaging Tom's destiny from some inevitable blind alley. The novelist relies, as it were, on our indulgent readiness for romanesque schemata of this kind.

The disappearance of the enigma of Tom's birth allows us to focus on the "true" subject of the novel, which, as advertised in the first chapter, is "human nature." Our main interest is riveted on the young protagonist whose ebullient vitality is endearing and whose clearly evident good nature conflicts with the neighborhood's prediction that he is born to be hanged. The nondetective suspense that the novel creates is now motivated by our concern for Tom's welfare, threatened as it is by his illegitimacy, his getting maligned and victimized, his lack of cagey prudence, and his opting for self-denying generosity in all the clashes between different codes of conduct (as when he chooses to lie to Allworthy rather than to betray Black George or to be gallant to Lady Bellaston rather than maintain the appearance of chaste faithfulness to Sophia). The reader's concern about the fate of Tom Jones creates the kind of suspense that John Gardner describes as "a dramatic equivalent of the intellectual process" that the novelist himself may have gone through in working out the ethical system of the novel. This suspense is "a serious business: one presents a moral problem—the character's admirable or unadmirable intent and the pressures of situation working for and against him . . . and rather than moving at once to the effect, one tortures the reader with alternative possibilities, translating to metaphor the alternatives the writer himself has considered. Superficially, the delay makes the decision—the climactic action—more thrilling; but essentially the delay makes the decision philosophically significant."[7] In so far as the happy ending of the novel is a conventional certificate and reward of virtue, the philosophical meaning of suspense lies in the problematic nature of virtue: why is it that Tom, despite his multiple sins and errors, deserves the sympathy and approbation that we feel for him? It is largely to work out an answer to this question that the novel needs leisure for putting together the gallery

of characters in pastoral, picaresque, and urban settings—characters
who form an ethical paradigm of "human nature."

Suspense is not a homogeneous experience; it tightens or relaxes in
accordance with the intrinsic interest aroused by various strands of
material, is punctured by comedy, and overlain by the vicissitudes of
information-processing response. While enacting, in general terms,
the philosophical tension of the novelist, the reader of *Tom Jones* is also
led through errors of perception similar to those of the characters.

As in *Nostromo*, we are lulled rather than led into these errors—
lulled, in the case at hand, by our sense of security and cooperation
with the narrator. This effect is achieved through the narrator's direct
addresses to the reader, especially in prefatory chapters, through
authorial comments on the action,[8] and through the handling of scene
and summary.

The imaginary relationship between the narrator and the reader of
Tom Jones develops, as it were, from standoffishness to friendship.
Various extended metaphors correspond to its successive stages. In the
opening chapter the narrator compares himself to an innkeeper and
the reader to a paying customer: they are on a cool business footing—
the host presents the bill of fare but the guest has not yet committed
himself. In chapter 2 the reader is still addressed in a take-it-or-leave-it
tone: "Reader, I think proper, before we proceed any farther together,
to acquaint thee, that I intend to digress, through this whole History, as
often as I see Occasion; Of which I am myself a better Judge than any
Pitiful Critic whatever" (1.2.28).[9] Yet in the third chapter the tone
becomes warmer. The first words of the chapter, "I have told my
Reader" (1.2.28) mark a turning point, and several lines further the
reader is addressed as "you, my sagacious Friend" (1.2.29). Coming in
a paragraph that contains an ironic reference to the fictionality of the
ensuing story, this flattering address intimates that the reader who has
not abandoned the book must have sufficient judgment to appreciate
it.[10] One can now think of oneself as a member of an elite audience,
even though one's attention may still be held merely by the wish to
know whence the baby came into Allworthy's bed. Such a self-image
of the reader will be further fostered by the metaphor of the theatre in
chapter 1 of book 7: after presenting a brief catalogue of the wrong
responses coming from the galleries, the pit, and the boxes, the narrator will pretend to confer privilege upon us by taking us "behind the
Scenes" (7.1.248) and thus almost bribing us into reserving judgment
of Tom's acts.

The process of molding the attitudes of the audience is well under way by chapter 4 of book 1. An individual reader now has a sense of intimacy, of exclusive dialogue, with the charmingly personal, witty, and wise narrator. One is pleased not to be guilty of the coarser responses outlined in the ironic authorial comments on Mrs. Deborah's fright on finding Allworthy in his nightgown: "Sneerers and prophane Wits may perhaps laugh at her first Fright; yet my graver Reader, when he considers the Time of Night, the Summons from her Bed, and the Situation in which she found her Master, will highly justify and applaud her Conduct; unless the Prudence, which must be supposed to attend Maidens at that Period of Life at which Mrs. *Deborah* had arrived, should a little lessen his Admiration" (1.3.30). The narrator disclaims the cynical humor of Restoration comedy as well as prudish exaggerations. At the same time he suggests that the "graver Reader" should be prepared to take into account all the factors in given situations—an important warning in a novel that must prevent its audience from an unqualified censure of Tom when he deceives Allworthy, abandons Molly, gets seduced by Mrs. Waters, or is kept by Lady Bellaston.

The friendly relationship with the deserving audience having been established, the narrator pretends to take the reader for a friendly stroll through the world of the novel. The metaphor of the inn is left behind—it will later be comically realized in the characters' adventures on the road in books 7 through 12. The new narrative situation is visualized in the following metaphor: "Reader, take Care, I have unadvisedly led thee to the Top of as high a Hill as Mr. *Allworthy*'s, and how to get thee down without breaking thy Neck, I do not well know. However, let us e'en venture to slide down together; for Miss *Bridget* rings her Bell, and Mr. *Allworthy* is summoned to Breakfast, where I must attend, and, if you please, shall be glad of your Company" (1.4.32-33).

By the end of the novel such leisurely pastoral walks will be replaced by a somewhat nervous coach ride, and it is as a fellow passenger that the narrator will take his leave of the reader in book 18, chapter 1. We now seem to be on almost equal terms with our genial companion, especially since we are repeatedly invited to suggest to ourselves (see, for instance, 4.14.158) different situations, drawing on experience, imagination, sagacity, or memories of scenes encountered earlier in the novel.

This invitation is often worded explicitly,[11] but its acceptance is insured by the handling of scene and summary. The summaries leave "vacant Spaces" (3.1.88) on the canvas, for the filling up of which preceding scenes provide guidelines.[12] For instance, the account of Mrs. Wilkin's reaction to Squire Allworthy's premature death-bed speech is curtailed in accordance with the "a-word-to-the-wise" principle: "Much more of the like Kind she muttered to herself; but this Taste shall suffice to the Reader" (5.8.187). After a vivid account of a row in George Seagrim's household, the end of the dispute is likewise briefly summarized: "A Council was now called, in which, after many Debates, *Molly* still persisting she would not go to Service, it was at length resolved, that Goody *Seagrim* herself should wait on Miss *Western*, and endeavour to procure the Place for her elder Daughter, who declared great Readiness to accept it" (4.9.140-41). By this time we are familiar with the dispositions and the language of the Seagrim women and feel competent to recreate the scene. We do not really exercise this illusory competence; rather, we remain satisfied with being credited with it and proceed to the next portion of the narrative under the impression of sharing the narrator's views of decorum and his lack of interest in the predictable scene.

The illusion of our competence is particularly strong in the cases of what may be called the "switching over" technique. This device is similar to the "camera stopping" described by Robert Alter.[13] Camera stopping consists in the use of authorial commentary to fill in a pause in the characters' conversation: the scene is frozen into a tableau for which the commentary serves as a legend. A famous instance of this method is in the scene of Lady Bellaston's visit to Tom while Honour is hidden behind the curtains in his room (15.7.622-23).

Unlike camera stopping, the switching-over technique involves a gap in the represented time: the narrator cuts a scene abruptly, summarizes parts of it, and offers his comments in lieu of the curtailed material. The comments often modify the tone of the discourse. For instance, in episode of Tom's quarrel with Squire Western, the Squire's violent abuse is "switched off" and replaced by the narrator's ironic commentary upon it: " 'I wull have Satisfaction o'thee,' answered the Squire, 'so doff thy clothes. At *unt* half a Man, and I'll lick thee as well as wast ever licked in thy Life.' He then bespattered the Youth with Abundance of that Language, which passes between Country Gentlemen who embrace opposite sides of the Question; with frequent application to him to salute that Part which is generally introduced into all Controversies, that arise among the lower Orders of the *English* Gentry, at Horse-races, Cock-matches, and other public Places. Allusions to that Part are likewise often made for the Sake of the Jest. And here, I believe, the Wit is generally misunderstood" (6.9.231). The character seems to be active both in and out of the limelight, yet offstage movements are not supposed to merit attention. This seems to apply to all offstage activities in the novel, as well as to inside views that would, it is suggested, demean the narrator and the reader: "It would be an ill Office in us to pay a Visit to the inmost Recesses of [Blifil's] Mind, as some scandalous People search into the most secret Affairs of their Friends, and often pry into their Closets and Cupboards, only to discover their Poverty and Meanness to the World" (4.3.120).

The impression that the characters are moving both in the foreground and the background prepares the audience to receive the ultimate happy-end disclosures not as afterthoughts but as planned though not always perceptible convergence of different planes of action. Yet our early impression of the characters' offstage predictability turns out to have been wrong. The ending shows that the illusion of our tacit mutual understanding with the narrator has masked important secrets harbored behind the familiar façades of Miss Bridget, Jenny Jones, Blifil, and Dowling: we are then forced to recognize that the motivation of people's actions is too complex for a mechanical application of surface conduct patterns. Our sense of synchronic competence turns out to have been deceptive: nontrivial developments (such as Blifil's conspiracy with Dowling during Allworthy's illness) have taken place out of the limelight; and even some of the onstage action (such as the complex entrances and exits in the Upton episode) have had a significance beyond our ken. The ending vexes us out of the belief in our synchronic competence, giving us a lesson parallel not only to that of the reckless Tom but also to that of the sedate Allworthy.[14]

In terms of belief in one's synchronic competence, Allworthy's experience is, indeed, more closely parallel to our own. At the beginning of the action he makes the correct guess about his sister's affair with Captain Blifil (comparable, in its function, to Emma's promotion of Miss Taylor's marriage); this can hardly fail to support his belief in his own perceptiveness. During Partridge's trial, therefore, Allworthy can all but claim omniscience, declaring, with perfect assurance, that "the Evidence of such a Slut as [Jenny Jones] appeared to be, would have deserved no Credit; but . . . he could not help thinking that had she been present, and would have declared the Truth, she must have confirmed what so many Circumstances, together with [Partridge's] own Confession, and the Declaration of his Wife, that she had caught her Husband in the Fact, did sufficiently prove" (2.6.76).

At the end of the novel Allworthy has to admit his mistakes—as Tom and the audience must do. As in *Bleak House* and *Emma*, the psychological basis of the error turns out to be universal: the novel reveals it in the most virtuous and prudent character as well as in the reader. The "prudence," which consists in the accurate perception and judgment of the characters of people, cannot be attained without a degree of humility and self-questioning, without, that is, an awareness of the inevitable limitations of one's perspective. It cannot, moreover, be attained without an awareness that one may sometimes turn out to be not an objective magisterial spectator but a slyly assessed target audience whose expectations and mental patterns a rogue or a rhetorician turns into a most effective instrument of deceit.

A rogue or a rhetorician . . . In *Tom Jones* the reader-novelist and the reader-character parallels are, as in *Emma*, supplemented by the analogy between the narrator's reticence and the characters' information-withholding conduct. The narrator's subterfuges reenact and combine with those of Miss Bridget, Blifil, and the Salisbury lawyer Dowling. The three characters practice, respectively, sham ignorance, half-truths, and hasty evasions.

At the beginning of the novel the narrator poses as a historian.[15] In this capacity he makes tongue-in-cheek pretense that information is not always easily available to him and that sometimes he has to take "uncommon Pains to inform [himself] of the real Fact" (9.7.395). He also pretends to merely narrate his material and not to control it; the qualities of Thwackum and Square, for instance, are presented as existing independently of himself and determining his attitudes: "Had not *Thwackum* too much neglected Virtue, and *Square* Religion, in the Composition of their several Systems; and had not both utterly discarded all natural Goodness of Heart, they had never been represented as the Objects of Derision in this History" (3.4.97). The powers that qualify the narrator as a historian are invention and judgment, where invention is understood not as an autonomous creative faculty but as "Discovery, or finding out; . . . a quick and sagacious Penetration into the true Essence of all the Objects of our Contemplation" (9.1.372). The narrator does not assume the privilege of supplying the objects of contemplation; his creativity is, as it were, limited to revealing the nature of those already given.

Toward the end of the novel, however, the narrator begins to merge with the novelist, the consciousness that is not merely recording the events but that has masterminded them. In book 16, chapter 6, we find that the characters are related to the narrator by quasi-filial ties—"I regard all the Personages of this History in the Light of my Children"

(16.6.660). Moreover, in book 17, chapter 1 it appears that his grown-up "Children" are not independent, that he still controls their destinies: "In Regard to *Sophia*, it is more than probable, that we shall somewhere or other provide a good Husband for her in the End, either *Blifil*, or my Lord, or Somebody else; but as to poor *Jones*, such are the Calamities in which he is at present involved, owing to his Imprudence, . . . that we almost despair of bringing him to any Good; and if our Reader delights in seeing Executions, I think he ought not to lose any Time in taking a first Row at *Tyburn*" (17.1.675).

This touch of narrative metalepsis[16] is as heavily ironic as the narrator's earlier disclaiming of omniscience, but the change in emphasis is significant. While weaving the mystery, the narrator wears the mask of a limited historian, but with the approach of the disclosures he flings off this mask and admits the fictional nature of his story. As a realist Fielding has by now largely completed his task. "Human nature" has been allowed to play its part, and, as a result of the events that so far have not been overtly interfered with, Tom has been brought to the brink of destruction. Life is harsh on the "good heart" that is not protected by prudence: as in Molière, comedy threatens to turn into tragedy, the most natural outcome of Tom's mistakes.

Therefore, the narrator's insistence on the fictional nature of his tale is well timed. It ironically reinforces the promise of a happy ending that art, though not life, may still provide. The "art" in question is not, however, Molière's kind of a frankly deus-ex-machina comic resolution,[17] appropriate as the supernatural may be to a mock-epic in prose: "This I faithfully promise, that notwithstanding any Affection, which we may be supposed to have for this Rogue, whom we have unfortunately made our Heroe, we will lend him none of that supernatural Assistance with which we are entrusted, upon Condition that we use it only on very important Occasions. If he doth not therefore find some natural Means of fairly extricating himself from all his Distresses, we will do no Violence to the Truth and Dignity of History for his Sake; for we had rather relate that he was hanged at *Tyburn* (which may very probably be the Case) than forfeit our Integrity, or shock the Faith of our Reader" (17.1.675-76). In other words, though he has finally admitted his omnipotence (after having disclaimed it for a long time), "Fielding" now relinquishes his control and calls our attention to his ingenious brand of artificiality. The ending, he suggests, is not the most artificial part of the novel—the whole story has been imperceptibly arranged into an elaborate pattern of coincidences and consequences, all well within the limits of the plausible, a pattern that turns artificiality into art. The narrator need not control the *fabula* any longer because by now the plot lines involving Partridge, Mrs. Waters (alias Jenny Jones), the Fitzpatricks, Mrs. Miller, and Squire Western have converged into one knot, and the denouement comes as a matter of course in a series of causally connected recognition scenes.[18] The subtlest artifice, the narrator seems to suggest, lies in the opening books, where, disguised as a historian, he made early arrangements for the late disclosures, conspiring with the information-withholding characters against the credulous inertia of a complacent audience.

Indeed, in the early chapters of the novel the sham ignorance of the mock historian plays up to the analogous behavior of Miss Bridget. The "historian" sometimes pretends not to know the details of the situations that he has actually masterminded; Miss Bridget likewise pretends to share her friends' curiosity about the origins of her son Tom and later judiciously assumes the conventional role of a gossip eavesdropping on Jenny Jones.

The narrator supports Miss Bridget's game by tentatively suggesting wrong motives for her conduct: "The usual Compliments having passed between Mr. *Allworthy* and Miss *Bridget*, and the Tea being poured out, he summoned Mrs. *Wilkins*, and told his Sister he had a Present for her; for which she thanked him, imagining, I suppose, it had been a Gown, or some Ornament for her Person. Indeed, he very often made her such Presents, and she, in Complacence to him, spent much Time in adorning herself. I say, in Complacence to him, because she always exprest the greatest Contempt for Dress, and for those Ladies who made it their Study" (1.4.33). The present that Allworthy has in mind is, of course, little Tom. Miss Bridget knows this but pretends she does not. The narrator bolsters her sham ignorance with his own, inventing a false though plausible conjecture ("I suppose") for her serene gratitude. The ensuing ironical observations about Miss Bridget's attitude to dress introduce an element of structural equivocation: on the first reading they are only perceived as a sally against Miss Bridget's manner of combining vanity with prudishness while they also serve as a conjuror's patter diverting the reader's attention from the subdued excitement of the scene.

The audience expects Miss Bridget to be disappointed with what her brother has to give her. The narrator evades the issue by a neat turn of phrase: "But if such was her Expectation, how was she disappointed, when Mrs. *Wilkins* . . . produced the little Infant!" (1.4.33). On the first reading the "if" clause is perceived as a link between the two paragraphs. On a rereading, however, it turns out to be an appropriate reservation: Miss Bridget would have been disappointed if such had been her expectation, which was not the case. The narrator's sham ignorance lays the groundwork for the enhancement of the dramatic irony on a repeated reading.

The narrator sometimes ironically disavows insight even when a direct censure of the character would not interfere with mystification. "This was a great Appearance of Religion," he says about Dr. Blifil and then comments: "Whether his Religion was real, or consisted only in Appearance, I shall not presume to say, as I am not possessed of any Touchstone, which can distinguish the true from the false" (1.10.47). He thus both aligns himself with the chorus of neighbors who keep gossiping about the main characters and misrepresenting their motives and distances himself from that chorus by a kind of epistemological humility that is quite earnest under its surface irony. In addition to playing the game of cognitive privilege, this technique activates our judgment and contributes to our false sense of security.

The limitation of privilege is removed later in the novel. In the last six books the narrator has no scruples about explaining the intrigues of Mrs. Fitzpatrick or Lady Bellaston: by this time active mystification is a matter of the past and sham ignorance is no longer called upon to prevent premature disclosures.

Pressing business is the leitmotif of the lawyer Dowling, whom Blifil bribes to suppress the secret of Tom's birth. While remaining offstage, Dowling is referred to as an attorney from Salisbury, who "seemed in a violent Hurry, and protested he had so much Business to do, that if he could cut himself into four Quarters, all would not be sufficient" (5.7.186).

The attorney is carrying the news of Miss Bridget's death and confession, but since Allworthy is too ill to receive him, the message is communicated to Blifil. The malice that Blifil bears Tom noticeably increases after the offstage interview, that is, on his learning that, as his half brother, Tom may have higher claims on Allworthy's property. Blifil suppresses this part of the news. When he tells Allworthy the rest of it and is asked about the messenger, the latter's haste is conveniently brought up again: "[Allworthy] now enquired for the Messenger; but *Blifil* told him, it had been impossible to detain him a Moment; for he appeared by the great Hurry he was in to have some Business of Importance on his Hands: That he complained of being hurried, and driven and torn out of his Life, and repeated many Times, that if he could divide himself into four Quarters, he knew how to dispose of every one" (5.8.190).

In another episode it is through the motif of haste that the mysterious attorney is identified as Mr. Dowling. As though checking his impulse to defend Tom from slander, Dowling precipitates his departure from Mrs. Whitefield's inn: "*Dowling* sat all this while silent, biting his Fingers, making Faces, grinning, and looking wonderfully arch; at last he opened his Lips, and protested that [Tom] looked like another Sort of Man. He then called for his Bill with the utmost Haste, declared he must be at *Hereford* that Evening, lamented his great Hurry of Business, and wished he could divide himself into twenty Pieces, in order to be at once in twenty Places" (8.8.330).

Haste is Dowling's means of evasion. The only time he seems to be at leisure to have a drink with Tom, he is so moved by the young man's story that he practically blurts out the secret of his parentage: " 'Ay! ay!' cries *Dowling*, 'I protest then, it is a Pity such a Person should inherit the great Estate of your Uncle *Allworthy*' " (12.10.504). Yet both Tom and the audience fail to attach significance to this slip of the tongue. It seems likely that on this occasion Dowling might have been tempted to say more, yet now it is Tom's turn to depart in haste. The narrator follows suit, not without a sly hint at a lost chance: "But we may possibly take some other Opportunity of commenting upon this, especially if we should happen to meet Mr. *Dowling* any more in the Course of our History. At present we are obliged to take our Leave of that Gentleman a little abruptly, in Imitation of Mr. *Jones;* who was no sooner informed, by *Partridge,* that his Horses were ready, than he deposited his Reckoning, wished his Companion a good Night, mounted, and set forward towards *Coventry,* tho' the Night was dark, and it just then began to rain very hard" (12.10.507).

At the end of the novel Dowling again pleads haste in order to evade an explanation with Allworthy, but this time the latter is not in a sickbed. Allworthy's insistence and a bolted door produce the disclosure, which has actually been at the tip of the attorney's tongue all along.

"In Imitation," as it were, of Dowling, the narrator sometimes excuses his withholding of information by the need to proceed to matters of greater urgency, as, for instance, in the case of Tom's leaving Dowling, about whom, one feels, the last word has not yet been said. In so far as this technique diverts our attention, it is analogous to Austen's finesse. However, the narrator of *Emma* is too reserved to enter into a friendly relationship with the reader, especially since such a relationship would have to be maintained despite the vicissitudes of mystification.

Another instance of withholding information under the pretense of haste prepares the groundwork for the eventual disclosure of Square's affair with Molly Seagrim. The narrator does not tell us about the relationship when it begins, but he intimates that not everything has yet been said about the devious tutor: "[Square], Master *Blifil*, and *Jones*, had mounted their Horses, after Church, to take the Air, and had ridden about a Quarter of a Mile, when *Square*, changing his Mind, (not idly, but for a Reason which we shall unfold as soon as we have Leisure) desired the young Gentlemen to ride with him another Way" (4.8.137). The parenthetical remark prepares us for the discovery of Square in Molly's closet: even though it does not completely dispel our sense that this discovery is an afterthought meant to extricate Tom from a moral predicament. The episode is a miniature model of the effect produced by the novel's major surprise gap: the artifice that comes to Tom's rescue has been contrived long before the episodes in which it takes effect.

According to a respectable convention, the third-person narrator, historian or otherwise, must not lay himself open to the charge of blatant misrepresentation—he is, as it were, always under oath. At a delicate moment he therefore resorts to equivocation: he makes us think that Jenny Jones is little Tom's mother without actually ever saying this. Jenny, he observes, saved her accusers trouble "by freely confessing the whole Fact with which she was charged" (1.6.37). She is accused of having given birth to Tom, and she does, indeed, plead guilty. The narrator tells us the truth though not the whole truth: he withholds the facts that the charge is unjust and the confession false; yet technically he remains not guilty of perjury.

This strategy seems to have been borrowed from Blifil, who excels in formulating statements that equally well express the ostensible meaning intended for the hearer and a quite opposite real purport. For example, when Allworthy warns Blifil that "he would, on no Account, be accessary to forcing a young Lady into a Marriage contrary to her own Will," Bilfil includes the following statement in his reply: "Sir, I promise you I would not myself, for any Consideration, no not for the whole World, consent to marry this young Lady, if I was not persuaded she had all the Passion for me which I desire she should have" (7.6.264). Allworthy takes this for an assurance that Sophia loves Blifil; out of context Blifil's words do allow such an interpretation. The reader, however, knows that Sophia's "passion" for Blifil is hatred and that, far from deterring him, this only heightens his expectations: "Indeed no one hath seen Beauty in its highest Lustre, who hath never seen it in Distress. *Blifil* therefore looked on this human Ortolan with greater Desire than when he viewed her last; nor was his Desire at all lessened by the Aversion which he discovered in her to himself. On the contrary, this served rather to heighten the Pleasure he proposed in rifling her Charms, as it added Triumph to Lust: nay, he had some further Views, from obtaining the absolute Possession of her Person, which we detest too much even to mention; and Revenge itself was not without its Share in the Gratifications which he promised himself" (7.6.263). The hint of sadism in Blifil grants a degree of truth to his diagnosis of Sophia's feelings for him. Formally, Blifil is not telling straightforward lies, but the language that he uses is calculated to conceal rather than reveal his thoughts.[19] He turns Allworthy from an objective tool of justice into a target audience that is misled by its own preconceptions. As shown above, in more ways than one "Fielding" does the same to the reader.

Not inconsistently with the complex personality of the historical author, the narrator passes judgment on (and perhaps expresses a slight embarrassment at) his use of half-truths similar to those of Blifil: "This excellent Method of conveying a Falsehood with the Heart only, without making the Tongue guilty of an Untruth, by the means of Equivocation and Imposture, hath quieted the Conscience of many a notable Deceiver; and yet when we consider that it is Omniscience on which these endeavour to impose, it may possibly seem capable of affording only a very superficial Comfort; and that his artful and refined Distinction between communicating a Lie, and telling one, is hardly worth the Pains it costs them" (7.6.264). In addition to making a theological point, the statement about the futility of equivocation anticipates rereadings, when the audience will largely share the ironic omniscience of the novelist.

In *Tom Jones*, by contrast to *Emma* or *The Sound and the Fury*, the amount of material affected by mystification is, relatively, too small to constitute a structurally built-in demand for a repeated reading. There is no compulsion of unfinished business in our return to the novel, yet, owing to our acquaintance with its behind-the-stage intrigues, the experiences of rereading it is still qualitatively different from that of the first reading.

The narrator of the novel seems to have foreseen our return and taken measures to prevent the illusion of his friendly treatment of the reader from seeming duplicitous in view of his half-truths and mystifications. Indeed, the narrator feels the need to apologize to the reader for temporarily (for the length of but a few pages) withholding information on minor matters, such as Mrs. Fitzpatrick's "very particular Friend[ship]" (11.8.464) with the Irish peer. In a conspiratorially ironic manner he comments that "This Circumstance . . . as the Lady did not think it material enough to relate to her Friend, we would not at that Time impart to the Reader" so as not to "interrupt her Narrative by giving a Hint of what seemed to her of too little Importance to be mentioned" (11.8.465).

The need for apology is, by the same token, even greater when the main secrets of the plot are revealed on the first reading. At the end of the novel the narrator has recourse to a hit-and-run technique—he bids farewell to the reader in the prefatory chapter of the last book, just before the disclosures, and then fades from the text: the novel closes with a sequence of dramatically presented scenes in which the element of "telling" is reduced to a minimum. Yet on a rereading the narrator's imaginary presence is quite massive again and the intimacy of his addresses to the reader can be perceived as hypocritic.

This side effect of reticence is neutralized by the impression that during our repeated journey through the novel the narrator is quite frank with us about his use of mystification. He now turns mystification into a new source of both dramatic and verbal irony, at the expense of the characters and at our own expense in so far as we have been victims of deceptions on the first reading. This is a new phase in the narrator-reader relationship. With an air of a fellow conspirator (which revives our sense of being an elite audience) the narrator calls our attention to all the little plots hatched offstage. Moreover, at these points the narrator (like Dowling) often seems to be uneasy and apologetic. Such an effect is absent in *Emma*, where it is unnecessary because the reserved disposition of the narrator precludes any suggestion of a broken promise.

The uneasiness of the narrator of *Tom Jones* manifests itself in subtle stylistic variations, which may or may not be consciously registered by the audience. Such variations often relate to a dialogue technique that belongs to the complex of methods making up Fielding's peculiar brand of heteroglossia.[20] The conversations of the characters of *Tom Jones* are recorded by means of three main types of discourse: direct, indirect, and "represented" (or free indirect) speech. Each of the three has a specific function.

Direct speech allows the characters to speak for themselves: the narrator's voice is not heard when direct utterances are sounded—such utterances verge on insets, miniature stories-within-stories, in which the colors grow denser than in the surrounding narrative and thus produce stylization.[21]

Conversely, in the case of indirect speech it is the narrator who reports the character's message in his own voice, as in the following example: "*Allworthy* bid him immediately call a Servant" (4.11.143). Fielding's indirect speech usually contains catalysts rather than kernels: requests or orders that are natural under given circumstances or communication of matters that the reader either expects (e.g., the horses are ready) or is already familiar with. Since the details thus conveyed are usually accurate—the narrator will not, as it were, tell a straightforward lie in his own voice—indirect speech implies the narrator's corroboration of the character's message.

In Fielding's novels the third type of discourse, represented (or free indirect) speech, combines the punctuation of direct speech with the morphology of indirect speech: Blifil "positively insisted, that he had made Use of no such Appellation: adding, 'Heaven forbid such naughty Words should ever come out of his Mouth'" (3.4.97). The use of quotation marks makes it clear that the words of the utterance belong to the character, but the use of the third-person pronoun shows that they are pronounced by the narrator, who dissociates himself from the utterance by means of quotations marks. The syntactic dependence of the character's utterance changes its would-be intonational pattern, often creating the impression of sarcastic parody.

When it comes to withholding information, however, Fielding changes his use of the three types of discourse. For instance, though matter-of-fact communication's—orders, servants' reports, etc.—are usually presented in indirect speech, there is a significant exception to this regularity. When the sick Allworthy is informed that a messenger (Dowling) has brought him some important news, he sends Blifil to talk to him, and his order is presented in direct speech: "'Go, Child,' said *Allworthy* to *Blifil*, 'see what the Gentleman wants. I am not able to do any business now, nor can he have any with me, in which you are not at present more concerned than myself. Besides I really am—I am incapable of seeing any one at present, or of any longer Attention'" (5.7.186). On a rereading we notice that here the narrator actually explains why Miss Bridget's death does not lead to the revelation of Tom's origin. Allworthy is ill, so he sends somebody else to attend to his affairs; and it is only natural that the deputy should be

Blifil, the heir to the bulk of his fortune. Direct speech highlights the point and turns the catalyst-type detail into an important kernel. Moreover, Allworthy's admission of his inability to handle the situation may be perceived as symptomatic: it applies, perhaps, to more episodes than one.

In the next chapter Blifil is called upon to react to the news of his mother's death. On the repeated reading we know that he has just learned that Tom is his brother and has decided to conceal the matter. His memorable statement to his tutors is presented in free indirect speech without quotation marks, a device common in the works of later novelists but rather unusual in *Tom Jones:* "The young Gentleman said, He knew very well we were all mortal, and he would endeavour to submit to his Loss as well as he could. That he could not, however, help complaining a little against the peculiar Severity of his Fate, which brought the News of so great a Calamity to him by Surprize, and that at a Time when he hourly expected the severest Blow he was capable of feeling from the Malice of Fortune. He said, the present Occasion would put to the Test those excellent Rudiments which he had learnt from Mr. *Thwackum* and Mr. *Square,* and it would be entirely owing to them, if he was enabled to survive such Misfortunes" (5.8.189). The choice of words is undoubtedly Blifil's; the introductory "he said" is omitted at the beginning of the second sentence yet the narrator does not mark the passage off by inverted commas. This is more than a technical matter. On a rereading we are aware that the harangue contains a great deal of truth: Blifil has indeed just received a shock (Tom has turned out to be a more dangerous rival than he had thought); and he does, indeed, intend to make the best of it by employing the rudiments (of self-serving casuistry and inventive malice) that his tutors have taught him. The narrator himself, however, is equivocating almost as much as Blifil. His refraining from the use of quotation marks, his wonted formal method of dissociating himself from a character's words, almost amounts to an admission of playing up to Blifil's reticence. On a repeated reading we know that we have been misled at precisely this point; yet we appreciate both the artistry of the equivocation and the fairness with which the narrator self-consciously reveals its mechanism. Moreover, we are shown that the dramatic irony of the episode is even more intricate than it appears on the first reading. Already then it is clear that Blifil breaks the sad news to Allworthy under the pretext of doing his duty but actually in order to precipitate his uncle's death and inherit his estate. Now we know that Blifil has additional motivation: if Allworthy lives long enough to learn the truth about Tom's identity he may (and eventually will) make him his principal heir.

Thus a change in the use of the three types of discourse adds to Fielding's irony a dimension that can be perceived only on a rereading. Verbal equivocation similar to that of Austen's and his own characters is another technique that produces this long-term effect. The narrator seems to wink at the reader[22] when he makes statements like "Who this Mrs. *Waters* was, the Reader pretty well knows; what she was, he must be perfectly satisfied" (17.9.704). On the first reading the words seem to mean that the Mrs. Waters who visits Tom in prison is the woman who seduced him in Upton and then left in the company of Mr. Fitzpatrick. The phrase "what she was" then reads as a sarcastic reference to the lady's conduct. On a rereading the commentary acquires an additional meaning: "That Mrs. Waters was Jenny Jones the reader pretty well knows; that she was not Tom's mother he must be perfectly satisfied"—calling our attention to the potentialities of the wilful handling of language by which we have been so successfully misled. The cautionary message of *Tom Jones* is milder than that of *Emma*; the mystification is almost watertight since clues to the "real story" are practically impossible to pick up on the first reading.

Indeed, though like *Emma* and *Bleak House*, *Tom Jones* has taken advantage of our tendency to remain "perfectly satisfied" with a single raison d'être for any narrative detail, here this reason is stronger and more consciously registered than in *Emma* and has a better aesthetic justification than in *Bleak House*. Thus, after Miss Bridget and Mrs. Wilkins have both watched the interview between Mr. Allworthy and Jenny Jones through a keyhole, we are told that "Mrs. *Bridget* gently reproved the Curiosity of Mrs. *Deborah,* a Vice with which it seems the latter was too much tainted, and which the former inveighed against her with great Bitterness, adding, 'that among all her Faults, she thanked Heaven, her Enemies could not accuse her of prying into the Affairs of other People'" (1.8.43). On the first reading, coming immediately after the Hogarthian lady has moved away from the keyhole, this remark is understood as part of the satirical pattern in which the hypocrisy of Miss Bridget and Mrs. Wilkins is reduced *ad absurdum*. On a rereading Miss Bridget turns out to be a character rather than a caricature. The narrator is understood to be signaling to us that here she is indeed interested in nobody's business but her own: she is Tom's real mother, and "the Affairs" on which she is spying through the keyhole directly concern her own history and situation.

The common denominator of the passages in which the narrative lays bare the mechanics of mystification is the triple suggestion that (1) *Tom Jones* offers a richer intellectual experience than could have been appreciated on the first reading; (2) that the motivation of people's actions is often much more complicated than the most acute general observations can provide for,[23] and (3) that mystification and its deconstruction have been performed for the reader's instruction as well as delight. Since the reader has been entrapped by the techniques parallel to those practiced by the characters, this experience on the first and its processing on the second readings make up a lesson both in the need for self-critical prudence and in the treacherous ways of the world. The discovery of the new dimensions of the text further suggests that this lesson is part of a moral-aesthetic architectonics whose principles the reader might find it rewarding to seek out.

A "bear-with-me" message is, indeed, conveyed by the tone of much of the authorial commentary as well as by such statements as "We warn thee not too hastily to condemn any of the Incidents in this our History, as impertinent and foreign to our main Design, because thou dost not immediately conceive in what Manner such Incident may conduce to that Design" (10.1.398). What on the first reading may sound as the novelist's somewhat immodest flaunting of his credentials, as for instance, his explanation, in chapter 1 of book 9, that he writes prefatory essays in order to convince the reader of his literary skill (since bare narratives of adventures can be concocted by hacks), turns out to combine with an understatement of his achievement, since the essay actually introduces one of the most intricate knots of the plot: no run-off-the-mill scribbler could devise the Upton episode with so much wit, elegance, control, and gusto. The intricacy of the plot maneuvers that insure the novel's happy ending can also be fully appreciated only on a rereading. They are a source of aesthetic enjoyment in its own right, but they are also evidence of the strength and suppleness of the mind behind the narrative. Once we are prepared to appreciate that we owe *Tom Jones* to superior intelligence rather than to happy histrionic craftsmanship, we are also better prepared to believe that the play of this intelligence is based on a "great, useful and uncommon" moral "Doctrine, which it is the purpose of this whole work to inculcate, and which we must not fill up our Pages by frequently repeating, as an ordinary Parson fills his Sermon by repeating his Text at the End of every Paragraph" (12.8.500).

The ironic inflation of the quality of the doctrine by the use of three adjectives, including "great," is a signal that the statement should be taken cautiously. Indeed, its reference to repetition is misleading: Fielding does not explictly formulate his doctrine, let alone repeat it—hence the critical disagreement about the presence, validity, and quality of this doctrine as well as about the form, explicit or implicit, in which it is presented.[24] The labor of distilling the moral philosophy of *Tom Jones* is left to individual readers. The scope of the present project does not allow me to present my view of it at length, beyond mentioning that, I believe, it revises Hume's combination of moral intuitionism and utilitarianism by claiming that, though not all people possess an innate moral instinct, in some its absence can be compensated for by the conscious commitment to the good of others,[25] and that such a commitment of the will must supplement even the best of natural inclinations while being held in check by reasonable prudence; Tom, indeed, is both naturally good and consciously committed to the good of others but has to learn the prudence that Sophia instinctively possesses alongside the other two virtues. Of the three constituents of Fielding's ethical paradigm, the conscious commitment to the good of others can, perhaps, be taught by example, but the need for prudence is the more effectively demonstrated if lack of it becomes apparent. The game of mystification in *Tom Jones* points to our own deficiency in this respect—after first enhancing our self-defeating belief in our competence.

"Human nature," offered to the mental equivalent of the reader's palate by the "bill of fare" at the beginning of the novel, is, according to the Augustan understanding, that which is generally true of various types of people. And yet the "taste" and the judgment to which the novel appeals lie not merely in an automatic application of the general to the particular but also in determining the measure of the applicability of any general rule to concrete circumstances, and in supplementing and correcting the rule itself.[26] This implies taking into consideration a vaster variety of data than are provided for by a generalization: the judgment of the reader must involve not only self-protective prudence but also "prudence" in the best sense of the word, namely "a rational faculty . . . which depends on the proper functioning of memory, intelligence, and foresight."[27] Yet "No Man is wise at all Hours" (3.4.97); even Squire Allworthy, the paragon of Christian humanistic virtues, occasionally fails to assess the true motives and characters of the people around him, even if he is sagacious enough to perceive his sister's attachments to Mr. Summer and Captain Blifil despite her dissimulations. Neither people nor books can be expected to adhere with perfect constancy to the ideals of reason, virtue, or harmony, as the case might be; and "if we judge according to the

Sentiments of some Critics, and of some Christians, no Author will be saved in this World, and no Man in the next" (11.1.435). The reader, whose perceptiveness, and hence "prudence," are likewise found wanting, is given a cautionary lesson—not only about the wiles that may lie in wait for him in society but also about his or her own naive "Self-Conceit" hidden under the "thin Disguise of Wisdom" (13.1.525-26).

The narrator of the novel seems to have assimilated such a lesson; therefore the ironic generalizations with which he interprets the characters' actions are often modified by suggestions of guesswork—"but, *perhaps*, these very Raptures made [Jones] forget" (12.4.483; my italics). He notes moreover, that by means of his comments, he makes a "short Appearance, *by Way of Chorus*, on the Stage" (3.7.106-7; my italics),[28] sallying forth as it were, from the *orchestra*, or, perhaps, from behind the stage where, by the middle of the novel, he has also metaphorically placed the reader. The analogies between his techniques of mystification and those of his characters likewise place the implied author "on the stage."[29]

Fielding can be imagined as an occupant of the Euripedean ground between the Aeschylean tragedy and the Lucianic New Comedy. In the words of Nietzsche's "The Birth of Tragedy," Euripides "brought the *spectator* onto the stage" when he "transferred the entire world of sentiments, passions, and experiences, hitherto present at every festival performance as the invisible chorus on the spectators' benches, into the souls of stage-heroes."[30] A parallel feat in the history of fiction is completed in nineteenth-century realistic novels. Fielding's larger-than-life heroes foreshadow it by serving as illustrations of "human nature," yet they still bear traces of their origin in a "dream" produced by a choric transport of the narrator, into which the audience is partly drawn.[31] The emotions of ordinary men and women are enacted by these stylized heroes; upon having been estranged, these emotions are, to some extent, vicariously reenacted by the audience. Yet the *intellectual* tribulations of the heroes are reenacted directly by the information-processing experience of the audience. As we become conscious of this nonvicarious experience, and particularly of its pitfalls, we place ourselves, as it were, not on the stage but rather in the imaginary *orchestra*, that secondary fictional world in which our communication with the novelist is taking place.

The shadowy in-between world of the "orchestra," in which the reader is led through the motions that parallel those of the characters on the stage, solidifies in some realistic nineteenth-century novels such as, among others, *Emma, Vanity Fair*,[32] and *Bleak House*. The characters' experience is then presented as a vast and firm "reality" given to the reader's perception; and self-referential reminders that this "reality" is an illusion conjured up by the novelist are kept away from the text, especially owing to the novelists' tendency to thematize the difference between reality and the characters' self-delusion.[33] In the "orchestra," the arena of the mind, the audience is made to grapple with its own errors and delusions.

In twentieth-century self-referential fiction the sense of the dramatic illusion is often frankly canceled by the text, either repeatedly or in what Nabokov called an "epilogical mopping-up."[34] At the same time, the shadowy world of each novel's "orchestra" tends to lose part of its specific distinctive features. The audience is given more freedom: as the burden of the quest for meaning is manifestly transferred from the text to the reader, the filming-site world of the "orchestra" merges with the spectators' benches and expands over indefinite spaces in which the partitions between aesthetic and ethical experience are almost completely erased.

PART THREE

The Permanent Suspension
of Information

CHAPTER SEVEN

A Passage to India
At an Angle to the Universe

> The test of a first-rate intelligence is the
> ability to hold two opposed ideas in the
> mind at the same time and still retain
> the ability to function.
>
> —F. Scott Fitzgerald, *The Crack-Up*

Among the significant developments of twentieth-century fiction is the increase in the number of novels that do not satisfy the reader's wish for what is deemed sufficient information about story events. The narratives of Fitzgerald's *The Great Gatsby*, Nabokov's *The Real Life of Sebastian Knight*, Fowles's *The French Lieutenant's Woman*, Walker Percy's *The Movie Goer*, Pynchon's *The Crying of Lot 49*, and, among others, the two novels discussed in the following two chapters of this book, permanently withhold instructions that could unambiguously stabilize our pattern recognition.[1] The resulting gaps usually emphasize the unavailability of certain kinds of knowledge and express a skeptical attitude that is alien to the Socratic optimism of the previous century's realistic fiction. The kinds of knowledge that the novels repudiate are different, as is the meaning of the repudiation. Permanent gaps can be read as expressions or explorations of the novelists' ethical or epistemological beliefs; the question may then arise whether the experience through which, as rhetorical techniques, they lead the audience is consonant with these beliefs.

The rhetorical effects of permanent gaps have a common denominator: on the first reading we expect the informational gaps to be filled eventually (since in fiction temporary gaps are still more usual than permanent gaps). We endeavor to anticipate the disclosures with our own surmises, but by the end of the first reading we are confronted with the narrative's refusal either to confirm or to refute our hypotheses. The conclusions that the latter discovery suggests constitute the main variable in the paradigm of the permanent gaps.

In the heyday of realistic fiction (when permanent gaps were often of the "did-they-or-didn't-they" kind) the resulting vagueness or ambiguity would tend to suggest that the withheld details are immaterial and should never have concerned us at all. The conclusion is moral rather than epistemological: for example, in Thackeray's *Vanity Fair* we come to understand that it is not important whether Becky does or does not become Lord Steyne's mistress since her behavior is equally bad in either case; our curiosity about the sordid detail is made to appear similar to the inquisitiveness of society gossips and eavesdropping servants. By contrast, in more recent works, for instance, in Henry James's "The Turn of the Screw" or in such a radical experiment as Nabokov's *Invitation to a Beheading*, the finality of a gap suggests that the ambiguity is an integral part of the theme.[2]

The rhetorical effect of a permanent gap thus involves our interest in the suppressed (actually, the nonexistent) portion of the *fabula* during the first reading and a resignation to its absence on a repeated reading. This chapter traces the effects produced by the central gap on the first reading of E.M. Forster's *A Passage to India* and then discusses features that come into relief on a rereading. It must, however, start with an examination of the nature and implications of the narrative stance that combines the general impression of omniscience with the withholding of information about the novel's pivotal event.

The voice of *A Passage to India* is that of a nondramatized third-person narrator; the focalization is variable. Though narrators of this kind tend to be perceived as "omniscient," their cognitive privilege is usually restricted in more or less consistent specific ways. Whereas *Tom Jones* and *Emma* display communicative rather than cognitive principles—their narrators are unwilling rather than unable to disclose certain details before they become common knowledge in the fictional worlds; the narrator of *A Passage to India* seems to claim limited powers of insight.

His main limitation concerns whatever takes place outside or below the range of an intelligent bystander's observation. He gives no more information about the characters than is available to themselves or to their observant friends, or he defines their behavior in an analytic-impressionist manner—as in the following instance: "[Mrs. Turton] was 'saving herself up,' as she called it—not for anything that would happen that afternoon or even that week, but for some vague future occasion when a high official might come along and tax her social strength. Most of her public appearances were marked by this air of reserve" (39).[3]

Whenever the narrator gives us a piece of information of which the personage himself may not be conscious (for example, noting that Aziz is "sensitive rather than responsive," 67), it pertains to permanent character traits that could be common knowledge. The narrator may likewise generalize and comment on characters as members of a group, observing, for example, that Indians take "the public view of poetry, not the private which obtains in England" (15), or registering the rise of mob instincts at the club where the members start "speaking of 'women and children'—that phrase that exempts the male from sanity when it has been repeated a few times" (183). No explicit statements, however, are made about subconscious phenomena. If a character does not know the cause or the nature of his state of mind, the narrator will not probe it. For example, the narrator does not overtly analyze the psychological processes that lead Aziz to suspect Fielding of an intention to marry Miss Quested, even though he suggestively describes the things reflected in the consciousness of Aziz and registers the moment when the suspicions surface: "But as he drove off, something depressed him—a dull pain of body or mind, waiting to rise to the surface. When he reached the bungalow he wanted to return and say something very affectionate; instead, he gave the sais a heavy tip, and sat down gloomily on the bed, and Hassan massaged him incompetently. The eye-flies had colonized the top of an almeira; the red stains on the durry were thicker, for Mohammed Latif had slept here during his imprisonment and spat a good deal; the table drawer was scarred where the police had forced it open; everything in Chandrapore was used up, including the air. The trouble rose to the surface now: he was suspicious; he suspected his friend of intending to marry Miss Quested for the sake of her money, and of going to England for that purpose" (279).

This self-imposed limitation of the omniscient narrator largely accounts for the persistence of the novel's main gap: we never learn what happened to Adela Quested in the Marabar caves because she does not attain the degree of self-knowledge that would permit her to define the nature of that experience. Eventually she seems to believe that no attack was made upon her, yet she is not convinced, and does not wish to be convinced, that she merely hallucinated in the cave. Ultimately she resigns herself to never learning the truth; and since her possible subconscious awareness of it is beyond the narrator's pale, he does not corroborate any guess that the audience might be inclined to make. Likewise beyond the pale of the narrator's self-imposed limitations is the ability to decide whether Adela's experience in the cave is morbidly psychological or of a mystical, spiritual kind.

Another restriction on the narrator's cognitive privilege is spatial: he does not record the things that happen simultaneously with but at some remove from those on which the camera eye is fixed. Events that take place simultaneously at a considerable distance from each other are described, but only in separate chapters: for instance, Aziz is shown playing polo on the Maidan in chapter 6, while the bridge party, described in chapter 5, is supposed to be in progress at the club. Within one episode, however, the narrator's vision never exceeds that of the participants: he can suggest that the thing that looks like a snake is actually a tree stump only when Adela Quested, on her way to the Marabar caves, discovers this with the help of her field glasses. When the main group of characters is returning from the expedition the field glasses are in the pocket of Aziz, and the remote object is ironically referred to as "the snake that looked like a tree" (160). Likewise, since the narrator remains with Mrs. Moore and Adela in the club, he cannot register whether it is Fielding or someone else who makes a pleasant remark and disappears into the darkness (24-25). The technique is reminiscent of the device of implied simultaneity that Dickens used to promote suspense in *Bleak House* and laid aside when no longer necessary. In *A Passage to India*, however, the spatial limitation of the camera eye is not a local rhetorical device but an aspect of the narrator's consistent cognitive principle. The narrator seems to be an invisible and slightly uneasy presence, sensitive, shrewd, capable of reading people's surface thoughts and responding to moods, yet sharing certain limitations of human vision and insight. Needless to say, a narrator of this kind is most appropriate to the spirit of the liberal humanism that finds itself on alien soil in the world of this novel.

The narrator's spatial limitation is made directly responsible for the novel's central gap: if the camera eye is focused on Aziz in one cave, it cannot register what is happening to Adela in another cave. No new device is employed to suppress information; indeed, the regularity of the procedure makes the gap appear almost inevitable. Moreover, it is Aziz and not Adela who attracts the focus of the camera eye at the crucial moment, because Adela has just asked her companion a tactless question: the narrator has hitherto never failed to explain how and why minor manifestations of indelicacy offend Aziz. The shift of focalization is, therefore, not fortuitous.

The limitations of the narrator's cognitive privilege provide him with a kind of alibi. If asked what happened to Adela in the cave, he could answer with Godbole's remark, "I cannot say. I was not present" (176). If the camera eye had followed Adela into the cave, or if it could have penetrated the stone walls, the narrator would have been in a position to tell us whether or not the guide, or some lurking Pathan, did actually assault Adela (at the beginning of the novel Ronny Heaslop convicts a Pathan of attempted rape, 50-51); and his refusal to inform us on this point would have been arbitrary. In the early manuscript version of the novel the narrator directly reports Adela's experience in the cave: her "hallucination" or what appears to be one, is presented in such a way that the reader, like the girl herself, may take it for an actual event, especially since the physical element in it is rather intense.[4] That Forster did not include the direct account of Adela's Marabar experience in the final version suggests his unwillingness to make it immediately clear whether or not a physical assault did take place.

There are reasons for this unwillingness, as the analysis of audience response on the first reading of the novel will show. However, alibi or no alibi, withholding the information about the nature of the event that is located at the very center of the novel is perceived as breaking a promise that even a mildly omniscient stance would hold out to the audience. The resulting disappointment of the reader diffusely reenacts the disappointments of the characters—a constantly recurrent motif and the pervasive mood of the novel.[5] At the same time, however, it offers a new promise—that depth psychology, the life of the spirit, or the vastness of the universe contain much more than is given to habitual perception or what Tennyson called our "matter-molded forms of speech." Forster's wary consciousness of the possibility of mystical insight seems to have grown more acute by the time of his writing *A Passage to India* than it was at the earlier stages of his career. The famous statement of Jean-Paul Sartre—that the novelist's technique usually relates back to his metaphysics[6]—is particularly well borne out by the narrative stance of this novel.

When we read the novel for the first time, the first hypothesis that offers itself where we become acquainted with Adela's complaint against Aziz is that an attack on her was actually made by the guide who accompanied her and Aziz to the caves. This theory is largely a result of the way in which the narrative exploits the selectiveness of our attention: it is Aziz rather than Adela who is placed at the center of our interest when a catastrophe is anticipated at the beginning of the novel.

At the end of chapter 1, the Marabar Hills are metaphorically described as threatening "fists and fingers" (9). The impression of a distant menace is reinforced in chapter 2, when Aziz, passing a pleasant evening with his friends, feels that it is "Delicious . . . to lie on the broad verandah with the moon rising in front and the servants preparing dinner behind, and no trouble happening" (10). The reference to "no trouble happening" is ironic; it produces an effect similar to that of the descriptions of the calm before the storm in sea stories.

We do not know what shape the trouble will take, but the above sentence connects it with Aziz who is, moreover, a recognizable version of the young protagonist who must learn caution through experience. His first appearance in the novel is marked by his releasing his bicycle before a servant can catch it (9); later he is shown yielding to "a wild desire to make an enemy for life" by provoking Dr. Panna Lal—only to repent afterwards: "Dr. Panna Lal was a person of no importance, yet was it wise to have quarrelled even with him?" (59-60). His lack of circumspection is coupled with fits of paranoia; he fears, for example, that his failure to attend the bridge party may strain his relationship with the authorities. An earlier episode in which Ronny Heaslop is barely prevented from reporting Aziz as a malcontent shows that the doctor's worries are not entirely unfounded. His position is vulnerable. Unlike Cyril Fielding, he does not "travel light" (121): he is rooted in his society and religion, has a young family to support, and therefore feels "placed" (121). Any "silly escapade" may bring "disgrace on his children" (103).

Aziz is made vulnerable by his wish to keep up appearances in the eyes of the people he likes. Due to the exaggerated rumors that Mrs. Moore and Miss Quested are displeased with his breaking, as it were, a promise made for the sake of friendly politeness, he undertakes to organize an expedition that, as the narrative suggests, "challenge[s] the spirit of the Indian earth, which tries to keep men in compartments" (127). The chosen site is the Marabar Hills—we recall that during Fielding's tea party Professor Godbole could not bring himself to mention something ominous about them (75-76). Without realizing the import of his words, Aziz also prophesies trouble: when Fielding and Godbole miss the train, he cries out that he is destroyed (131) and later, planning the timetable for the picnic, reserves one hour "for misfortunes" (139). Aziz, furthermore, accepts responsibility for everything that happens: even when his two friends miss the train through their own fault, he says, "I am to blame. I am the host" (132). Words, especially those not meant in earnest, words that are gestures rather than actions, acquire an ominous life of their own in *A Passage to India*. It takes Mrs. Moore's early emotional responsiveness or Fielding's experience to overcome (not completely in the case of the latter) the difference between what Forster presents as the Indian and the English semiotic systems.[7] It is not surprising, therefore, that in addition to being used with virtuoso skill, language is warily thematized in this novel.[8]

As the account of the Marabar picnic unfolds, the reader's formerly vague forebodings crystalize: some misfortune seems imminent before the end of the day. At first, however, the expedition appears to be a success: the host's only mistake is allowing too many people into the first cave. The crush largely accounts for the faintness of Mrs. Moore: it has the power to explain her faintness rationally, suggesting that the ideological shift that it initiates in her is a side effect of fright and physical strain. The shock she receives does not add to our concern about Aziz: the relationship that these two characters have established seems to preclude any possible misunderstanding. It is only in retrospect that we are able to estimate the magnitude of the blow dealt her by the Marabar echo: throughout the novel Forster's style urbanely underplays the moral and physical suffering of his characters—testing, as it were, Godbole's notion that, unlike good and evil, individual suffering "is a matter of no significance to the universe" (178). The acuteness of this suffering emerges mainly from its effect on the characters' subsequent conduct, their breakdowns, and their mutedly irrational collisions with one another.

One of the central emotional events whose importance for the plot we are practically made to overlook on the first reading is Adela's realization that she does not love her fiancé. The evidence that links the trouble that is expected to befall Aziz with Adela's mental and emotional life is downplayed; its full force emerges only in retrospect, toward the end of the novel.

When a string of associations leads Adela to conclude that she is committing herself to a loveless marriage, she stops in surprise, with a "doubtful" expression on her face. The word "doubtful" does not convey the intensity of her shock. As in many instances throughout the novel, an emotional state is rendered figuratively: "The discovery had come so suddenly that she felt like a mountaineer whose rope had broken." Here, as in Nabokov's novels, profound emotion and mystical insight constitute catachretic gaps[9] that can only be bridged by meta-phor, extended comparison, or similar translexical devices. Since the word "so" refers to "suddenly," the simile seems to emphasize the suddenness rather than the terror of the discovery. The three exclama-tions that follow, "Not to love the man one's going to marry! Not to find it out till this moment! Not even to have asked oneself the question until now!" express not Adela's panic but her self-reproach for having deviated from moral theory (Adela's mind is repeatedly described as "theoretical," 46, 151). The anticlimactic conclusion that this is "Some-thing else to think out" (152) points to her attempt to calm herself in what will later be described as "her hard school-mistressy manner" (244). She appears to succeed in remaining rational, and the thought that love may not be "necessary to a successful union," or, at least, that love is not everything, subdues her excitement. It is only on a rereading that one is likely to interpret her stopping again, frowning, and raising the subject of marriage in her conversation with Aziz (152) as a sign that she has only a surface control of her agitation. The narrator's cognitive principle, however, prevents him from delving beneath that surface.

The string of Adela's verbalized thoughts does not prepare us for a possible onrush of morbidity. Moreover, the trajectory of the camera eye effectively finesses against the importance of her emotional state: only a couple of minutes elapse between Adela's realization that she does not love Ronny and her ordeal in the cave, but the accounts of the two incidents are separated by a very long portion of the text devoted to other matters so that by the time we learn about the charge that Adela makes against Aziz our memory of her thoughts on the threshold of the cave has grown dim.

There is an obvious underdrift of trouble in the episodes that precede the announcement of the charge, but at first we are misled about the nature of this trouble. Together with Aziz, who panics ("This is the end of my career," 155), we think that Adela has gotten lost. The egocentricity of Aziz and his treatment of the guide (whom he beckons "gently" and then slaps on the face) do not augment our sympathy for him; still, it is questionable whether at this point we are concerned about the predicament of Adela who may have really gotten lost, or, by way of inertia, about the possible consequences of this mishap on the life of Aziz.

Our perplexity does not last long: Aziz discovers "the simple and sufficient explanation of the mystery": Miss Quested has joined the people in the car that he has just seen driving up to the hills—"friends of hers, no doubt, Mr. Heaslop perhaps." For a moment the words "no doubt" and "perhaps" create the suspicion that Aziz is engaged in wishful thinking (this passing thought is not irrelevant for subsequent developments). We are soon reassured: "He had a sudden glimpse of her, far down the gully—only a glimpse, but there she was quite plain, framed between rocks, and speaking to another lady. He was so relieved that he did not think her conduct odd" (155). The last words, however, enhance the impression that Adela's conduct is, indeed, odd; and the discovery of her damaged field glasses adds to our uneasiness. As Fielding suspects on joining the party, "something [has] gone queer" (157). The foreboding now turns into an enigma: what has happened to change Adela's conduct?

Meanwhile no answer is forthcoming because Adela is out of the range of the camera eye. What with Fielding's worries and the recklessness of the elated Aziz, the account of the journey back to Chandrapore builds up suspense. A further delay takes place when the policeman who meets the party at the station refuses to divulge the charge on which he arrests Aziz. It is only in the following chapter that the cause of the arrest is stated, and our reaction to Mr. Turton's periphrasis ("Miss Quested has been insulted in one of the Marabar caves") is similar to Fielding's—"not Aziz" (163). Since the narrative has accounted for all the movements of Aziz in the caves, we know that Fielding is right in believing that the charge against Aziz must rest "upon some mistake" (164). The "simple and sufficient" explanation that comes to mind is that Adela must have been attacked by the guide, who has been elusive and unreliable, and that the muddle is caused by mistaken identities.

The alternative possibility, namely of Adela's having hallucinated, is first suggested in the next chapter, when McBryde notes that an echo had disturbed her and Fielding insinuates that it might have made her nervous (167). Our recollection of Godbole's pregnant reticences and of the devastating effect of the echo on Mrs. Moore support this possibility. Yet the echo could merely account for the frightened young woman's failure to make sure who followed her into the cave; it need not yet be regarded as evidence that no attack took place.

The hallucination hypothesis gains further strength with Godbole's cryptic remark that "If a young lady has sunstroke, that is a matter of no significance to the universe. . . . If she thought her head did not ache, she would not be ill, and that would end it" (178). The hint, however, has only a moderate impact since it is made in the middle of a theological discussion; therefore, we still tend to favor the notion that Adela was attacked by the guide. On resigning from the

club, Fielding gazes at the Marabar Hils in the distance and reformu-
lates the enigma in accordance with this rational surmise: "What mis-
creant lurked in them, presently to be detected by the activities of the
law? Who was the guide, and had he been found yet? What was the
'echo' of which the girl complained?" Like ourselves, Fielding anticipates a satisfactory solution: "He did not know, but presently he would
know. Great is information, and she shall prevail" (190-91). On a rereading these words will be perceived as a heavily ironic commentary on
the Socratic optimism of the rationalist tradition in Western thought.

On the first reading, however, the clues to the mystery seem to be
forthcoming at any moment. This is implicitly though vaguely promised by the "omniscient" stance, but such a conventional promise is
partly neutralized by the narrator's cognitive principle. The "truth"
remains beyond the narrator's reach. Adela does not provide it when
telling her story in the McBrydes' bungalow because she is unable to
"think the incident out" (194). We then hope that Mrs. Moore's intuitive understanding may help Adela overcome her confusion, but Mrs.
Moore does not oblige. Our hopes revive when Adela is giving evidence at the trial because she seems to attain a clear vision of what
happened; yet in a penultimate moment the vision is cut short by the
commotion in the courtroom.

The hypothesis that the attack took place only in Adela's mind
keeps gaining strength but is never sanctioned by the text. Adela first
refers to the assailant as a shadow, which connotes unreality: "there
was this shadow, or sort of shadow, down the entrance tunnel, bottling
me up." But then she talks about a man: "I hit at him with the glasses,
he pulled me round the cave" (193), and the assailant regains sub-
stance. When Adela first considers the possibility of having made a
mistake, it is not clear whether she thinks that the attack never took
place or that the assailant was not Aziz. It is only during the trial scene
that the case for hallucination becomes stronger because Adela is obviously overcome by an odd psychic state: "A new and unknown
sensation protected her, like magnificent armour. She didn't think
what had happened or even remember in the ordinary way of memory,
but she returned to the Marabar Hills, and spoke from them across a
sort of darkness to Mr. McBryde. The fatal day recurred, in every
detail, but now she was of it and not of it at the same time, and this
double relation gave it indescribable splendour" (227).

Reliving the past in the present, Adela is detached from both, and
this detachment, which produces an unwanted aesthetic experience
that she did not have during the actual expedition, protects her not only

from the awareness of the eager audience in the courtroom but from a repetition of the mistake that she made at the Marabar Caves. She is now alert to the string of exquisite images from which she was diverted by her worries on the "fatal day": "Why had she thought the expedition 'dull'? Now the sun rose again, the elephant waited, the pale masses of the rock flowed round her and presented the first cave; she entered, and a match was reflected in the polished walls—all beautiful and significant, though she had been blind to it at the time" (227-28).

Asked whether Aziz followed her into the cave, she cannot reply until he "enter[s] the place of answer" (228). Instead of going into the cave, as she did during the expedition, she now stays to wait for him, and when she does not see him entering the cave, she has to admit this to the court. Symbolically, the account of her experience implies a transcendence, an achievement of a view from beyond or outside the self, yet the matter-of-fact tone of the subsequent narration prevents the audience from lingering on these shifty metaphysical grounds.

Indeed, in addition to suggesting that Adela is, surprisingly enough, given to mystical experience, the scene also allows us to interpret this experience as psychological rather than spiritual and thus, by extrapolation, provides for the possibility of Adela's having hallucinated. We are also reminded of the fact that just before entering the cave she was disturbed by the thoughts of her engagement: "She had thought of love just before she went in, and had innocently asked Aziz what marriage was like, and she supposed that her question had roused evil in him" (227). It now seems likely that, in fact, the worry roused something in herself, whether or not it should be called evil. During the trial she also feels "the heat strike her face" (228) at the entrance to the cave. Had this detail been presented in the direct account of the expedition, the suggestion of a sunstroke (later supported by Godbole's innuendos) might have prepared us for something morbid to follow—much as a later reference to Fielding's "tender romantic fancies" awakened by "the buttercups and daisies of June" (282) on his return to England prepares us for the news of his marriage. Although the heat is mentioned several times in the account of the excursion, Adela does not seem to feel it: she is conscious of hardly anything except boredom and the doubts concerning her engagement.[10] It is, therefore, only during the trial episode that the possible effect of the heat on her state of mind is brought to the reader's attention.

Yet even after the trial the rational hypothesis of the guide's involvement is not completely ruled out: the guide is still missing, the initial impressions concerning him linger, and, moreover, a Western reader (whom the novel primarily addresses; great numbers of Indian readers reject it outright) is rather reluctant to believe that an intelligent and "reliable" (136) young woman like Adela could so confuse illusion and reality as to become irresponsible to the point of betrayal. It is, as it were, less disturbing to have an obscure felon commit the crime than to have the "schoolmistressy" Adela imagine one and act on that fancy. This preference, however, will soon come in for harsh criticism.

When Adela discusses her experience with Fielding after the trial, we expect these two sensible people to come up with a solution of the Marabar enigma. Not only is this expectation frustrated again, but Hamidullah, who breaks in on the dialogue, reinterprets the whole problem on a racial basis. For him the obscure guide becomes representative of all downtrodden Indians:

> "I gather you have not done with us yet, and it is now the turn of the poor old guide who conducted you round the caves."
> "Not at all, we were only discussing possibilities," interposed Fielding.
> "An interesting pastime, but a lengthy one. There are one hundred seventy million Indians in this notable peninsula, and of course one or other of them entered the cave. Of course some Indian is the culprit, we must never doubt that." [243]

Since Fielding has for some time functioned almost as the reader's spokesman, Hamidullah's reproach applies to the audience as aptly as to Fielding. It reinterprets our suspicion of the guide as evidence of racial or cultural prejudice. Indeed, it now seems that the Western audience of the novel is not immune to Anglo-Indian attitudes: as in *Bleak House*, we are made to discover, or at least suspect, in ourselves the same tendencies that the novel criticizes in its characters. "The racial problem can take subtle forms" (158). It is not impossible that unacknowledged racism does underlie Adela's wondering, at the outset of the picnic, whether after one year in India newcomers become as rude as the *sahibs* of the civil station. And it is probable that suppressed racism is betrayed by her hysterical request that Miss Derek should keep away the Indian chauffeur (168), if Miss Derek's testimony is to be credited. And it is certain that conscious racism underlies the complacent self-righteousness of Ronny Heaslop, about whom the novelist makes the oft-quoted and oft-criticized[11] remark that "One touch of regret—not the canny substitute but the true regret from the heart—

would have made him a different man, and the British Empire a different institution" (51). (Ronny's last words in the novel, in his letter to Fielding, typically blame all the British troubles on "the Jews," 308). But it also may be that Adela is merely tactless and insensitive to the racial implications of her remark. By analogy, our suspicion of the guide or a Pathan is not based on an anti-Indian bias or on any misconceived literary archetype of a licentious Oriental male—it is the outcome of a mild case of narrative entrapment. Nevertheless, it is obviously the rationalist attitude (likewise promoted by the tone of the novel) that makes us reluctant to embrace the hallucination hypothesis. And rationalism is culture bound and hence to some extent xenophobic. We may now become somewhat ashamed of having suspected the guide (whether vicariously sharing Fielding's discomfiture or whether under a parallel influence of Hamidullah's rebuke), even though in terms of "hard fact" such a suspicion is not entirely unjustified. As in the world of *Bleak House*, injustice on a grand scale is thus related to liabilites of individual attitudes—which the rhetoric of the novel extends even to the possible intellectual preferences of the reader.

And yet Hamidullah is unjust; in the ensuing episode he is even somewhat brutal, which suggests that the two English people on the scene, as well as the Western rationalist audience, may be both perpetrators and victims of injustice.[12] In a situation like that of the British in India (and analogous situations are numerous and familiar), any indelicacy may be turned into evidence of racial, national, or cultural prejudice. Fielding's misunderstandings with Aziz repeatedly illustrate this rule, but now the audience is made to face it as part of its own experience.

From now on we no longer expect the novel to confirm our first suspicion, but the inherited fictional conventions (promoted, to a degree, by the detective element of the novel) make us look forward to the closure of the gap, even if it would mean sanctioning the hallucination theory. Like Fielding, we "don't like it left in the air" (263). Whenever Miss Quested appears in the narrative, we expect her to have reached a definite conclusion about the Marabar incident and to enlighten us accordingly. Yet another string of disappointments is in store for us. "Let us call it the guide," says Adela. "It will never be known. It's as if I ran my finger along that polished wall in the dark, and cannot get further" (263). Even after Adela leaves Chandrapore it remains possible that some belated evidence may come to light—but it does not. Neither does Godbole provide us with an insight to cling to.

A further opportunity for disclosure seems to present itself when we are made to half believe that Fielding is about to bring Adela back as his wife, yet this turns out to be a mistake. Our expectations are revived one last time when Aziz discovers Adela's letter, yet our curiosity still remains unsatisfied, and the novel seems to illustrate its statement that "Life never gives us what we want at the moment that we consider appropriate" (25). It makes us reenact, as it were, the chronic disappointment of the people who live in a world where the request "Come, come, come" (80) is never granted.

The dissatisfaction of the novel's characters is not overwhelming because they do not spend their whole lives calling "Come, come, come." The routine of their lives in their social "cocoons" (132), brightened by rare moments of pleasant human contact, numbs their need for a more complete fulfillment. Neither is the dissatisfaction of the audience particularly intense, because after Hamidullah's bitter remarks the Marabar enigma largely loses its power.

One reason for the flagging of our interest in the enigma is the influence of the narrator's consistent cognitive principle: we are subliminally aware that no information can come from him directly; therefore we become almost resigned to its absence. Another strong reason for the waning of hermeneutic interest is connected with our awareness that the disclosure can no longer affect the life of Aziz, with whom we have been most concerned throughout the debacle. However, the imminent parting of Fielding and Aziz, the impossibility of a lasting friendship between them, adds to the mild frustration caused by the permanence of the novel's major gap. In all likelihood, this combined disappointment accounts for the note of dissatisfaction that recurs in even the most favorable critical discussions of the novel.[13] It is, however, not a consequence of artistic failure but an integral part of the cognitive response to A Passage to India. With a touch of self-consciousness, the narrative traces its own origins, like the origins of all art, to the eschatological alertness associated with the failings of the familiar world: "If this world is not to our taste, well, at all events there is Heaven, Hell, Annihilation—one or other of those large things, that huge scenic background of stars, fires, blue or black air. All heroic endeavour, and all that is known as art, assumes that there is such a background, just as all practical endeavour, when the world is to our taste, assumes that the world is all" (207-8). Instead of catering to the mental set of his rationalist Western audience, the novelist infects it with his own uneasiness.

Thus the novel stubbornly resists attempts at rationalistic explication. An aftertaste of our dissatisfaction with the inconclusiveness of its hermeneutic code induces us to reassess the mystery on a repeated reading, turning it from an element of the plot to a crucial component of the theme.

The handling of information does not cause as striking a difference between the first and the repeated readings of *A Passage to India* as it does in most of the other novels discussed above. Whereas on a rereading of *The Sound and the Fury* and *Nostromo* we uderstand the *fabula* in a way that, because of the diffusion of information, is impossible on the first reading, in *A Passage to India* the *fabula* can be constructed on the first reading with almost the same success as on the second. Moreover, the dramatic irony that suffuses a rereading of *Emma* is but incidental on a rereading of Forster's novel: as in *Emma*, it concerns a secret affair—that between Miss Derek and Mr. McBryde.

The superintendent of police is not surprised that a native, Aziz, has been "found out" because he considers all Indians to be "criminals at heart"—just because they have been born below the thirtieth latitude (166-67). On a repeated reading there is a touch of satisfaction in our awareness that he too will, in a way, be "found out." More important, the episode suggests that if McBryde had not been Miss Derek's lover, she might not have taken the confused Adela directly to his bungalow, and the charge against Aziz might not have been made. The Marabar caves set evil loose in Chandrapore, or something like evil ("love in a church, love in a cave, as if there is the least difference," grumbles Mrs. Moore, 202); and, in accordance with Godbole's statement that everyone is implicated in an evil action, the whole cast of the novel's characters turns out to have a part in the catastrophe. Major Callendar gives Aziz a day off; the Turtons lend the ladies a carriage to go to the station; the Nawab Bahadur helps to provide an elephant; Godbole prolongs his prayers and, together with Fielding, misses the train; and now it seems that the whole incident might have been hushed up but for the adventurous Miss Derek. She enjoys the excitement of a scandal, especially since starting the bureaucratic machine prolongs her stay in Chandrapore with the McBrydes. Ironically, it is this prolonged stay that brings her affair into the open and creates a scandal.

"When evil occurs, it expresses the whole of the universe. Similarly when good occurs," says the sage Godbole (178). Forster's plot, however, does not claim to express the whole universe—it restricts itself to depicting a view of the fabric of social relationships in the British Raj. And not the whole fabric—the beautiful punkah wallah in the courtroom may somehow be involved in the psychological background to Adela's conduct or in the metaphysical denial of isolation, yet he remains supremely unaware of whatever is passing in the room and eventually even fails to notice that the trial has ended. Without denying the comprehensiveness of Godbole's maxim in metaphysical terms, Forster obliquely reminds us, in this and some other episodes, that there are classes in Indian society that the novel cannot embrace. The culture-bound English rationalist tradition of this genre shares the limitations of the missionaries, no matter how liberal they attempt to be: "We must exclude someone from our gathering, or we shall be left with nothing" (38). In a sense, the dissatisfaction that permeates *A Passage to India* is Forster's dissatisfaction with the genre in which he has so far worked, the novels of the so-called "Great Tradition." Though *A Passage to India* anticipates the tendencies that will become manifest in the Nouveau Roman and in American post-modernist fiction,[14] it remains largely imprisoned within the inherited conventions and only breaks out of them with the help of the thematic texture around the mystery at the center of its plot.

The difference that the permanent gap causes between the first and the repeated reading relates to the interpretation rather than to the explication of the novel. On a rereading our awareness of the permanent character of the gap directs our attention to the symbolism of this gap and to the patterns of the motifs and verbal echoes, which, by contrast with the undiscriminating "Ou-Boum" of the Marabar Caves, may not rise to a symbolic status yet insistently suggest the possibility of previously unappreciated meanings. These patterns are largely eclipsed by the hermeneutic code on the first reading. Now the threshold of our attention to them is significantly reduced.[15]

We may now notice, among other things, that the word "gap" itself is one of the lexical items that echo throughout the novel. It is associated with the motifs of incompleteness, discomfort, dissatisfaction: "gaps" are never properly filled in. Thus, Miss Derek is called to "fill up a gap in the cast" of *Cousin Kate*, but she "lack[s] the necessary experience, and occasionally [forgets] her words" (40). The "one serious gap in his life" which Aziz hopes to fill by his friendship with Fielding (60) reopens at the end of the novel. Fielding "leave[s] a gap in the line" (171) when he throws in his lot with the Indians rather than with his countrymen. Symbolically, in the last scene of the novel, Fielding and Aziz issue "from a gap" between the rocks (322) to face the cosmic verdict on their friendship.

Since we are aware of the outcome of the plot, a rereading is not spurred by an interest in "what happens next" (which, judging by *Aspects of the Novel*, Forster would not fail to take into account[16]). As a result, we become less concerned for Aziz and much more attentive to Adela's experience before she enters the cave. To the intensity of this experience we now duly attach the significance that was underplayed on the first reading. If by the end of the first reading we reject suspicion of the guide as distasteful, we now also treat the hypothesis of the guide's involvement as less probable than the theory that the attack was entirely a matter of Adela's subjective experience.

Our awareness of the central permanent gap also alerts us to the presence of minor permanent gaps that did not attract sufficient attention on the first reading, either because we expected them to be eventually filled or because we were inclined to explain them away as cases of coincidence. What sort of information does Godbole withhold during Fielding's party? What makes Mrs. Moore shudder and say "A ghost!" (97) on hearing about the accident that the Nawab Bahadur really attributes to a specter? Why does Adela think that Mrs. Moore has affirmed the innocence of Aziz when the old lady's opinion has not been voiced? Is it "a trick of his memory or a telepathic appeal" (290) that makes Godbole link the image of Mrs. Moore with the image of a little wasp that the old lady had been gentle to in Chandrapore (35)?[17] Since the element of coincidence is otherwise infrequent in the novel, it does not seem valid to explain the last three gaps in this rationalistic way. "Telepathy" might do better, especially in Mrs. Moore's case, yet it is a "pert, meagre word" (263), which merely gives a name to phenomena that resist reason and science. "The secret understanding of the heart" would be still more to the point, yet with his usual urbane irony Forster does not allow us to forget that it may be pathos rather than philosophy or truth (19-20). The insufficiency of rational and metaphorical solutions leaves a margin for the explanation of the events in spiritual, cautiously supernatural terms;[18] yet the narrator does not really encourage us to seek one. On the first reading he interferes with our possible awareness of this margin by implicit promises that information "shall prevail," for instance, by fostering our suspicion of the guide's guilt—a finesse that functions rather like the model of the village of Gokul during the Hindu Festival, "divert[ing] men from the actual image of the God, and increas[ing] their sacred bewilderment" (287). On a rereading the narrator appears to be reconciled to the presence of the unknown. He does not venture beyond the mere awareness of the mystery. The Marabar Hills symbolize the unknowable in the face of which both Western rationalism and Oriental mysticism are helpless, but they also symbolize man's separation from man,[19] the failure of personal relationships. In other words, they remain a vehicle of the novel's moral as well as its cautiously metaphysical thematics.

Both these symbolic meanings of the Hills converge in turning them into an indiscriminate echo of the silence that stands for what is not available for satisfactory verbal expression. Not a single character of the novel feels competent to talk about the Hills—they are, in themselves, a sort of language that none can understand. As soon as Fielding has expressed his belief in information ("Great is information and she shall prevail") while standing on the verandah of the club, the Marabar Hills reassert themselves, reminding him of the mystery: "It was the last moment of the light, and as he gazed at the Marabar Hills they seemed to move graciously towards him like a queen, and their charm became the sky's. At the moment they vanished they were everywhere, the cool benediction of the night descended, the stars sparkled, and the whole universe was a hill" (191). A string of impressions and thoughts brings Fielding to the painful realization that despite his reasonable achievements he will never understand or live up to vague but no less important other values: "And he felt dubious and discontented suddenly, and wondered whether he was really and truly successful as a human being. After forty years' experience, he had learnt to manage his life and make the best of it on advanced European lines, had developed his personality, explored his limitations, controlled his passions—and he had done it all without becoming either pedantic or worldly. A creditable achievement, but as the moment passed, he felt he ought to have been working at something else the whole time,—he didn't know at what, never would know, never could know, and that was why he felt sad" (191).

It has been frequently suggested that *A Passage to India* contains Forster's admission of the failure of liberal humanism.[20] The passage above, however, does not confirm such a view. Liberal humanism is, essentially, an ideology. It may not lead to political or even moral victories when confronted with adversaries that do not play by its rules, but that is of less significance than the fact that, like the doctrine of nonviolence, it can only be effective as a way of life rather than as a strategy. And as a way of life it is unsatisfactory only if divorced from genuine kindness (or love or charity) or dominated by entrenched rationalism. Lack of genuine warmth of heart is what makes it ineffective in the case of Adela Quested; lack of eschatological alertness, or openness to the possibly transcendent "something else," is what gives Fielding his sense of failure. It is rationalism rather than liberal humanism that is confronted with oriental mysticism in Forster's novel.[21]

But the latter is also found wanting; the Hindu mystic Godbole seems equally helpless in the face of the mystery symbolized by the Marabar Hills.[22] The account of the festival at Mau suggests that mysticism offers no clearer insight into the soul and the universe than do science and reason: "But the human spirit had tried by a desperate contortion to ravish the unknown, flinging down science and history in the struggle, yes, beauty herself. Did it succeed? Books written afterwards say 'Yes.' But how, if there is such an event, can it be remembered afterwards? How can it be expressed in anything but itself? Not only from the unbeliever are mysteries hid, but the adept himself cannot retain them. He may think, if he chooses, that he has been with God, but as soon as he thinks it, it becomes history, and falls under the rules of time" (288). Godbole himself appears to be sharing some of the narrator's doubts. It does not become clear whether the "strange thoughts" aroused by the festival are the thoughts of the narrator or of Godbole: the sentence in which they are mentioned effects a transition between the narrative commentary and the account of Godbole's experience: "No definite image survived; at the Birth it was questionable whether a silver doll or a mud village, or a silk napkin, or an intangible spirit, or a pious resolution, had been born. Perhaps all these things! Perhaps none! Perhaps all birth is an allegory! Still, it was the main event of the religious year. It caused strange thoughts. Covered with grease and dust, Professor Godbole had once more developed the life of his spirit. He had, with increasing vividness, again seen Mrs. Moore, and round her faintly clinging forms of trouble" (290).

The account of the festival throws a retrospective light on Godbole's behavior at Fielding's tea party and on his peculiar reticence concerning the Marabar caves. Godbole is most cautious of all the characters of the novel; his "knack of slipping off" (192) is self-protective. His cautiousness, however, is associated not with fear of trouble that can result from straining the social fabric of Chandrapore but with the personal limitations that he mentions to Aziz: "Never be angry with me. I am, as far as my limitations permit, your true friend" (305). Obviously some limitations are imposed on the friendship between Godbole and Aziz by their religious differences, occupations, and social status—this is the meaning in which another Hindu, the assistant magistrate Mr. Das, uses the word in his apology to Aziz ("Excuse my mistakes, realize my limitations," 267). Yet Godbole means more than that. His specific limitation is a lack of psychic energy, similar to Mrs. Moore's fatigue. What makes Godbole steady and reliable ("all his friends trusted him, without knowing why," 176) is acknowledgment and acceptance of his limitations. He knows that his capacities are small (291); therefore he does not undertake to confront his doubts or risk personal commitments. Cautiousness keeps him from joining the expedition to the Marabar Caves: he misses the train because he prolongs his morning prayers—deliberately or with an unconscious purpose. And something more than cautiousness prevents him from even talking about the caves at Fielding's party: his own experience of them some time in the past must be assumed to have been as dangerous as the echo of Mrs. Moore.

In a sense Godbole acts upon the narrator's own cognitive principle: he does not talk about the realms of experience that he does not properly understand. Yet he seems to know that his failure to warn his friends against the expedition is an evil, and since, according to his theology, evil is the absence of God, he suddenly presents Fielding and his guests with a religious song the burden of which is the prayer to Krishna to "come, come, come." As he explains later, this is an evening song; and the fact that it is sung in the evening not only expresses Godbole's sense of the fitness of things but also suggests that the song is an earnest prayer. Aware of his participation in an evil act, Godbole persistently repeats that Krishna does not respond to his appeal:

> "But He comes in some other song, I hope?" said Mrs. Moore gently.
> "Oh no, he refuses to come," repeated Godbole, perhaps not understanding her question. "I say to Him, Come, come, come, come, come, come. He neglects to come." [80]

The narrator's sly "perhaps" ironically suggests that Godbole understands Mrs. Moore's question well enough but chooses to answer in his own way, meaning, perhaps, that Krishna neglects to come to him, among others, at the moment. The word "perhaps" is used in a similarly ironical manner in connection with the Marabar echo: "Professor Godbole had never mentioned an echo; it never impressed him, perhaps" (147). Here the hesitation expressed by the word "perhaps" suggests that it is equally probable that Godbole was too violently affected by the echo to make it a subject of drawing-room talk. Yet he could just as well have been baffled by some other feature of the hills that "rise abruptly, insanely, without the proportion that is kept by the wildest hills elsewhere" and "bear no relation to anything dreamt or seen" (124). Evidently, Godbole's theology makes little provision for a phenomenon of this kind.

The above interpretation of Godbole's conduct is, of course, preeminently rationalist; a metaphysical approach to the novel, in terms, for instance, of Plotinian theology, would yield a totally different though not more comprehensive reading.[23] What matters, however, is that the text provides support, albeit not ultimate sanction, for both the opposites, making the one incomplete without the other and relating both to the novel's pivotal permanent gap.

Both Godbole and the narrator are wary: having "explored [their] limitations" they know better than to treat mystery as a tourist attraction. Godbole can refer to it in the presence of Mrs. Moore, but during his dialogue with Fielding on the evening of the Marabar picnic, he constantly finds himself obliged to deny his interlocutor's reductive reformulations (175-79). The English men and women of the novel are safer if mystery does not turn into a matter of their daily intercourse with the world but remains the "huge scenic background" made up of "stars, fires, blue or black air" (208) and as remote as these. Some of them will never notice this background, but others, like Mrs. Moore, are aware that "Outside the arch there [seems] always an arch, beyond the remotest echo a silence" (52). Adela and Fielding wonder whether there are "worlds beyond which they could never touch" or whether "everything that is possible enter[s] their consciousness" (263). Our own awareness of the mysterious background is enhanced by the numerous minor gaps in the fabric of the literal narrative: mystery erupts through them like light (or darkness) through the holes in a canvas on which a genre scene is painted.

We are not allowed to dwell on this background for any length of time because the narrator, having slipped into "strange thoughts," promptly (though somewhat regretfully) shakes them off for the sake of realistic trivia:

> Some kites hovered overhead, impartial, over the kites passed the mass of a vulture, and with an impartiality exceeding all, the sky, not deeply coloured but translucent, poured light from its whole circumference. It seemed unlikely that the series stopped here. Beyond the sky must not there be something that overarches all the skies, more impartial even than they? Beyond which again . . .
>   They spoke of *Cousin Kate*. (39-40)

"If you don't know, you don't know; I can't tell you," the narrator seems to say to us together with Mrs. Moore (200). The Marabar Hills, arches beyond arches, and realms of experience to which words like "telepathy" or "hallucination" do not quite apply, are only manageable when kept in the background. The presence of a permanent gap symbolically suggests that an attempt to reach out to them is futile and dangerous. Symptomatically, Adela is discouraged by Fielding when she tries to explain her experience as mystical rather than psychological. "My belief," says Fielding, "is that poor McBryde exorcised you. As soon as he asked you a straightforward question, you gave a straightforward answer, and broke down." He is wrong—since McBryde and Adela had rehearsed their straightforward questions and answers before the trial—but Adela does not contradict him. With their thoughts running in different channels, Fielding uses the word "exorcise" figuratively, whereas Adela is quite ready to accept it in its literal sense—"I thought you meant I'd seen a ghost" (240). She wishes to reinterpret her experience as a modern version of providential interference, an experience of a spiritual, supernatural, rather than morbidly psychological, nature. But she knows that for Fielding the acceptance of the supernatural is tantamount to intellectual dishonesty. Therefore, when he asks her what happened in the cave, she answers ambiguously, "Let us call it the guide," feebly hinting at a special kind of guidance. Fielding's staunch rationalism enhances her sense of an impasse. "I am up against something," she says to him, "and so are you" (263).

Thus, on the first reading, the novel goads us into attempts to close its gap in a rational manner, but though we focus on the realistic foreground, the constant elusiveness of information makes us wonder whether this realistic fictional world "is all." The doubt, combined with our awareness of the permanent gaps, activates a rich complex of symbols and motifs on a repeated reading and suggests meanings beyond rationality and verisimilitude. The permanence of the gap brings into relief what Forster calls "fantasy," which "implies the supernatural but need not express it."[24] Yet fantasy is always kept in check—like everything else in the world where questions are not answered and invitations not accepted, where emotions are, or have to be, controlled, where pleasant gatherings are interrupted or marred by tactlessness or misunderstanding, where there is no complete truth or perfect joy, where not a single feeling remains unalloyed, where disappointment and dissatisfaction that accompany control are the common denominator of all experience. And since in itself "disillusionment cannot be beautiful" (211), it is compensated for aesthetically, by a rhythm and patterning more elaborate than in any other of Forster's novels, by "cameo" dialogues (278), gentle irony, and subtle suggestiveness of character portrayal—all of which is not dissimilar to the Indians' use of language to express or create a mood rather than communicate a statement.

Whereas in *Nostromo, The Sound and the Fury,* and *Absalom, Absalom!* the handling of information brings into relief the central themes, in *A Passage to India* it emphasizes not the main theme, that of personal relationships, but a secondary one, that of the mystery against which these relationships are played out.[25] It is this subsidiary theme, however, that sets *A Passage to India* apart from Forster's other novels, all of which deal with personal relationships. It has been noted that in *A Passage to India* "the real and the symbolic worlds coexist independently instead of blending into one another and becoming a whole."[26] I believe that this is an aesthetic achievement rather than a failure. The novel presents the real world against the background of a mysteriously symbolic one; the limited vision of the people who live in this or similar worlds cannot blend the two and become "one with the universe" (208). The narrator, who is almost a tangible human presence, cannot accomplish such a feat. Like Cavafy in Forster's famous verbal portrait, he remains standing "at a slight angle to the universe."[27]

CHAPTER EIGHT

Absalom, Absalom!

"Happen Is Never Once"

> From the point of view of a world wholly
> determined by the operation of blind
> forces, play would be altogether super-
> fluous. Play only becomes possible,
> thinkable and understandable when an
> influx of *mind* breaks down the absolute
> determinism of the cosmos. The very
> existence of play continually confirms
> the supra-logical nature of the human
> situation.
>
> —Johan Huizinga, *Homo Ludens*

William Faulkner's *Absalom, Absalom!* (1936) displays more pronounced modernist tendencies than *A Passage to India*, as well as tendencies currently identified with post-modernism.[1] It repeatedly untells its own story, raises new enigmas upon offering clues to old ones, and "writes" its characters out of their presence so consistently[2] that Derrida could say, with Freud, that some poets have been there before him. Yet it can hardly be doubted that *Absalom, Absalom!* is a humanist novel that restores some central humanist verities to meaning and turns this meaning into an intense private experience for its audience. In the final count most great novels do this—each in its own way. *Absalom, Absalom!* does it by way of involving the audience in the game played by the characters, a game which, like any game, both limits and asserts individual freedom.

One of the main conditions of this game is the novel's permanent gap. If by the end of *A Passage to India* our guess about what happened in the Marabar caves practically amounts to a conviction that is not sanctioned by the text, in *Absalom, Absalom!* the major mysteries seem to be solved in the text yet remain unsanctioned by the reader. The residual uncertainty stems from the permanent suspension of a piece of information that, though minor in itself, could decisively close the novel's central gap.

The central gap is a murder mystery. Henry Sutpen, son of plantation owner Thomas Sutpen, brings home a fellow student, Charles Bon, for a college vacation. Charles becomes engaged to Henry's sister Judith, but Thomas Sutpen vetoes the marriage without divulging his reasons, except, possibly, to Henry. In a gesture of defiance Henry leaves home with his friend. The engagement is not broken off, but four years later Henry prevents the marriage on which he has insisted by shooting Charles at the gate of Judith's house. One must assume that Thomas Sutpen has a strong reason for rejecting the suitor, yet it is not clear whether it is the same reason for which Henry kills his friend Bon. Several decades later Quentin Compson produces the staggering suggestion that the accomplished gentleman Charles Bon was the underbred Thomas Sutpen's part-Negro son. Since this fascinating theory explains a number of moot points in Sutpen's relationships with the other characters, we are willing to accept it, yet we are never told how Quentin comes by his knowledge. The absence of "hard facts" that could testify to the truth of Quentin's theory forms the minor gap. Because this minor gap is never closed in a satisfactory way, that is, because we never find out exactly how Quentin learned about Bon's origins, the novel's major gap, the motive for Henry's killing of Bon, likewise remains open.

Shreve McCannon thinks that Quentin, his roommate at Harvard, has learned about Bon's origin from Judith's black half sister Clytie during his nocturnal visit to Sutpen's Hundred with Miss Rosa.[3] Quentin, however, does not really corroborate this surmise:

> "Your old man," Shreve said. "When your grandfather was telling this to him, he didn't know any more what your grandfather was talking about than your grandfather knew what the demon was talking about when the demon told it to him, did he? And when your old man told it to you, you wouldn't have known what anybody was talking about if you hadn't been out there and seen Clytie. Is that right?"
> "Yes," Quentin said. "Grandfather was the only friend he had."
> "The demon had?" Quentin didn't answer, didn't move. (274)[4]

Quentin's "Yes" is not an answer to Shreve, whose question he does not seem to hear. During the nocturnal encounter to which Shreve refers (369-71), Clytie does not volunteer any information to Quentin. Since their dialogue is not curtailed, we cannot infer that anything not recorded in the text passed between them—except, perhaps, by way of intuitive awareness inspired by the expression of Clytie's face (in the latter case it is not at all clear whether we are invited to credit this awareness—so many other characters of the novel think that they "know" things intuitively and are proved wrong). On the other hand, we are not "shown" Miss Rosa's and Henry Sutpen's meeting of the same night, nor are we told what Quentin and Miss Rosa talked about on their way back to Jefferson. All we are given is a stylized cameo dialogue between Quentin Compson and Henry Sutpen:

> *And you are—?*
> *Henry Sutpen.*
> *And you have been here—?*
> *Four years.*
> *And you came home—?*
> *To die. Yes.*
> *To die?*
> *Yes. To die.*
> *And you have been here—?*
> *Four years.*
> *And you are—?*
> *Henry Sutpen.* (373)

Technically speaking, Quentin might have got his facts from Henry in the parts of the scene that are not accounted for in the text. Or he could have gotten them from Miss Rosa if she had been taken into Henry's confidence.[5] Both possibilities, however, conflict with character psychology. Judging by Miss Rosa's harsh words to Jim Bond, Charles Bon's grandson, ("You ain't any Sutpen! You dont have to leave me lying in the dirt!" 371), she is ignorant of the blood tie between Sutpen and Bon—otherwise she would have known that Jim Bond is a Sutpen just as she knows that the black Clytie is a Sutpen, Thomas Sutpen's child. It is likewise difficult to believe that the secret could have been revealed during the Quentin-Henry interview: their dialogue has a finished crab-canon form, frozen by Henry's fatigue and Quentin's mental paralysis and centering on the words "To die."[6] As noted above, the impossibility to determine whether Quentin learned the secret of Bon's birth from a reliable source or whether he imagined or guessed it[7] renders the novel's central gap permanent: if the theory is based on guesswork, it may, for all we know, be nothing but a projection of Quentin's or his culture's obsessions.

Quentin's insights are presented as a workable assumption that is not, however, to be credited without reserve. We are, nevertheless, challenged to join the detective game, continue it beyond the point where Shreve and Quentin stop, and, fully aware of the fictionality of the characters, achieve a better view of the story than those dramatized in the text. First, however, we must establish the rules of this game.

The rules seem to be encoded in (a) the structure of the novel and (b) the attitudes taken by its fictionalized players. The audience is, actually, given a degree of freedom in the choice of rules because the structure of the novel can accommodate different schemes and because the attitudes of the characters are ambivalent. Critical discussions of the point in view and character psychology of *Absalom, Absalom!* are, in fact, attempts to determine by what rules the reconstructive game of the novel is to be played. The analysis offered below is no exception.

The most important component of the structure of *Absalom, Absalom!* is its complex point of view. With its numerous acts of story-telling telescoped into one another this novel belongs to the so-called box-method narratives. Its master discourse, the outer "box," is presented by an undramatized third-person narrator, whose voice is heard most distinctly in the description of Quentin's visit to Miss Rosa and of the scenes in the Harvard dormitory.

Like the narrator of *A Passage to India*, the "Faulkner" of *Absalom, Absalom!* observes a consistent cognitive principle. He disowns any direct knowledge of Thomas Sutpen and his affairs. Though he presents the Jefferson of 1833 in the authoritative manner of a historian ("Jefferson was a village then: the Holston House, the courthouse, six stores, a blacksmith and livery stable, a saloon frequented by drovers and peddlers, three churches and perhaps thirty residences," 32), he refers all the facts about Sutpen either to Quentin's "twenty years' heritage of breathing the same air" (11), or to General Compson, Miss Rosa, or hearsay. Even Sutpen's portrait, on which the narrator projects the information about the Haitian debacle, is presented as part of the memory of the community:

> That was all the town was to know about him for almost a month. He had apparently come into town from the south—a man of about twenty-five as the town learned later, because at the time his age could not have been guessed because he looked like a man who had been

sick. Not like a man who had been peacefully ill in bed and had recovered to move with a sort of diffident and tentative amazement in a world which he had believed himself on the point of surrendering, but like a man who had been through some solitary furnace experience which was more than just fever, like an explorer, say, who not only had to face the normal hardship of the pursuit which he chose but was overtaken by the added and unforeseen handicap of the fever also and fought through it at enormous cost not so much physical as mental, alone and unaided and not through blind and instinctive will to endure and survive but to gain and keep to enjoy it the material prize for which he accepted the original gambit. [32]

The narrator seems to place himself in Quentin Compson's generation and to have no access to the events that took place half a century before. While Quentin is irresistibly attracted to the Sutpen story, the third-person narrator endeavors to maintain a wary detachment: Medusa's head should only be glanced at in a mirror. Since Miss Rosa's last visit to Sutpen's Hundred and Clytie's burning of the mansion are the final events of the saga, the narrator reports them as imagined by Quentin, refusing, as it were, to present the Fall of the House of Sutpen without mediation. Quentin's meeting with Henry Sutpen is also presented in a mediated way, through an account of Quentin's memories. "I do not know. I was not there," the narrator of *Absalom, Absalom!* seems to say, as does the one of *A Passage to India*. As a result he cannot give us any information to confirm or refute Quentin's hypothesis. The cognitive principle of the narrator of *Absalom, Absalom!* is thus a link between the mimetic content and the form of the novel.

The account of Quentin's visit to Sutpen's Hundred shows the whole extent of "Faulkner's" reluctance to present the story of Sutpen's family without mediation. At the beginning of the novel Miss Rosa tells her version of the story to Quentin, and Quentin accompanies her to the old house several hours later. However, though Miss Rosa's narrative act is presented as part of the fictional present, the expedition that followed it is recounted only at the very end of the novel where it takes the form of the fictional past—because it is no longer the story of Quentin but that of the Sutpens. The episode is introduced as a memory that Quentin relives in all the particulars of emotion and sensation: "Now Quentin began to breathe hard again, who had been peaceful for a time in the warm bed, breathing hard the heady pure snowborn darkness. She (Miss Coldfield) did not let him enter the gate. She said 'Stop' suddenly; he felt her hand flutter on his arm and he thought, 'Why, she is afraid.' He could hear her panting now, her voice almost a wail of diffident yet iron determination: 'I don't know what to do. I dont know what to do.' ('I do,' he thought. 'Go back to town and go to bed.') But he did not say it" (364).

And yet this attribution of the focus is somewhat artificial, perhaps deliberately so. Shreve is familiar with the facts, which means that Quentin has already told him about the visit to Sutpen's Hundred. It is therefore unlikely that he should go over the episode in his mind for a second time. And indeed, several lines later the episode begins to read not as Quentin's memories but as a direct account of the event. Then a further distortion of chronology takes place: Quentin's encounter with Henry Sutpen (372-73) is presented as a flashback, as the contents of Quentin's memories on coming home after the fatal visit; we are supposed to believe that lying in his bed in Cambridge Quentin remembers not the event itself but his memories of the event, placing the third-person narrator at a triple remove from the action. This, however, is too great a demand on our credulity if we notice the novelist's sleight of hand. The account of the visit to Sutpen's Hundred must, in my opinion, be understood as "pseudo-diegetic":[8] the narrator distances himself from the product of his own imagination by ascribing it to the memories of a character. The technique may be compared to that of Nabokov's "Terra Incognita," where hotel-room wallpaper shows through the tropical scene conjured up by a dying man's delirium—the imagination of the author showing through the imagined imagination of the character.

In a number of other cases, the attribution of the focus is even more problematic: a stretch of the narrative seems to be presented through the consciousness of a character, but this character is not clearly identified. At the beginning of the Harvard series, for instance (181-216), it is often impossible to distinguish Quentin's memories from the third-person narrator's intrusions and from the oral discourse of Quentin or Shreve. A narrative block that formally consists of a single two-and-a-half page sentence begins as a record of Quentin's thoughts (181) but ends as the speech of Shreve, whose words Quentin confirms. Another narrative block starts as Shreve's second-person narration: Shreve seems to be addressing Quentin (212-15) and (accurately?) recounting the facts that he has heard from him before, but it becomes apparent that Quentin is not really listening, as his friend's words strike on his "resonant strings of remembering" (213). It is not clear whether the subject matter of the narrative is supposed to represent that of Shreve's speech or that of Quentin's memories aroused by it. The confusion suggests the idea of the "happy marriage of speaking

and hearing" (316)—there are no other happy marriages in the novel—
as well as the fact that whatever is supposed to be happening in the
dormitory at this moment, the imagination at work on the story is that
of the third-person narrator rather than of Quentin or Shreve. The
stretches of discourse where focalization is problematic are, in fact,
pseudo-diegetic. To avoid this heavy word, I shall henceforth refer to
them as "distanced narratives." Their function is (a) to avoid the
authoritative manner of the omniscient narrative, and (b) nevertheless,
to distinguish the imaginative contribution of the third-person narrator
from that of the characters.

"Distanced narrative" is used to present Henry Sutpen's last meeting with his father and his subsequent conversation with Charles Bon.
The two scenes seem to be passing in front of Shreve's and Quentin's
eyes, yet on closer examination it is evident that the narrator never
makes the fantastic assertion that Quentin and Shreve simultaneously
imagine the scenes in an identical way or else reconstruct them through
accurate extrasensual perception. The diegetic account of the fictional
present smoothly yields to a pseudo-diegetic representation of the
wartime episode in Carolina, italics in the text marking the transition
that occurs in the middle of a lengthy period:

> Shreve ceased again. It was just as well, since he had no listener.
> Perhaps he was aware of it. Then suddenly he had no talker either,
> though possibly he was not aware of this. Because now neither of them
> were there. They were both in Carolina and the time was forty-six
> years ago, and it was not even four now but compounded still further,
> since now both of them were Henry Sutpen and both of them were
> Bon, compounded each of both yet either neither, smelling the very
> smoke which has blown and faded away forty-six years ago from the
> *bivouac fires burning in a pine-grove, the gaunt and ragged men sitting or*
> *lying about them, talking not about the war yet all curiously enough (or*
> *perhaps not curiously at all) facing the South where further on in the darkness*
> *the pickets stood—the pickets who, watching to the South, could see the flicker*
> *and the gleam of the Federal bivouac fires myriad and faint and encircling half*
> *the horizon and counting ten fires for each Confederate one.* [351]

The narrator does not really attribute the focalization of the ensuing
two scenes to Quentin and Shreve but suggests that at this point they
feel that they have achieved empathy with the figures of Henry and
Bon as created by their imagination. The same is true of the episode that
explains why Henry consented to Bon's wiring the letter which Judith
would later entrust to Quentin's grandmother (346-50).

Had these scenes been presented without being (seemingly) attributed to Quentin and Shreve, "Faulkner" would have implicitly assumed responsibility for the accuracy of the facts that they contain. We would have accepted the episodes with that willing suspension of disbelief which, by force of convention, precludes doubt in the cognitive reliability of the omniscient narrator. The semblance of focalization discourages us from accepting the narrator's insights as the ultimate truth. On the other hand, since it is impossible to attribute the focalization to any single character, the concerns embodied in the "distanced narrative" appear to be those of the narrator himself, rather than those of the personages.

By contrast, the personal or ideological interests of the characters are expressed in the stretches of discourse that seem to be narrated in the first person by Miss Rosa, Mr. Compson, Quentin, or Shreve. Here the focalization is unambiguously attributed to one of the four characters; and at first glance the narratives seem to be intercalary stories-within-stories of a traditional kind. It has often been observed, however, that as soon as these narratives gain momentum, they shed all traces of the focalizers' individual idiom. For instance, it is only in the preliminaries to her act of story-telling that Miss Rosa talks "in character," while the dense sexual connotations that infuse her monologue are later incompatible with the image—though not with the psychology—of the stiff lady sitting straight in her hard chair: [9] *"Perhaps I couldn't even have wanted more than that, couldn't have accepted less, who even at nineteen must have known that living is one constant and perpetual instant when the arras-veil before what-is-to-be hangs docile and even glad to the lightest naked thrust if we had dared, were brave enough (not wise enough: no wisdom needed here) to make the rending gash"* (142-43).

Just as parts of Miss Rosa's discourse do not fit into the narrative situation that frames them, so the monologue of Mr. Compson, which is supposed to be uttered before the speaker is acquainted with Quentin's theory, anachronistically projects an awareness of Sutpen's blood ties with Bon, making the reader wonder how Mr. Compson could have failed to anticipate Quentin's insights. For instance, admitting his inability to comprehend what kind of man Judith's sweetheart must have been, Mr. Compson calls him "a myth, a phantom: something which they engendered and created whole themselves; some effluvium of Sutpen blood and character, as though as a man he did not exist at all" (104). Though Mr. Compson apparently means to say, figuratively, that each of the Sutpens saw not the real Bon but a creature of his or her imagination, on a rereading the literal sense of these words comes to the fore: Bon, indeed, may have been an effluvium of Sutpen's blood and character, "engendered" by him, created by his betrayal, and treated "as though as a man," a suffering and identity-seeking individual, "he did not exist at all." Several pages later Mr. Compson comes so close to Quentin's theory that he describes Bon as a Telemachus, a "mental and spiritual orphan whose fate it apparently was to exist in some limbo halfway between where his corporeality was and his mentality and moral equipment desired to be" (124). It may also be added that if really spoken out loud, Mr. Compson's narratives of chapters 1 through 4 would demand a much greater interval of time than the few late afternoon hours during which they are supposed to take place.

Verisimilitude is also called into question by the stylistic similarity of all the "first-person" narratives: Shreve sounds like Mr. Compson,[10] and Quentin like both of them, and like General Compson and Thomas Sutpen in their narratives, and sometimes even like Miss Rosa. The structural reason for these stylistic affinities, as well as for Miss Rosa's sexual undersong, is that the clearly focalized narratives (which I shall henceforth call the "nested narratives"[11]) are in fact presented by the authorial third-person narrator (to whom, following a convention, I shall henceforth often refer as the "omniscient" narrator) "with" the focal characters—the way the first three sections of *The Sound and the Fury* are told "with" the Compson brothers. In *Absalom, Absalom!*, unlike *The Sound and the Fury*, the focal characters are engaged in narrative acts and may, with some reservation, be called narrators; but what the reader hears is not the voices of these speakers but the voice of the omniscient narrator carrying out their narrative acts in their stead. The technique may be compared to Fielding's "switching over": the omniscient narrator "switches off" the character's direct utterance (soon after the introductory block) and fills the resulting gap in the representational time with his own speech. The resemblance of the two methods is not immediately apparent because, unlike Fielding, who, by passing from direct utterance to narrative commentary, makes it clear at what point the "switch" takes place, the narrator of *Absalom, Absalom!* does not indicate definite borderlines between the direct speech of a character and the passages where his own voice takes over. The narrator does not dissociate himself from the focalizers of nested narratives—just as in a crucial scene in *Tom Jones* the narrator does not dissociate himself from the information-withholding Blifil.

Nested narratives are not faithful records of the focal characters' monologues. They are the omniscient narrator's rendition of the focalizers' attitude to the narrated events. Miss Rosa's "lover's discourse,"[12] for instance, is not her own rhetoric but the omniscient narrator's attempt to convey the true nature of her involvement with Sutpen and his children. Likewise, Mr. Compson's anachronistic equivocations are the omniscient narrator's analysis of psychological self-revelation: though Mr. Compson fails to achieve Quentin's insights unaided, subliminally he is aware of the significance inherent in the story. Quentin's theory merely turns the moral meaning into a literal one, realizing, as it were, the father-son metaphor. Each of the nested narratives contributes to the imaginative reconstruction of the past events, at the same time revealing the concerns and the disposition of the focalizer. The omniscient narrator, who presents these narratives to the reader, brings each individual disposition into a higher relief than the character himself might have done.

In terms of its approach to the Sutpen saga, the master narrative structurally replicates the nested narratives. Such a relationship between "Faulkner's" discourse and that of the character-narrators is expressed almost graphically in the *mise-en-abîme* image that presents Quentin's somewhat oversimplified version of determinism:

> "Yes," Quentin said. "The two children" thinking *Yes. Maybe we are both Father. Maybe nothing ever happens once and is finished. Maybe happen is never once but like ripples maybe on water after the pebble sinks, the ripples moving on, spreading, the pool attached by a narrow umbilical water-cord to the next pool which the first pool feeds, has fed, did feed, let this second pool contain a different temperature of water, a different molecularity of having seen, felt, remembered, reflect in a different tone the infinite unchanging sky, it doesn't matter: that pebble's watery echo whose fall it did not even see moves across its surface too at the original ripple-space, to the old ineradicable rhythm.* (261)

The historical event is irrecoverable—the pebble has sunk to the bottom of the deep waters of human experience of which language forms only the surface ripples. Each dramatized view of Sutpen's story is a concentric circle of ripples; the penultimate circle is that of the narrator who transmits the agitation to the reader, the furthermost circle. The characters who are most intensely affected by Sutpen's actions—like Henry Sutpen, on whom everybody places the burden of responsibility—manifest the least propensity to narrate; the further a character finds himself from the heart of the matter, the weaker his intuitive understanding of the tragedy and the greater the use he has to make of language, "that meager and fragile thread, . . . by which the little surface corners and edges of men's secret and solitary lives may be joined for an instant now and then before sinking back into darkness where the spirit cried for the first time and was not heard and will cry for the last time and will not be heard then either" (251). At the same time, the issues raised in such a character's nested narrative are broader. While Miss Rosa's concerns lie only with Sutpen's relationship with his family and with herself, Mr. Compson is interested in the relationship between the Sutpens and the rest of the community; besides, his imagination is engaged by Bon's dependent, devoted, and uncomplaining mistress, the polar opposite of the Mrs. Compson of *The Sound and the Fury*.[13] Quentin is obsessed by the idea of incest and also poignantly interested in Sutpen as a man who, having once discovered himself, with shame, at the wrong end of the Southern social hierarchy, eventually takes his revenge on his society by becoming its apotheosis.[14] Shreve, who, if we remember *The Sound and the Fury*, is "not a gentleman," enviously focuses on the sophisticated Bon and at the same time expresses an intelligent outsider's wish to place specific Southern problems into perspective: *"Tell about the South. What's it like there. What do they do there. Why do they live there. Why do they live at all"* (174).

Since the third-person narrator seems to have insisted on avoiding direct contact with the Sutpen tragedy, his circle is further removed from the center of commotion than that of the characters; it is less intensely agitated, its vibrations are of smaller amplitude, but it is broader in circumference. The distinctive concerns of this narrative are largely embodied in the "distanced" stretches of the discourse; as I shall attempt to show, they are likewise bifurcated and tend to even broader generalizations than those of the nested narratives. The formulation of these concerns (the interpretive activity) is one of the tasks imposed upon the audience, the ultimate circle of the ripples.

Yet interpretation is only a part of the ludic activity in which the audience becomes involved. The nature of our second task is suggested by a further analogy between the master discourse and the nested narratives: if all the character-narrators tell what they know firsthand and then engage in an imaginative reconstruction of what they do not know, the third-person narrator recounts the contributions of all the characters and then also adds something of his own. Are we not invited to do the same?

The pattern works in the following way. The nested narratives fall into two parts: (a) empirical material, which the focal character has obtained as a narratee, an eavesdropper, a spectator, or a participant in the narrated events; and (b) paraleptic material,[15] that is, scenes that the focal character did not witness and is, therefore, not competent to present in a dramatic manner. *Absalom, Absalom!* constantly flouts the convention according to which a first-person narrator should not "show" the scenes he or she has not observed but summarize them, making due reference to the source of information. Here all the focal characters rebel against the limitations of their angle of vision and assume the very prerogatives of omniscience that the third-person narrator takes great pains to disclaim.

The spurious theories of the characters are credited for a long time on the first reading because we often fail to realize the paraleptic character of the scenes. Sometimes when a scene begins we no longer remember to which character the focus is attributed (because they all often sound alike), or we miss the moment where the discourse over-steps the limits of the focal character's competence. Miss Rosa's narrative, for instance, smoothly and gradually moves from the "telling" (summary references to Sutpen's contests with his Negroes) to the "showing" of the following paraleptic scene:

the spectators falling back to permit [Ellen] to see Henry plunge out from among the negroes who had been holding him, screaming and vomiting—not pausing, not even looking at the faces which shrank back away from her as she knelt in the stable filth to raise Henry and not looking at Henry either but up at *him* as he stood there with even his teeth showing beneath his beard now and another negro wiping the blood from his body with a towsack.

. . . .

"'Don't lie to me, Thomas,' Ellen said. 'I can understand your bringing Henry here to see this, wanting Henry to see this; I will try to understand it; yes, I will make myself try to understand it. But not Judith, Thomas. Not my baby girl, Thomas.'

"'I dont expect you to understand it,' he said. 'Because you are a woman. But I didn't bring Judith down here. I would not bring her down here. I dont expect you to believe that. But I swear to it.'

"'I wish I could believe you,' Ellen said, 'I want to believe you' [29-30]

As in *Nostromo*, we are made to overlook the narrative shift at the moment when it takes place. Only at the end of the scene are we reminded that Miss Rosa was "not there to see the two Sutpen faces this time—once on Judith and once on the negro girl beside her—looking down through the square entrance to the loft" (30). The scene turns out to be not the account of a dialogue (which, for all we are supposed to know, may not have taken place at all) but the omniscient narrator's somewhat stylized rendering of Miss Rosa's view of the relationship between Ellen and Thomas Sutpen as well as of Judith's mysterious self-assertion. Other paraleptic scenes are, likewise, ultimately accepted as the *"Might-have-been[s] that [are] more true than truth"* (143). By showing events supposed to be characteristic though not necessarily actual, they present analyses of the characters' psychological, moral, or cultural motivation.

The tension between the credibility of the analyses and the arbitrariness of the imaginative reconstruction of events is never so strong as in Quentin's account of Sutpen's confidences to General Compson. When Sutpen visits Quentin's grandfather during the war, he seems to disclose to him a great deal of information—yet to withhold the fact that Bon is his part-Negro son. In Quentin's paraleptic presentation, Sutpen seems to be about to make this disclosure when he is interrupted by General Compson's indignant outburst against his oversimplified morality:

"I merely explained how this new fact rendered it impossible that this woman and child be incorporated in my design, and following which, as I told you, I made no attempt to keep not only that which I might consider myself to have earned at the risk of my life but which had been given to me by signed testimonials, but on the contrary I declined and resigned all right and claim to this in order that I might repair whatever injustice I might be considered to have done by so providing for the two persons whom I might be considered to have deprived of anything I might later possess: and this was agreed to, mind; agreed to between the two parties. And yet, after more than thirty years, more than thirty years after my conscience had finally assured me that if I had done an injustice, I had done what I could to rectify it—" and Grandfather not saying "Wait" now but saying, hollering maybe even: "Conscience? Conscience? Good God, man, what else did you expect? Didn't the very affinity and instinct for misfortune of a man who had spent that much time in a monastery even, let alone one who had lived that many years as you lived them, tell you better than that? didn't the dread and fear of females which you must have drawn in with the primary mammalian milk teach you better? What kind of abysmal and purblind innocence could that have been which someone told you to call virginity? what conscience to trade with which would have warranted you in the belief that you could have bought immunity from her for no other coin than justice?" [264-65]

The verisimilitude of this scene is questionable. It would be more natural to expect Quentin's grandfather to wait for Sutpen to divulge the last bit of his secret, unless, like Quentin and later Shreve, he understands this secret without its being put into words. In that case it remains unclear why the secret is not among the information that General Compson is supposed to have transmitted to Quentin's father, unless, breaking the rules of the game, one might suggest that it is withheld in order that the story might be told.

The problem, however, becomes irrelevant if the scene is understood not as a reconstruction of the dialogue as it is supposed to have taken place but as Quentin's analysis of the moral reality underlying it. This analysis is presented in the form of a morality play, where Sutpen stands for "that innocence which believe[s] that the ingredients of morality [are] like the ingredients of pie or cake and once you [have] measured them and balanced them and mixed them and put them into the oven it [is] all finished and nothing but pie or cake [can] come out" (263). General Compson represents a more sensitive, yet also a more cynical and ultimately demoralizing view, which is later endorsed by Quentin's father (and which Quentin may be projecting upon the grandfather). The scene dramatizes the conflict of two personified world views that Quentin rejects but cannot renounce.

If the paraleptic scenes in the nested narratives are little morality plays staged by the characters, the scenes presented in the third-person narrator's "distanced" discourse are dramatizations staged by "Faulkner" himself. On the other hand, the "hard facts" of the nested narratives correspond to "Faulkner's" direct accounts of narrative situations and of the nested narratives. The third-person narrator goes part of the way recounting the story after the focalizers, but then, like Sutpen and practically all the other tellers, "back[s] up and start[s] over again with at least some regard for cause and effect even if none for logical sequence and continuity" (247). He takes the story out of the focalizers' hands, shapes it to suit his concerns, and completes those parts of the Sutpen saga that are short-circuited by the impasse that reduces the character-narrators to silence in different parts of the novel. Yet he too leaves moot points and self-contradictions—for the audience to deal with.

For instance, the reader is called upon to explain how Clytie, who has never been away from home, could find Charles Bon's son in the French quarter of New Orleans,[16] why Bon replaced Judith's picture with that of his mistress and son, why Sutpen refused to recognize Bon as his son, or why he provoked Wash Jones into killing him. In looking for answers to such questions we engage in the activity that combines elements of the explication and interpretation of the text: our reconstructed *fabula* "facts" will rest on circumstantial evidence alone and will therefore be largely dependent on our interpretation of the novel. But that is the predicament of the character narrators as well: none of them are cognitively reliable.

Indeed, Miss Rosa assumes that the photograph found on Bon's body is the picture of Judith; it never occurs to her that Bon may have substituted for it a portrait of someone else (his mistress and son, of whose existence Miss Rosa is not aware). Mr. Compson first offers the bigamy-threat theory and then rejects it—whether as incomplete or as spurious, failing to see that this initial theory is reconfirmed by Quentin's suggestion that Bon had Negro blood: if Bon is a "Negro," then Henry cannot dismiss his marriage to the octoroon as morganatic. Shreve tampers with the memory of the community to suit the ethical patterns that he wishes to impose on the events—he finds it more convenient to think, for instance, that it was not Henry who carried the wounded Bon out of the battle, but the older man who saved the life of the younger, thus preserving the loved obstacle without which his course would have been less heroic. Moreover, Shreve furnishes Sutpen's house with "crystal tapestries" and "Wedgwood chairs," (to him "Wedgwood" sounds like furniture, 178), cannot help calling Miss Coldfield "Aunt Rosa," and allows his imagination to realize the metaphor of calculated morality by conjuring up the image of emotional ledgers kept by Bon's lawyer. Quentin anachronistically refers to Sutpen's birthplace as "West Virginia" (220)—in *The Sound and the Fury* he is shown daydreaming during a history lesson—and lapses into another anachronism when he puts the words "my first marriage" into Sutpen's mouth (248) long before the second marriage that they presuppose has taken place. It seems that even the third-person narrator is guilty of similar misrepresentations when he projects an awareness of Quentin's theory onto Mr. Compson's description of Bon and of the story of Judith's relationship with Bon's son (192-204). The very style of "Faulkner's" discourse, with its marathon sentences, strings of attributes, and negative/positive similes, expresses a groping uncertainty, a struggle against the inability to comprehend and express things "for which three words are three too many, and three thousand words that many words too less" (166). The narrator is bound to face a cognitive impasse whichever way he turns—unless, of course, he admits the fictionality of his own and the focalizers' tale, the fact that, like the characters, he is "creating . . . out of the rag-tag and bob-ends of old tales and talking, people who perhaps had never existed at all anywhere" (303). Like Miss Rosa, he projects what he knows upon the side of the picture that is not turned to him. Needless to say, this is also the predicament of the audience.

Indeed, the story of Henry's and Bon's love for each other seems to be a projection of the homosexual attraction of Quentin and Shreve.[17] Bon's wrapping Henry into the cloak at the bivouac seems to be inspired by Shreve's getting the overcoat for Quentin in the fictional present, as well as by the cloak that, according to Mr. Compson, was used for duels in New Orleans. Shreve's story of how Bon's mother refused to accept the false news of Sutpen's death is a projection of Miss Rosa's refusal to reconcile herself to the fact that Sutpen died without first admitting that he had been wrong.[18] The imagination is thus denied complete autonomy: it is the captive djinn that is conjured up by the rubbing of Aladdin's lamp. The role of the lamp is played by symbol-making patterns of relationships at one's disposal; the picture "projected" onto the blanks largely replicates these patterns. The audience, is, however, given a choice of patterns that it may reproduce in its imaginative filling of the blanks.

The bifurcation in the concerns of the furthermost circle of ripples, the novel's audience, is associated with the difference of the effect that the novel produces on the first and on the repeated readings. *Absalom, Absalom!* opens with a mass of diffused information, from which there presently emerge blurry contours of the violent/docile, God-/demon-like Sutpen and his mysterious children, who *"should have been the jewels of his pride and the shield and comfort of his old age, only . . . they destroyed him or something or he destroyed them or something"* (9). The audience is presented with what seems to be a frame for a weird jigsaw puzzle: "in 1833 . . . [Sutpen] first rode into town out of no discernible past and acquired his land no one knew how and built his house, his mansion, apparently out of nothing and married Ellen Coldfield and begot his two children—the son who widowed the daughter who had not yet been a bride—and so accomplished his allotted course to its violent (Miss Coldfield at least would have said, just) end" (11).

A movement toward the resolution of the puzzle proceeds in three stages. First, Mr. Compson suggests that Sutpen's son Henry and his prospective son-in-law Bon quarreled over the latter's octoroon mistress (the bigamy-threat theory). Then it is suggested that Bon must have been Sutpen's son (the incest-threat theory), and finally that Bon must have been part Negro (the miscegenation theory). The bigamy-threat hypothesis makes us think that the murder mystery has been solved (more or less like the mystery of Tom's origin in the first book of *Tom Jones*). This provisional solution permits the narrator to prepare us for Quentin's incest-threat theory without letting us make the premature guess ourselves—a procedure reminiscent of Austen's techniques in *Emma*.

The bigamy-threat theory finesses a number of cryptic facts such as the presence of the blasé Bon among the freshmen of a backwoods college, Sutpen's uncharacteristic avoidance of a direct conflict with his daughter's suitor, or the existence of a Sutpen child older than Clytie. We are prevented from anticipating Quentin's interpretation of these moot points. In effect, the narrator prepares us in much the same way as in Mr. Compson's paraleptic tale Bon prepares Henry for the disclosure of his morganatic marriage. The method is aptly described by Mr. Compson's *mise-en-abîme* metaphor of a plate on which a picture is being projected. The plate is the listener's (or reader's) mind, upon which the teller acts with "calculation, the surgeon's alertness and cold detachment, the exposures brief, so brief as to be cryptic, almost staccato, the plate unaware of what the complete picture would show, scarce-seen yet ineradicable" (111). It is on such a plate, as it were, that the frame of the jigsaw puzzle appears in the opening pages of the novel.

A careful preparation for the incest-threat theory is, indeed, necessary lest it may sound like a grafting of the *Nicholas Nickleby* kind of poetic justice onto the uncongenial body of an American novel. To heighten our receptivity to Quentin's suggestions at the right moment, the narrative forces us to formulate his hypothesis for ourselves:

> It was at this point that Shreve went to the bedroom and put on the bathrobe. He did not say Wait, he just rose and left Quentin sitting before the table, the open book and the letter, and went out and returned in the robe and sat again and took up the cold pipe, though without filling it anew or lighting it as it was. "All right," he said. "So that Christmas Henry brought him home, into the house, and the demon looked up and saw the face he believed he had paid off and discharged twenty-eight years ago. Go on."
>
> "Yes," Quentin said. "Father said he probably named him himself. Charles Bon. Charles Good" (265).

The two friends talk about the possibility that Bon was Sutpen's son without putting it into so many words, and we are left to draw the inference ourselves, prompted by Shreve's sudden realization. Shreve understands Quentin's hints before we do yet his discourse leaps to the next link in the logical chain, leaving it for us to "back up" and supply the link, "Bon was Sutpen's firstborn," that has been elided. To some extent, we reenact the experience of Shreve, who guesses Quentin's meaning without waiting for it to be formulated, and perhaps even the experience of Quentin, who may have derived his insight from the look of tragic awareness on the faces of Clytie and Henry Sutpen. This rhetorical procedure also seems to be modeled on the strategies that Mr. Compson ascribes to Charles Bon. In the paraleptic New Orleans episode, Charles tells Henry how his townsmen settle their mortal conflicts, exposing him to the idea of a duel (which, with the two combatants wrapped up in the same cloak, looks almost like fratricide) in order not to have to say to him "Why should we fight?" Henry himself is led to ask "What would you—they be fighting for?" (113) before he is allowed to see the octoroon. Charles thus makes Henry give utterance to an idea that would have been dangerous if it had come from himself, and Henry is induced to accept the idea as his own. This device, which the omniscient narrator seems to have borrowed from Quentin and Bon, takes advantage of the reader's belief in his own sagacity, and, rather like the Elton debacle in *Emma*, leads the audience into a trap. Indeed, just as Shreve forms a false surmise about the sex of Milly's baby, so the reader is diverted from evidence of the miscegenation theory.

Unlike the reader, in this episode Shreve understands the whole meaning of Quentin's hints about Bon, and so he imagines Bon's mother betraying a "desperate urgency of fear" upon Charles's reference to "a little speck of negro blood" in his mistress (308). Henceforth Shreve and Quentin continue their imaginative reconstruction of the story, always keeping in mind the fatal drop of Negro blood in Charles Bon, yet never mentioning it. One may note that this kind of oblique conversation is also carried on by other characters: the little Sutpen's Tidewater neighbors talk about social inequality "though it [is] never once mentioned by name, as when people talk about privation without mentioning the siege, about sickness without naming the epidemic" (231); Miss Rosa talks about the insult she received from Sutpen without specifying what the insult was; and, finally, Quentin talks about Sutpen's reaction to the birth of his last child without even mentioning (what to him is a self-evident fact) that this child was a girl and not the desired male heir.

The miscegenation theory is therefore finessed, just like the incest-threat theory before it, even though a considerable number of narrative details can only be explained as evidence of Bon's part-Negro origin: the yet-undisclosed secret that has caused the break-up of Sutpen's first marriage, the ease with which Sutpen legally dismisses his first wife, and his stubborn reluctance to discuss the matter. There is even a verbal echo that points to an analogy between Bon's relationship with his mistress and Sutpen's with his first wife: according to Mr. Compson, if Bon wanted to persuade Henry that by marrying Judith he would not commit bigamy, his "trump" would be, "Have you forgot that this woman, this child, are niggers?" (118). Later on, when Quentin recreates Sutpen's confidences to General Compson, he also mentions the "last trump" (274), which "the demon" is making up his mind to use. On the first reading, however, this analogy and other challenging details are eclipsed by the stunning effect of the incest-threat theory, for which the reader almost shares credit with Quentin. Just as the confession of Jenny Jones in Fielding's novel makes us believe that the mystery of Tom's birth is no longer relevant, so in *Absalom, Absalom!* the quasi-disclosure of blood-ties between Sutpen and Bon seems a sufficient explanation of the murder mystery. We do not expect any more sensational discoveries. It now seems that the remaining loose ends can be accounted for within the existing framework. Then, as in *Tom Jones*, we find out that the mystery has transformed itself into a surprise gap. The effect of what we eventually assume to be the final disclosure, namely, the effect of the miscegenation theory, is thus enhanced by the element of surprise.

This effect consists in a powerful emphasis on the theme of racial injustice. We have watched Henry struggling to reconcile himself to the idea of incest, and we have believed that the ancient taboo ultimately proved stronger than his love for Bon and Judith, that it made him kill Bon in order to prevent incest. Then, all of a sudden, in the middle of a "distanced" scene, we learn that Bon is supposed to have been part Negro. A few pages later Bon's words, *"So it's the miscegenation, not the incest, which you cant bear"* (356), change our whole view of the situation. Now that Henry has painfully and tortuously brought himself to consent to the incestuous marriage, it appears that a tiny admixture of Negro blood is less pardonable in Bon than virtual bigamy and conscious incest: the tragedy of the Sutpen house has been caused by sheer blind and primitive racial intolerance.

Thus the distribution of information in *Absalom, Absalom!* brings the theme of racism into high relief at the end of the first reading. Unlike *A Passage to India*, Faulkner's novel does not induce the reader to "simulate" the racist attitudes of his characters, but it does make us reenact a more general kind of error of attitude, one of which racism is a variant. This is the tendency to use people as means to ends, without considering the feelings and desires, irrational as they may be, to which every individual is entitled. The analogous tendency in audience response to the first reading consists in regarding the personages active in the fictional present as sources of information, as fictional means to be a quasi-detective end, rather than as characters in their own right.

As in most of the novels discussed above, the text itself is responsible for promoting this attitude. Since at the beginning of the novel all the missing pieces of the Sutpen puzzle seem to refer to the fictional past, we treat the fictional present, in which Quentin Compson talks to Miss Rosa, as a functional narrative situation. Only at the end of the novel does the fictional present of the opening chapters turn out to play an important part in the novel's *fabula*.

The hermeneutic code, which consists of all the plot details and narrative techniques associated with the murder mystery, is, of course, the major factor in deflecting our interest from the fictional present and the characters engaged in it, yet the influence of the mystery is also reinforced by camouflage techniques reminiscent of those employed in Austen's *Emma*. As it becomes clear only toward the very end of the novel, Miss Rosa has invited Quentin to her house in order to persuade him to take her to Sutpen's Hundred so that she might find out who or what is hidden there. Not only is her intuition of a secret presence in the mansion withheld from the reader, but even the prospect of the expedition is jammed on the first reading by the camouflage of the one detail that could have alerted us to the fact that the old story is not yet finished.

This detail is Miss Rosa's motive for summoning Quentin and telling him the story. Quentin thinks that she wishes to have the story told so that posterity should be able to understand the tragic downfall of the South—this is one of the reasons for his own future narrative act. He later rejects this hypothesis, recollecting that Miss Rosa is a poetess of sorts and would not need to delegate such a task. The excuse offered by Miss Rosa herself, her hope that the story would appear in print with her own name mentioned kindly, is more plausible, and, like Austen's equivocations, to some extent true. On a repeated reading it is accepted not as a downright lie but as one of the "might-have-beens that are more true than truth" since it reminds one of Judith's entrusting Bon's letter to Mrs. Compson in order to leave some memory behind ("Because you make so little impression, you see," 127). On the first reading we are satisfied with Miss Rosa's excuse, or at least we accept the narrative situation as conventional. The anticipation of the dramatic development that is to take place several hours later is further veiled by a number of stylistic devices. For instance, instead of saying that Quentin keeps wondering why Miss Rosa should tell him the things that he already knows, the narrator says that "It would be three hours yet before he would learn why she had sent for him because part of it, the first part of it, Quentin already knew" (11). This non sequitur construction circumvents the need for a phrase like "he wondered why," lest the reader be tempted to ask "why indeed?" Information is promised and then delayed—legitimately, because Quentin also has to wait for it. Furthermore, the sentence effects a smooth transition to a string of facts about Sutpen, thus finessing against Miss Rosa's subterfuges. Later, part of the delayed information is smuggled into the narrative, but in such a way that on the first reading we fail to recognize its importance: "'But why tell me about it?' [Quentin] said to his father that evening, when he returned home, after she had dismissed him at last with his promise to return for her in the buggy" (12). We have no way of knowing that the "promise to return for her in the buggy" is what Miss Rosa wanted all along. Not only is this detail denied emphasis but it seems to have made its way into the text apropos, attached and subordinated to the fact that "she dismissed him at last." Even Mr. Compson's explanation, "It's because she will need someone to go with her . . . and she chose you because your grandfather was the nearest thing to a friend Sutpen ever had" (12), is virtually lost on the reader, because the emphasis is shifted from the question "why does she want to tell the story?" to the question "why to Quentin?" As a result, the fictional present does not distract our attention from the Sutpen saga: Miss Rosa interests us as a former agent rather than the present teller or a possible present agent of her tale. Quentin likewise seems to be a mere receptacle of information, a narratee who provides a formal link between Miss Rosa's and Mr. Compson's narrative acts. Even when Miss Rosa makes the startling suggestion (at the end of chapter 5) that something is still hidden in the mansion, the expectation of the discovery is perceived as one more point of interest among many: we do not wish to learn the epilogue of the old story before we hear the story itself.[19]

Moreover, when the account of the fictional present appears

drawn-out, we are liable to resent the delay (as happens with some episodes of *Bleak House*). Our response then parallels the impatience of Shreve, who resents Quentin's breaking off the story of Sutpen at the point where Sutpen himself stops telling it to General Compson ("All right. Dont bother to say he stopped talking now; just go on," 258). In effect Shreve forgets Quentin's emotional involvement with the story and eventually drives him into a state verging on a nervous break-down.

In *Absalom, Absalom!* the analogy of moral tendencies displayed by the characters and the audience is all the more important in view of the reader's role as the furthermost circle of agitated ripples spreading from the center. Our somewhat impatient reading is not unlike Quentin's perusal of Bon's letter, which for him is "not like a something impressed upon the paper by a once-living hand but like a shadow cast upon it which had resolved on the paper the instant before he looked at it and which might fade, vanish, at any instant while he still read" (129). It is not for nothing that the reading of letters in the novel is imagined as consuming them, as reducing them to ashes.[20] Listening to another's story, or rather forcing the other to tell it, is in some cases just as manipulative as forcing another to listen. The reader's tendency to concentrate on the tale and neglect the teller reflects analogous attitudes in the world of the novel—Shreve is not the only listener who becomes unconscious of the teller's feelings. Quentin himself is another. He sometimes forgets even the very presence of the teller because he is carried away by the image of Sutpen that crystallizes in his own imagination: at times, his "listening would renege and hearing-sense self-confound and the long-dead object of [Miss Rosa's] impotent yet indomitable frustration would appear, as though by outraged recapitulation evoked, quiet inattentive and harmless, out of the biding and dreamy and victorious dust" (7-8). The word "renege"[21] can also be read as a metaphor for our own experience on the first reading, when we focus on the story and often forget who is supposed to be telling it at a given moment.

By the end of the first reading it becomes clear that Sutpen's story does not end with the death, disappearance, or degeneration of the last Sutpens but continues as the story of Quentin Compson ("happen is never once"), who gets entangled in it despite his self-protective better judgment. By a kind of inertia, however, we still read the account of the nocturnal expedition to the mansion not for the sake of what it may reveal about Quentin's involvement with the past but in the hope of discovering how his theory of Bon's origins will be confirmed by "hard fact." The episode is anticipated earlier in the novel: Shreve seems to think that Quentin derived his insights from his contact with Clytie. Yet the account of Quentin's meeting with Clytie does not satisfy our curiosity because it gives no hint of a sudden insight. Our hopes, however, are rekindled by the opening of another informational gap: Quentin decides to see for himself what is hidden in one of the rooms of the house. Yet immediately afterwards he is shown departing—the narrative has elided a portion of the represented time: " 'But I must see too now. I will have to. Maybe I shall be sorry tomorrow, but I must see.' So when he came back down the stairs (and he remembered how he thought, 'Maybe my face looks like hers did, but it's not triumph') there was only Clytie in the hall, sitting still on the bottom step, sitting still in the attitude in which he had left her. She did not even look at him as he passed her" (370-71).

We are not told what Quentin has seen; there is only a veiled intimation that he has carried out his decision to pursue the secret. This arbitrary delay protracts suspense and seems to promise a momentous revelation. We wish to know why Quentin is agitated when he comes home—not because we are concerned for his state of mind but because we are interested in what he found in the house or how he discovered Bon's origin. Just as we are satisfied on the first count, we are also faced with a major disappointment: the dialogue between Quentin and Henry Sutpen sheds no light on the past. Our hope to find an unambiguous solution to the problem of the source of Quentin's information lingers while we read the remaining few pages of the novel, only to be crushed by the open ending. As in the case of *A Passage to India*, our understanding of the novel now depends on the way we cope with our thwarted expectation.

It is when Quentin turns out to be a participant of the story, the person who is coerced into taking Miss Rosa to Sutpen's Hundred and who thereby unwittingly precipitates the destruction of the remaining inhabitants of the mansion, that our interest in him as a character in his own right is fully awakened. The ending of the novel, with Quentin's monosyllabic utterances and final hysterical outburst, defers the satisfaction of this interest to a repeated reading. Like *The Sound and the Fury*, *Absalom, Absalom!* has a built-in demand for a rereading: the first chapters of the novel are expected to provide formerly overlooked clues to Quentin's psychology, to the long-term effects of his experience, to the genesis of his insights, and perhaps to their validity. We also wish to test Quentin's theories against the material that we read before we were acquainted with them, and though this continues the detective interest of the first reading, Quentin now competes with Thomas Sutpen for the role of the novel's central figure.[22] This refocusing of interest is the proper response to the persistence of the gap, especially since it lays the basis for a broader view of the novel's thematic concerns. Our disappointment at not being given a clinching bit of information that would sanction Quentin's theories has occurred after a series of promises and delays—reenacting, in miniature form, Thomas Sutpen's own frustration. In his single-minded preoccupation with his design, Sutpen regards all setbacks as delays, till at last he has no more strength left to pursue his goals. One of his failures lies in his refusal to accept defeat, reassess his goals, and radically change his course. Not even the Civil War, which destroys the society he has aspired to join, is sufficiently final for Sutpen; it does not turn him away from his obstinate quest. An inability to achieve a drastic reorientation, a recurrent Faulknerian theme, likewise destroys the chances of a spiritual survival for the other characters—Miss Rosa, Ellen Sutpen, Mr. Compson, or Bon's son. These characters cannot release their stubborn grip over their obsolete social identities and move on. The audience, by contrast, has to move on, giving up one set of expectations, forming another, and following it up on a repeated reading.

In his account of the levity that covers Quentin's and Shreve's "youthful shame of being moved," the third-person narrator notes that the two of them are engaged, without knowing it, in "that best of ratiocination which after all [is] a good deal like Sutpen's morality and Miss Coldfield's demonizing" (280). In other words, they are engaged not so much in the reconstruction of "the career of somebody named Thomas Sutpen" (247) but in the search for the hubris, for what Sutpen calls the "mistake" (263) that has lead to the failure of his "design" despite the superhuman energy with which he has pursued his goals. If they do not really find this "mistake" it is because they fail to look for it in themselves, in their tendency to erase the individuality of the other, reducing the other merely to a source of information or a kind of silent psychoanalyst whose presence is required for self-projection in speech.

In his total commitment to his design, Sutpen is an extreme exponent of this "mistake." He becomes an apotheosis of the Old South not only in that he has more swiftly and violently risen to a position of prominence among the planters. His disregard of the ethical imperative that forbids treating people as means rather than as ends in themselves is an expression of the basic hubris of slaveholding society. Yet practically all of the novel's characters share this attitude to some extent: Henry wishes to use Judith for his own union with Bon, Bon wishes to use both the brother and the sister in order to exert pressure on Sutpen, Bon's mother (in Shreve's story) wishes to use her son as an instrument of uncanny revenge, and Miss Rosa uses Quentin for her own similar bit of revenge (she seems to be fully expecting to find Sutpen himself hidden in the old mansion, since she has never accepted his having died without first admitting that he was wrong; therefore after having found Henry her face does not express triumph, 370). Her attitude to Quentin reenacts ("happen is never once") Sutpen's tendency to reduce people—slaves, dependents, wives—to instruments in the achievement of his grand design, maiming their lives in the process. Even Shreve cannot resist the contagion: while physically taking care of Quentin, he cannot help prolonging and exacerbating his mental torments.[23]

Quentin also appears to be tainted by another aspect of Sutpen's "innocence"—the inability to allow for depth and complexity of feeling in other people. In the world of *Absalom, Absalom!* failure to respect others as ends in themselves is associated with the failure to recognize their autonomous and incalculable individualities. Of all the spiteful remarks that Shreve makes at the end of the novel, the most keenly true is the one about Quentin's failure to understand Miss Rosa ("You dont know. You dont even know about the old dame, the Aunt Rosa," 362). Quentin is, indeed, powerless against the old lady, whose handwriting he does not recognize "as revealing a character cold, implacable, and even ruthless" (10), not only because of his gallantness but also because his understanding of her is limited and biased. Though he has listened to Miss Rosa's confessions, he is still unable to go beyond her social façade in attempting to predict her conduct:

> He could almost see her, waiting in one of the dark airless rooms in the little grim house's impregnable solitude. . . . She would be wearing already the black bonnet with jet sequins; he knew that: and a shawl, sitting there in the augmenting and defunctive twilight; she would have even now in her hand or on her lap the reticule with all the keys, entrance closet and cupboard, that the house possessed which she was about to desert for perhaps six hours; and a parasol, an umbrella too, he thought, thinking how she would be impervious to weather and season since although he had not spoken a hundred words to her in his life before this afternoon, he did know that she had never before tonight quitted that house after sundown save on Sundays and

Wednesdays for prayer meeting, in the entire forty-three years probably. Yes, she would have the umbrella. [88-89]

On a repeated reading we know that this description lacks a crucial
detail: in the folds of her inevitable umbrella Miss Rosa will have
concealed a torch and a hatchet for breaking into the Sutpen mansion.
The "apple-pie morality," which Quentin shares, to some extent, with
Sutpen, makes no provision for the ferocity of frustrated feelings.
Quentin's notion of a Southern lady does not take into account the existence of needs that even a gentlewoman will go to great lengths to satisfy, or the touch of the "moral brigandage" (260) that underlies, in fact,
the whole society but is very much in the character of a woman who combines entrenched conventionality with occasional flashes of ruthless
and defiant self-assertion. The episode is endowed with a touch of dramatic irony that qualifies Quentin's insights as partial and immature.

It is therefore not unjustified to doubt the completeness of Quentin's imaginative reconstruction of the past events, even if one assumes
that his major insights may be accurate since they knit together all the
loose ends of Sutpen's story. The novel, indeed, shows the precise
point at which Quentin and Shreve discontinue the reconstruction of
Thomas Sutpen's portrait.

While listening to and then telling ("Let me play a while now," 280)
the story of Sutpen's and Wash Jones's deaths, Shreve keeps wondering why Sutpen should have abused Milly on the birth of their child.
Shreve somehow too automatically assumes that Milly gave birth to a
son and that Sutpen's unpredictable conduct may have had some
complex motivation. Then he suddenly realizes that Sutpen's final act
of suicidal brutality was provoked by a sheer fortuitous touch of
destiny—the sex of the newborn baby. Shocked by the absurdity of a
world view that makes the fate of several people depend on biological
dice, Shreve feels like putting an end to the whole game:

> *"Will you wait?"* Shreve said. "—that with the son he went to all that
> trouble to get lying right there behind him in the cabin, he would have
> to taunt the grandfather into killing first him and then the child too?"
> "—What?" Quentin said. "It wasn't a son. It was a girl."
> "Oh," Shreve said. "—Come on. Let's get out of this damn icebox
> and go to bed." [292]

It is at this moment, emphasized by being placed at the end of the
section, that Shreve comes to an impasse. He understands that the

birth of a daughter instead of a son explains Sutpen's conduct; yet he is so disgusted with the "demon's" blind stubbornness in a poignant test situation that the sympathy he has felt for Sutpen as a heroic seeker of far-off aims yields to a revulsion for a heartless incorrigible fanatic. Though the two friends continue to play with the story for a while, from then on they are concerned only with Henry and Bon: Shreve, who takes the lead, refuses to give another thought to the exact motives for Sutpen's neglect of his firstborn son and his lastborn daughter. Neither does he give Quentin a chance to return to the subject.

Up to this point Shreve's game of reconstruction has followed the rule set in Mr. Compson's approach to historiography: "Have you noticed how so often when we try to reconstruct the causes which lead up to the actions of men and women, how with a sort of astonishment we find ourselves now and then reduced to the belief, the only possible belief, that they stemmed from some of the old virtues" (121). In accordance with this rule, Shreve explains, for instance, that Bon's motive for placing the picture of his mistress and son into Judith's case was his wish to assuage Judith's grief. A critic of the novel may explicate this detail in a more realistic way: "Defiance and counter-retaliation are the cause of [Charles Bon's] removing Judith's picture from his wallet and replacing it with that of his octoroon wife (Shreve's foolish interpretation of this act gives ironic heightening to its real poignancy). Charles's gesture says, in effect, that if he is to be none of theirs, they will be none of his."[24] In their search for meaning both the critic and the character engage in practically the same game of imaginative reconstruction. The critic has more psychological insight, yet the character, Shreve, adheres more closely to the midrashic rule of tracing the actions of people to some of the "old virtues." Joining the game, I would offer a third interpretation of Bon's gesture: it could have been an appeal to Judith to remember and protect his mistress and child whom he would not be able to protect himself (my "Aladdin's lamp" here is Ellen's dying appeal to Rosa to protect her children). This, indeed, seems to be the message that Judith herself extracts from the substitution of the photographs in the metal case.

For all of Mr. Compson's cynicism and Shreve's flippancy, both wish to put only the most noble construction on the events of the past. A gentleman, as J.L. Borges makes a character say in "The Shape of the Sword," can only fight on the losing side. Shreve, however, abandons the seemingly losing cause too soon, giving up attempts to humanize Sutpen's image. His outrage reenacts the outrage of Miss Rosa and Wash Jones, and, like these two characters, he fails to do justice to

Sutpen's personality. This is the time for us, the audience, to say, like Shreve, "Let *us* play a while now."

If we play by Mr. Compson's rule, we shall interpret Sutpen's actions not as blindly insane or bigoted but as motivated, indeed, by an "old virtue," the reductionist "apple-pie" conscience that has, since the beginning of his career, made him seek "a sort of balance of spiritual solvency" (40). Although in the morality-play scenes staged by Quentin's imagination Sutpen remembers his struggles against remorse ("his conscience had bothered him somewhat at first but . . . he had argued calmly and logically with his conscience until it was settled," 262), Quentin and Shreve fail to bring Sutpen's conscience to bear upon his conduct in the two major crises. It is the audience who must fully reconstruct Sutpen's motivation, rebelling against the authority of the text the way Quentin rebels against the narrative authority of his father and Shreve against that of Quentin.

The omniscient narrator likewise rebels against the narrative authority of Shreve, if only by emphasizing the moment at which Shreve turns away from Sutpen and his sons. "Faulkner" continues to play the game of reconstruction beyond the point where the nested narratives give it up, and his insights, expressed in "distanced" scenes, are offered for the interpretation of the reader. The reader's task is to establish the motives for the acts that take place in the morality plays staged by the omniscient narrator.

The most prominent of the "distanced" scenes are those emphasized by the unwonted use of the present tense—Henry's last meeting with his father (351-55) and his subsequent conversation with Bon (355-58). These are the penultimate acts of Bon's tragedy, when the fatal shot is not heard but anticipated, and the moral positions of Henry and Bon are defined with the maximum explicitness and just barely avoiding the stridency of melodramatic apotheosis.

The first of these two episodes reveals the essence of the hubris of the South, already exemplified in Miss Rosa's and Quentin's attitudes to each other: the reduction of individuals to abstractions. Sutpen regards Bon not as his eldest son, not as a man who has saved Henry's life, not even as a person who can be dealt with directly but as an obstacle to be removed. He does not discuss Bon with Henry but merely plays his last "trump," revealing that his Haitian wife was part Negro. Sutpen does not hate or fear Negroes: his racism is ideological, superimposed. He accepts the values of the society that he wishes to defeat by joining and therefore disqualifies anyone with a drop of

Negro blood from being connected with the dynasty that he plans to found.[25] The nature of Sutpen's mistake is elucidated by Bon in the second interview: "*—And he sent me no word? He did not ask you to send me to him? That was all he had to do, now, today; four years ago or at any time during the four years. That was all. He would not have needed to ask it, require it, of me. I would have offered it. I would have said, I will never see her again before he could have asked it of me. He did not have to do this, Henry. He didn't need to tell you I am a nigger to stop me. He could have stopped me without that, Henry*" (356). The poignancy of Bon's plea is enhanced by a sense of futility: Sutpen does not acknowledge Bon because he fails to understand the need for such a recognition, to understand that this recognition, rather than marriage with Judith or blackmail or property or revenge, is Bon's aim. Richard Poirier, whose essay " 'Strange Gods' in Jefferson, Mississippi" has stimulated the best critical studies of *Absalom, Absalom!*, remarks that Sutpen "fails to realize that Bon is demanding only the same sort of recognition denied him as a boy at the plantation door."[26] Later critics, however, persistently talk about Sutpen's "refusal" to acknowledge a part-Negro son. If Sutpen's tragic fault were indeed a refusal to acknowledge Bon rather than the symptomatic failure to understand the need for such an acknowledgement, the thematic core of the novel would have been the indictment of racial discrimination. This would harmonize with the major impression that, as noted previously, we carry away from the first reading, but it would not provide for a thematic connection between the Sutpen-Bon plot line on the one hand and the Sutpen-Miss Rosa and Sutpen-Wash Jones plot lines on the other. The thematic concerns of the novel are broader: racial discrimination is presented as merely one aspect of the failure to sympathize with and respect other human beings, the failure which blinds Sutpen to Bon's wish to assert himself and makes him impervious to Miss Rosa's sense of dignity, which blinds Quentin to the distinction between personality and role, and which temporarily blinds Judith to Charles Etienne's need for acceptance and love.

As Quentin says earlier in the novel, Sutpen's trouble is his "innocence" (220). His brand of innocence is an inability to even suspect the independent inner life of an individual behind social functions and moral abstractions. If Sutpen fails to see that the only thing required of him is a simple uninhibited gesture of parental acknowledgement, it is largely because instead of trying to understand his eldest son he engages in weighing moral alternatives, calculating, as Mr. Coldfield, another suicide, might have done, "a demand balance of spiritual solvency" (50). This is what Quentin and Shreve neglect to take into account. Sutpen knows that he must either admit bigamy and thus destroy the life he has built for himself or disclose the part-Negro origin of his first wife so that the marriage can be considered legally invalid. That, however, would mean promulgating Bon's Negro origins and so ruining his life, as it later ruins the life of his son Charles Etienne. Unlike Doc Hines of Faulkner's *Light in August*, Sutpen does not wish to destroy the physical and social well-being of his part-Negro descendant. However, this is where his consideration for Bon ends: he lacks the imagination to understand that Bon may have other than material needs, more complex than blackmail or vengeance. Having turned the people around him into his instruments, Sutpen may, by force of habit, take Bon for no more than an instrument of his mother's revenge.

He tries to conceal Bon's origins to the last (just as Judith later tries to persuade Charles Etienne to go to the North where he may pass for a white man), in the hope that this, like his providing for his abandoned wife, will give him a sense of having behaved with equity. Sutpen must persuade himself that he is, and has been, fair. He never completely succeeds in doing so, which is one of the reasons why he cannot face Bon.[27] Quentin and Shreve do not understand this, just as Miss Rosa fails to understand that it is the wish to be fair that makes Sutpen propose a trial marriage to her instead of seducing her, as he later seduces Wash Jones's granddaughter. Likewise, Quentin and Shreve fail to understand that Sutpen's suicidal taunting of Wash Jones is prompted not only by the realization that his design can never be achieved but by the sense that for once in his life he has been blatantly unfair, and, being the kind of man he is, there is nothing he can do to restore his spiritual solvency. He cannot live, as Bon does, with a consciousness of his own injustice: his Puritan mind cannot come to terms with culpability and shame.

The difference between the two moral stands (Bon, significantly, is a Roman Catholic) is well defined by Mr. Compson's paraleptic imagination, according to which Bon, "this cerebral Don Juan who, reversing the order, [has] learned to love what he [has] injured" (108), refuses to deny his feelings for the abandoned woman or his appreciation of her loyalty. Ready to reject but not to repudiate, he would offer Henry and Judith not just himself but also a heavy onus of guilt,[28] with which the conscience of the Sutpen children might not be able to cope— Mr. Compson's rejected bigamy-threat theory, therefore, is another "might-have-been that is more true than truth." Sutpen's refusal to accept guilt is a graver fault than the cause of the guilt itself, because it proceeds from a denial of an independent inner life and the need for self-assertion in all the people with whom, in his own naive way, he endeavors to be fair. Sutpen's "innocence" covers all the spheres of relationship between people; and slavery and racial prejudice are among the crudest but also the most powerful expressions of this paradox-ridden "old virtue" responsible for the rise and the fall of the plantation society.

As shown above, on the first reading, the three-stage manner of presenting Quentin's solution of the mystery channels our attention to racial problematics when it "surprises" us by the miscegenation theory. As our understanding of the novel's theme broadens and bifurcates on a rereading, we still remember that racial prejudice is one of the most tenacious manifestations of the "innocence" of the South. This is borne out by the story of Judith. According to Mr. Compson, rather early in her life Judith understands an individual's wish to assert his identity: in a metaphor ascribed to her and associated with one of the meanings of Sutpen's "design," people try "to make a rug on the same loom only each one wants to weave his own pattern into the rug" (127). Yet the "distanced" narrative at the beginning of the Harvard series (the focalization seems to be attributed to Mr. Compson, but vaguely and quite inconsistently) shows Judith denying this right to Charles Etienne, who is brought up without manifest affection in her house and kept always between the whites and the blacks and away from either.[29] Later, however, faced with the harm done to Charles Etienne, in the third-person narrator's little morality play Judith finally brings herself to reject her own belief in racial segregation: "*I was wrong. I admit it. I believed that there were things which still mattered just because they had mattered once. But I was wrong. Nothing matters but breath, breathing, to know and to be alive*" (207).

Her attitude now echoes Charles Bon's slightly cynical professions of undiscriminating humanism[30] (and both echo Mr. Compson's intonations in both *Absalom, Absalom!* and *The Sound and the Fury*): "There is something in you that doesn't care about honor and pride yet that lives, that even walks backward for a whole year just to live; . . . the old mindless sentient undreaming meat that doesn't even know any difference between despair and victory" (349).

Yet neither Bon nor his son indulge that "mindless sentient meat"; neither of them acts out the cynical principles that are the polar opposite of Sutpen's apple-pie morality and that are equally destructive in their denial of an individual's need for self-assertion. It is in self-assertion that Bon pursues paternal acknowledgment, marriage with Judith, or death at Henry's hand; it is because of the same emotional need that his son flings his mixed origins in the faces of the white and the black and refuses to go to the North where he would stop being what he is. Judith finally recognizes that this is the only way in which Charles Etienne can live with himself, and, having learned her lesson, she offers him the affection that has been withheld too long. She acknowledges him as her nephew in a contrite act of recognition that her father had failed to perform. Then she dies nursing the sick Charles Etienne, whether with Charles Bon's fatalistic indifference or with fulfillment in *Liebestod*, as the reader might choose to believe.

Such an interpretation of Judith's story, however, is completely beyond our reach on the first reading, if only because the story is told before Sutpen's biography and Quentin's theories are presented. Thus the temporary withholding of information defers our understanding of the motifs out of which the episode is spun, whereas the permanent withholding of information, which draws us into the game of reconstruction on a rereading, goes a long way towards activating and defining these motifs.

As in *Bleak House* or *Emma*, on the first reading of *Absalom, Absalom!* the audience reenacts the characters's major error of attitude, the Sutpen-like "innocence" that neglects the psychological complexity of individuals behind their roles and functions. Yet we ultimately adjust our perception when we blend the stories of Sutpen and Quentin Compson into one, treating both the characters with equal attention though with different kinds of interest. The two competing protagonists exemplify two kinds of fictionality. Sutpen is an emphatically fictional character in whose creation we are invited to participate. No statement made about him can be true or false but only compatible or incompatible with other statements, especially with the one about the "old virtues" to be sought in history. The reconstruction of his story, prematurely discontinued by Quentin and Shreve, is a game that we can play of our own accord, provided we determine the rules. Quentin, on the other hand, partakes of a less fictional quality of a personage whose secrets are to be respected. Our sense of their reality owes to opposite phenomena: Sutpen is convincing because with a due effort of imagination we can learn all we wish to know about him, while Quentin appears real precisely because we do not know everything about him,[31] just as he does not know everything about Miss Rosa. We seem to be invited to throw imaginative bridges over the gap in Sutpen's story, yet not over the gap in the story of Quentin: Sutpen, and all he stands for, is the "blackbird" of which Faulkner hopes the reader may achieve the fourteenth and true vision.[32] Such a vision must use Quentin's theories as workable yet incomplete assumptions, as a basis for further reconstruction and interpretation, always remembering that it is not on the literal but only on the moral plane that the gap may be successfully closed, always remembering, moreover, that we are engaged in a game.

The game is, of course, a serious business, but it sets us free from the determinist chain of processes that constitute living in the world.[33] Nor do we submit to another determinist chain when Faulkner's novel coerces us to join its detective game—if only because it is our own interpretive activity that determines, or rather sets, the rules by which we play. Needless to say, the rules that I have suggested above seem to me to be the closest to the spirit of the game within the novel's world, especially since the old humanistic belief that people must be treated as ends in themselves rather than as means to ends, a belief that gained authority when it took the shape of Kant's practical imperative[34] without becoming less difficult to implement consistently, is the basis of Faulkner's moral vision and the terminus of his epistemological games.

Concluding Remarks

There never was a war that was
    not inward; I must
fight till I have conquered in myself what
    causes war
    —Marianne Moore, "In Distrust of Merits"

In recent decades the study of literature has been regaining the inter-disciplinary dimension that came under attack during the fifties and sixties. Yet the intrinsic analysis that New Criticism placed in the very centre of the critical endeavour has not been rendered obsolete by the current wavering of the belief in the hermetic unity, mandatory consistency, or centripetal coherence of a work of art. Apart from being a direct engagement of the mind with the text and the collective field-work without which "narrative crossings"[1] can turn into mechanical applications of the problematics of other disciplines, intrinsic analysis is necessary for the development of any literary scholar's authentic voice.

My approach to the seven novels discussed above is a method of intrinsic analysis that can open up to issues of ethical theory. I believe that a novel's place in the cultural history and in the history of ideas can also, in principle, be more precisely defined by determining the role that it assigns to its "implied" audience. And this role consists of the trials and errors of the first reading, of the nature of the reorientation undergone on rereadings, and of meaningful analogies between audience response and the experience of the fictional characters. Conversely, our ideas of the novel's place in literary history can be tested and perhaps modified by the examination of the encoded audience response.

Yet the main impulse behind this book has been not the promotion of intrinsic analysis so much as inquiry into the relationship between the aesthetic and the moral elements in one's response to literature. Augustine, the philosopher who collapses the distinction between a written text and the Book of Life, warns the audience against the "pernicious sweetness" of the unwise and the authors against letting "what should be said escape us while we are thinking of the artistry of the discourse" but concedes the value of artistry for holding attention.[2] Many centuries later Kant's rebellious disciple Arthur Schopenhauer, who adopts, *ad hoc*, the metaphor of the book,[3] endows the moment of aesthetic contemplation with moral value since it amounts to "the momentary silencing of all willing,"[4] thus checking the ominous progress of the Will which, for the duration of this moment, our consciousness ceases to objectify. The seductiveness of Schopenhauer's aesthetic theory has not been reduced by time, whether or not the other aspects of his doctrines have retained cogency. Modern literary criticism, however, finds it difficult to discuss aesthetic experience and its sources, if only because the traditional language of such discussions, the notions of "beauty," "harmony," and "congruence" are felt to be worn and culture bound. The writers for whom the aesthetic is a major avowed concern may ironically demystify its recognition but not elucidate it: Nabokov, for instance, frequently observed that aesthetic experience lodges not in one's head but, so to say, in one's spine. It is, however, not impossible to discuss aesthesis in terms other than beauty and harmony—for instance, in terms of play and balance, where play is understood as the back-and-forth movement (as in "the play of light and shade"[5]) and balance as a sustained act of skill in the face of danger. In the reading of fiction the aesthetic consciousness of balance and play enters into conflict with the attention to the subject matter of the narrative, but this conflict is, in its turn, aesthetic, since it results in a to-and-from movement of attention, a play of the reader's mind, its sallying forth to pure enjoyment and its return home to the defamiliarized, renewed cognitive and moral experience.

The narrative devices that I have discussed may be regarded as building blocks of the ethics of form: while indirectly conveying the novelist's attitude to his material they both provide aesthetic enjoyment and influence the cognitive and ethical experience of the reader. It is probably the moments of "aesthetic bliss" that produce the intensity of the feeling that literature and scholarship are all important humanistic endeavours. As the experience subsides and the books are laid down, the tacit communications with the aesthetic realm become a matter of the past that blends with one's daily activities; it is not "cancelled" like Tennyson's "trance," but it certainly is "stricken through with doubt." The present century has amply demonstrated of what little avail learning and highbrow culture can turn out to be. The best works of literary art fall flat against the psyche of a mass killer who is not averse to shedding a delicious tear over a sentimental passage in a novel. And they will not be needed for the improvement of those in whom Fielding would see an innate "Good Heart." Does the covertly didactic element of literature address only that limited class of readers who, like Fielding's young Nightingale, could yet be swayed one way or another, their hearts yearning for the right place and their sense of expediency raising obstacles in their progress to that out-of-the-way location?

A literary scholar has to idealize his or her work—through a belief in the moral value of discrimination, perceptiveness, and self-critical attention to the reading of texts, as well as through a belief in the ethical value of the moments of aesthetic transport. Not that one should become oblivious to the essential futility of this idealization. Academic study of literature in welfare societies is aware of its oscillation between the luxuriance of a hothouse plant and the stamina of a boat against the current. There are questions of life and death that it simply cannot affect. But perhaps, in its own way, academic study can keep trying, because it cannot evade its context, the problem of the educational value of art.

In our eventful century millions of people discovered in themselves the same attitudes as the ones that caused—or resulted from— a variety of moral/political aberrations and quasi-legitimized crimes. "How could we ever believe that, think that way, feel that way?" is the question that has troubled people on practically every meridian. Eloquently reticent novels raise parallel questions and are, therefore, isomorphic with the baffling aspects of reality in which we strive for a stable foothold. These novels provide models of the mechanics through which, in a seemingly disinterested process of reading, one is led to assume, temporarily, the very attitudes that one finds erroneous when displayed in the fictional worlds. The effect of these novels can, thus, be described by the conventional notion of catharsis—the eliciting of the potentially dangerous tendencies in our own mental and moral makeup and their ultimate rejection and reassessment.

Yet the term "catharsis" may be understood to mean ordering or clarification rather than cleansing.[6] I do not with to suggest the necessity for some sort of an inner purge or for a new kind of vigilance. *Nihil humanum* should be totally expunged from our inner lives: morality is, mainly, a matter of action; it concerns not all the thoughts and attitudes that flow through our minds but only those that we turn into the basis for our conduct. The choice of such attitudes, however, is bound to be improved by the freedom that results from the growth of self-critical awareness.

The manipulative withholding of make-believe information in the seven novels discussed may be regarded as symbolic of the self-contained silence of the text that, as Stanley Cavell put it, "should be interpretable politically as rebuke and confrontation and interpretable epistemologically as the withholding of assertion, . . . as if the withholding of assertion, the containing of the voice, amounts to foregoing of domination." The experience of reading is liberating when the interpretation of the text yields to one's being interpreted by the text—a process that, in Cavell's terms, should be guided by three principles: "First, access to the text is provided not by the mechanism of projection but by that of transference . . . second, the pleasures of appreciation are succeeded by the risks of seduction; and third, the risks are worth running because the goal of the encounter is not consummation but freedom."[7] Turning from the text to a critical view of one's own reading is an act of freedom both from the sway of the text and its author and from the invisible text inscribed in one's own mind by habits of perception and inchoate thought, the text that overlaps but need not be identical with what an individual may wish to regard—or create—as the authentic self.

Notes

Note: For publication facts for works cited, see Works Cited, 210-20.

CHAPTER ONE. Introduction

1. According to Milhail Bakhtin, the genre of the novel is distinguished from previous narrative genres by its "heteroglossia," which is a "stylistic three-dimensionality . . . linked with the multi-language consciousness." Heteroglossia may involve the presence of several languages in the same text, the use of several stylistic registers, and/or the presence of different ways of incorporating "the word of another." As a heteroglot genre, the novel reflects the contact of cultures as well as the artist's awareness of the extent to which we all live in a world made up of the words of others. See Bakhtin, *Dialogic Imagination*, 11.

2. Gardner, *On Moral Fiction*, 117.

3. See Martha C. Nussbaum, *Fragility of Goodness*, 13 ff.

4. Booth's *Company We Keep* authoritatively rehabilitates ethical criticism that has, for various reasons, suffered an eclipse—no matter what case can be made for ethical concerns having always been with us.

5. It must be added that the microscopic rhetorical analysis of Old Testament verses in Sternberg's *Poetics of Biblical Narrative* yields insights vastly beyond narratological concerns.

6. For discussions of various approaches to reader-response criticism see Suleiman and Crosman, *Reader in the Text*; Tompkins, *Reader-Response Criticism*; Holub, *Reception Theory*; and Freund, *Return of the Reader*.

7. Pushkin, *Eugene Onegin*, trans. by Vladimir Nabokiv, 1:102.

8. D.H. Harding, "Psychological Processes," 147.

9. Both the selections, published by Norton in 1980 and 1981, respectively, have been put together by the translator, John Glad. A fuller English language edition of Shalamov's stories, without cuts or explanatory insertions, is to be hoped for.

10. See Erlich, *Russian Formalism*, 242; Rimmon, *Concept of Ambiguity*, 30. This distinction is practically the same as Seymour Chatman's one between "story" and "discourse." See *Story and Discourse*, 19; I use the Russian terms so that other meanings of the word "story" do not interfere.

11. See, for instance, Culler, "Fabula and Sjuzhet," 27-37.

12. See Fish, "Literature in the Reader," 123-62.

13. Fish, "Interpreting the Variorum," 465-85.

14. For the discussion of the status of the "story" along these lines see Rimmon-Kenan, *Narrative Fiction*, 7-8.

15. The formalist assumption that the narrative "presents" or "describes" things that preexist it is, in fact, the position of classical rhetoric. The early nineteenth-century rhetorician Pierre Fontanier, for instance, uses the term "authorial metalepsis" for those infrequent cases when, as in Delille's *Trois Règnes de la Nature*, the writer pretends to produce that which he, "essentially, merely retells or describes." *Les Figures du Discourse*, 128, my translation.

16. A sentence in a fictional narrative can be regarded as a performative speech act that masks itself as a constative speech act. The distinction between these two kinds of speech acts in ordinary language was first introduced by Austin in *How to Do Things with Words*; see also his "Performative Utterances." Among the most important further developments of the theory are Searle, *Speech-Acts*; Benveniste, "Analytical Philosophy and Language"; Cavell, *Must We Mean What We Say?* 1-43; Pratt, *Toward a Speech Act Theory*; and Felman, *Literary Speech Act*.

17. The view of a literary work as a scheme to be "concretized" has been most fully and lucidly developed in Iser, *Act of Reading*, esp. ix-xii, 19, and 62-68.

18. On indeterminacy see Iser, *Act of Reading*, 24, 49, 66, 167-179, 181-185; on the function of blanks in activizing the perceiver see Gombrich, *Art and Illusion*, 174.

19. Sternberg, *Expositional Modes*, 70.

20. See Rifaterre, "Describing Poetic Structures," 215.

21. Rifaterre, "Describing Poetic Structures," 216.

22. Ibid.

23. Iser, *Implied Reader*, 282.

24. On art as prolonging perception cf. Shklovsky, "Art as Technique," 12.

25. Rifaterre, "Describing Poetic Structures," 215.

26. Nabokov, *King, Queen, Knave*, 9-10.

27. Fish, "Literature in the Reader," 145. In his later work Fish concluded that the primacy given to the reader conflicts too radically with the need to limit subjectivity. His way of solving this problem, however, is more useful for cultural, new historicist studies than for narratology. He claims that "it is interpretive communities, rather than either the text or the reader, that produce meanings and are responsible for the emergence of formal features. Interpretive communities are made up of those who share interpretive strategies not for reading but for writing texts, for constituting their properties. In other words these strategies exist prior to the act of reading and therefore determine the shape of what is read rather than, as is usually assumed, the other way around." *Is There a Text in This Class*, 14.

28. Eco, *Role of the Reader*, 8.

29. In *Rhetoric of Fiction*, 156, Booth mentions the "postulated reader," yet later criticism has adopted the term "implied reader"—the counterpart of Booth's "implied author" (151) which is not the historical author but the system

of norms implicit in the text; see also Rimmon-Kenan, *Narrative Fiction*, 86-89; and Wilson, "Readers in Texts."

30. "A reading's object is the singular text; its goal, to dismantle the system of that text. A reading consists in relating each element of the text to all the others, these being inventoried not in their general significance but with a view to this unique usage. . . . In the work of reading the critic will tend to put certain parts of the text provisionally between parentheses, to reformulate others, to complete or to add where he feels there is a significant absence. . . . Instead of replacing one text by another, reading describes the relation of the two." Todorov, *Poetics of Prose*, 237-38.

31. "This is very important," Fitzgerald wrote to Maxwell Perkins in January 1925. "Be sure not to give away *any* of my plot in the blurb. Don't give away that Gatsby *dies* or is a *parvenu* or *crook* or anything. It's a part of the suspense of the book that all these things are in doubt until the end." *Letters*, 176.

32. See Fish, "Literature in the Reader," 125. Austin eventually replaces his distinction between constative and performative speech acts by the observation that every speech act has three aspects: (i) locutionary (constative), (ii) illocutionary (performative), and (iii) perlocutionary (affecting the recipient—i.e. rhetorical); see *How to Do Things with Words*, 94-107. Approaching a literary text from the position of a semiotician, hence viewing it as a system of signs rather than a sequence of speech acts, Eco makes a similar distinction, though changing the order of (ii) and (iii)—the text tells at least three stories: "(i) the story of what happens to its *dramatis personae*; (ii) the story of what happens to its naive reader; (iii) the story of what happens to itself as a text (this third story being potentially the same as the story of what happens to the critical reader)." *Role of the Reader*, 205. Fish's reader-response analysis synthesizes (ii) and (iii).

33. Borges, *Labyrinths*, 75.

34. See, Barthes, *S/Z*, 19.

35. Ibid., 18-19.

36. Indirect support for this observation is the hierarchy of human needs outlined in Maslow, *Motivation and Personality*, 35-51. Maslow regards the need to know and understand, to which the hermeneutic code of a novel primarily appeals, as more fundamental than the need for self-realization and the aesthetic need. *Motivation and Personality* does not throw much light upon "the aesthetic need"—which is not surprising if one believes, with Kant, that in its pure form aesthetic experience is totally disinterested. It is, however, an issue in modern debates on aesthetics whether a pure disinterestedness of response is possible. Perhaps the effect of the work of fiction is based on a constant oscillation between moments of self-forgetful disinterested aesthetic response on the one hand and, on the other, a response based on gratification or nongratification of needs, intellectual, practical, or psychological, as the case might be.

37. Grossvogel accounts for the force of informational gaps (mystification) by viewing them as emblems of the "unknown affecting man, creating a state of being that he cannot accept and towards which he is forever tensed." *Mystery and Its Fictions*, 4.

38. Gardner, *On Moral Fiction*, 128.

39. Roughly, the term "voice" is applied to the person who is supposed to be performing the narrative act, whereas the "focus" is the character who provides the center of vision; see Genette, *Narrative Discourse*, 186-89. To avoid possible confusion I sometimes use the words "focal character" or "focalizer" instead of "focus."

40. On deliberate disruptions of this convention see Toker, "Self-Conscious Paralepsis."

41. See Sternberg, *Expositional Modes*, 99-102.

42. "An *analepsis* is a narration of a story-event at a point in the text after later events have been told." Rimmon-Kenan, *Narrative Fiction*, 46. The opposite phenomenon is *prolepsis*.

43. In "Flawed Crystals," Nussbaum modifies her earlier generalized claim that formal features are not content neutral by demonstrating why the *specific* narrative techniques of an individual novel are an optimal way of exploring the *specific* ethical issues raised by that novel.

44. See Richards, *Principles of Literary Criticism*, esp. 234: "All our activities react upon one another to a prodigious extent in ways which we can only as yet conjecture.

Finer adjustment, clearer and more delicate accommodation or reconciliation of impulses in any one field tends to promote it in others. A step in mathematical accomplishment, other things being equal, facilitates the acquisition of a new turn in ski-ing."

45. In *Into the Whirlwind*, memoirs of prisons and labor camps of the Stalin period, Ginzburg comments on the ennobling effect of solitary confinement (56). Yet in her solitary confinement she passed the time reciting to herself, from her phenomenal memory—and in a grimly ideal absence of "noise"— long stretches of some of the best of Russian poetry.

CHAPTER TWO. *The Sound and the Fury* / The Milk and the Dew

1. On "realistic motivation" see Sternberg, *Expositional Modes*, 246-50.

2. Cf. Cohn's description of the novel's first three sections as autonomous "memory monologues" in which "the present moment of locution is a moment emptied of all contemporary, simultaneous experience: the monologist exists merely as a disembodied medium, a pure memory without clear location in time and space." *Transparent Minds*, 247.

3. On the distinction between narrative "voice" and "focus" see note 39, chapter 1.

4. Cf. Faulkner's remarks about telling Caddy's story *"with"* the three brothers and then by himself. Gwynn and Blotner, *Faulkner in the University*, 1.

5. For a discussion of clues that helps us identify time-layers, see Stewart and Backus, "'Each in Its Ordered Place'"; and Vickery, *Novels of William Faulkner*, 32-34.

6. All page references in this chapter are to Faulkner, *The Sound and the Fury*.

7. See also Bleikasten, *Most Splendid Failure*, 69.

8. For the most satisfying analysis of Luster's motivation see Davis, *Faulkner's "Negro,"* 76-83.

9. Faulkner claims that he wanted to have the text of the novel printed in different inks in order to help the reader identify time-layers but that was too costly; see Gwynn and Blotner, *Faulkner in the University,* 94. However, in Benjy's section he often neglects the cheap printing device that indicates the borderlines between different scenes, i.e., the alternation of italics with the regular type face (see, for example, 40, 46, and 53). Obviously, confusion here is not a case of *malum necessarium.*

10. In Genette's nomenclature such a technique is called "paralipsis." See *Narrative Discourse,* 195.

11. Howe likewise suggests that Benjy's section does not reproduce the flow of a disturbed memory but conveys the impression of an underdeveloped mind; see, *William Faulkner,* 162.

12. Quentin seems to be trying to live in the Bergsonian *durée* rather than in time. Unless he frees himself from the consciousness of the passage of time, the appointed hour of suicide will arrive, and death be the only way of getting out of time; see Lowery, "Concept of Time," 71-72; and Johnson, "Theory of Relativity," 227. Faulkner's relationship with Bergson is discussed, in more detail, in Douglass, *Bergson, Eliot, and American Literature,* 118-65.

13. Cf. Irwin's psychoanalytic interpretation of Quentin's suicide, *Doubling and Incest,* 44 and 116 ff.

14. This theme may be disquieting in its simplicity, yet psychologists would not question its importance. Maslow, for instance, notes that "considering all the evidence now in hand, it is probably true that we could never understand fully the need for love" no matter how much we know about such prepotent needs as the hunger drive; moreover, "from a full knowledge of the need for love we can learn more about general human motivation." *Motivation and Personality,* 21.

15. Caddy is "too beautiful and too moving to reduce her to telling what was going on" and so "it would be more passionate to see her through somebody else's eyes." *Faulkner in the University,* 1. The word "see" (*"see"* her" rather than "present her") may suggest a conscious concern with the attitude of the reader.

16. Cf. Thompson, "Mirror Analogues," 90.

17. Davis interprets Quentin's relationship with Dilsey in racial terms: "the white girl reaches out for Dilsey as a mother substitute and rejects 'the nigger' who could never be her mother." *Faulkner's "Negro,"* 93. Yet it is no less important that Dilsey cannot satisfy Quentin's emotional needs because her psychic energy is all but exhausted. This aspect of Dilsey's portrayal distinguishes her from the "mammy" stereotype of Southern fiction.

18. In *Quest for Failure,* 151, Slatoff discusses the ambivalence of our attitude to Caddy as an instance of Faulkner's typical irresolution.

19. This is the phenomenon of "foregrounding": the "foregrounded" manner of presentation competes with the mimetic contents for the attention of the reader; see Ejkhenbaum, "How Gogol's 'The Overcoat' Is Made," 122-58; and "The 'Skaz' Illusion," 160-66.

20. Wagner's "Jason Compson," 556-60, contains an excellent study of the scenes of Jason's childhood yet overstates its defense of the adult Jason. Another interesting reassessment of Jason's character is made in Kartiganer, *Fragile Thread*, 14-16.

21. For some of the interpretations on which the scope of the paper does not allow me to dwell see Adams, *Faulkner: Myth and Motion*, 215-48; Sartre, "On *The Sound and the Fury*; and Collins, "Christian and Freudian Structures."

22. By ignoring the symbolism of the episode we reenact the attitude of the children, who, as Faulkner noted, see the "lugubrious matter of removing the corpse from the house," their first encounter with death, "only incidentally to the childish games they [are] playing." Jeliffe, *Faulkner at Nagano*, 103.

23. See Cohn's discussion of analogous cases in Quentin's section, *Transparent Minds*, 251-53.

24. Cf. the discussion of "the primacy effect" in Sternberg, *Expositional Modes*, 99 ff; and Perry, "Literary Dynamics," 53.

CHAPTER THREE. *Nostromo:* "Shaded Expression"

1. Schwarz, *Conrad*, 136.

2. "The repertoire consists of all the familiar territory within the texts" such as "references to earlier works, or to social and historical norms, or to the whole culture from which the text has emerged—in brief, to what the Prague structuralists have called the 'extratextual reality.'" Iser, *Act of Reading*, 69.

3. Cf. Guerard, *Conrad the Novelist*, 175.

4. All page references in the text of this chapter are to Conrad, *Nostromo*.

5. For a detailed discussion of the way abstract ideals are allowed to subsume the private selves of the characters of *Nostromo*, see Schwarz, *Conrad*, 133-56.

6. Borges, *Labyrinths*, 6.

7. The term is Genette's; see his *Narrative Discourse*, 116.

8. See Ford, *Joseph Conrad*, 225.

9. Nostromo's reasons for deciding to steal the silver are discussed in detail in Gillon, *Eternal Solitary*, 132-33.

10. Guerard, *Conrad the Novelist*, 180.

11. Conrad uses the Dickensian technique of making most of the characters of a novel share, in different degrees, a quality of which one of the characters is the most pronounced exponent. Adopting Kierkegaard's distinction, see Kierkegaard, *Either/Or*, 1:50-51—such a relationship between the characters could be called "representative" and opposed to, among others, the relationship of "embodiment" ("Incarnation"), where a certain quality is wholly concentrated in a single character.

12. See Saveson, *Joseph Conrad*, 24-31.

13. According to Shalamov's experience of Stalin's labor camps, a person cannot commit suicide after his exhaustion and demoralization have gone beyond a certain point: it is extra rations or an unexpected gesture of kindness that enable the prisoners to rally and, if that is their wish, commit a suicidal

action; see, for instance, "Quiet" in *Kolyma Tales*, 81-89. The conduct of Conrad's characters lends implicit support to Shalamov's observation. Significantly, Decoud kills himself while his food supply still keeps him from starving.

14. This "reluctance of the imagination" is a prophetic touch in a novel written at the beginning of the century in which millions of people would claim ignorance of the atrocities routinely committed in their society.

15. On the role of the title character and the reader's expectations related to him, see Cooper, *Conrad and the Human Dilemma*, 110.

16. According to Karl, the "split" is the result of Conrad's "lack of staying power," see "Significance of Revisions," 129-44. This would make it another case of a potential weakness turned to rhetorical advantage.

17. The parallel between our frustration on Captain Mitchell's eruption into the narrative and the experience of the characters of the novel was first observed by Daleski, who notes that "the form of the novel may be said to point to its fundamental thematic concerns—to the thwarting of the conventional expectations that are aroused by the reactivation of the San Tomé mine; and the thwarting, as far as almost all the main characters are concerned, of the expectations that are bred by their assumption of conventional roles." *Joseph Conrad*, 117-18.

18. Hewitt has shown that in *Nostromo* "almost every paragraph causes us to modify our judgements and reconsider our assumptions," *Conrad: A Reassessment*, 51-54. One should add that this effect is never registered as consciously as in the case of the "split."

19. See Conrad, *Victory: An Island Tale* in *The Works of Joseph Conrad*, 15:4.

20. See, in particular, Moser, *Joseph Conrad: Achievement and Decline*, 87 ff.

21. Berthoud, however, regards Mrs. Gould's conduct at Nostromo's deathbed as her "single lapse," *Joseph Conrad: The Major Phase*, 126.

22. Conrad, *A Personal Record: Some Reminiscences* in *The Works of Joseph Conrad*, 11:xxviii.

23. Conrad seems to have shared, though not without reservations, the Nietzschean belief in the value of monumentalist history: "fame is something more than the tastiest morsel of our egoism . . . : it is the belief in the solidarity and continuity of the greatness of all ages and the protest against the passing away of generations and the transitoriness of things." Nietzsche, "On the Uses and Disadvantages of History for Life" in *Untimely Meditations*, 69.

24. Borges, *Labyrinths*, 137.

25. The abandoned mine is forced on Charles Gould's father six years after the death of Guzman Bento (51). Charles is fourteen at the time (55); he is over twenty when his father dies (57) and about thirty at the time of the Sulaco revolution. However, the Avellanos had left Europe eight years before the revolution (147), and it was after their return to Costaguana that Don José was arrested by Guzman Bento—who, according to the above data, should have been dead long before.

26. In *Joseph Conrad*, Daleski shows that self-possession, which is among Conrad's major concerns, is made possible by a capacity for temporary abandon. The need for letting go in order to hold on also extends to other moral values and even political beliefs in Conrad's works.

CHAPTER FOUR. *Bleak House:* "Not Quite so Straight, but Nearly"

1. Van Boheemen's study of the theme of obscure parenthood and search for identity in *Bleak House* in *Novel as Family Romance,* 101-31, uses the psychoanalytic framework in an attempt to trace the cultural "blueprints" in the construction of the "fictions of identity." Van Boheemen's book suggests that the literary convention of obscure births is deeply rooted in cultural problematics, yet it overstates its case when noting that "orphanhood, as loss of parents, loss of origins and identity . . . summarizes the thematic and structural concerns of *Bleak House*" (102).

2. For discussions of the thematic significance of, respectively, the concealed relationships and of the detective plot of *Bleak House,* see Donovan, "Structure and Idea in *Bleak House,*" 186-201; and Garrett, *Victorian Multiplot Novel,* 52-59. In a totally different conceptual framework, D.A. Miller, *The Novel and the Police,* 66-81, shows the links between the Chancery and the Detective Police and hence the inevitable birth of the detective interest in *Bleak House.*

3. See note 34, chapter 1.

4. This is an intellectual variety of "catharsis": a heightening and eventual discharge of an attitude rather than of an affect. In a chapter devoted to this novel, Thurley points to the elements of the tragic vision more profound than mere criticism of legal abuses and social injustice; see *The Dickens Myth,* 172-202.

5. Problems of Dickens's serial publication are discussed in Coolidge, *Dickens as a Serial Novelist.* It must be emphasized that Dickens's narrative choices are never solely determined by the need to coerce the interest of the audience.

6. The concept of the omniscient narrative is frequently associated with the idea of divine omniscience—see the discussion of this analogy in Scholes and Kellogg, *Nature of Narrative,* 272. Yet few narrators perceived as omniscient exercise an unlimited cognitive privilege—penetrate walls, see what is happening in different places at the same time, read the innermost thoughts of taciturn people, delve into their subconscious, etc. Most often the privilege is restricted by some specific cognitive principle associated with the aesthetics, metaphysics, or moral philosophy of the individual work.

7. Grenadier, "The Mystery and the Moral," 304.

8. All page references in the text of this chapter are to Dickens, *Bleak House.*

9. The realization of metaphors is discussed in Toker, "Between Allusion and Coincidence," 180-81.

10. I use the word "suspense" to refer to the intensity of the audience's interest in one line of development. Sternberg's distinction between "suspense" and "curiosity" as interest in the narrative future and the narrative past is justified in descriptivist terms rather than in terms of audience response: Faulkner's *Absalom, Absalom!,* for instance, is a clear example of suspense, with its accompanying hopes and fears, produced not by interest in the narrative future but by the enigma in the fictional past. See *Expositional Modes,* 65. In *Poetics of Biblical Narrative,* Sternberg restates his distinction between curiosity

and suspense but adds that suspense arises "when conflicting clues project two future scenarios, and dies with the enactment of either in the plot" (261). Yet the two possible scenarios often hinge on closing a gap that concerns an event in the fictional past.

11. Episodic intensification is exploration of the potentialities of separate episodes without much regard for the relevance of the resulting local felicities to the work's overall design. Harvey, "Chance and Design in *Bleak House*," defends *Bleak House* from such a view yet notes that this novel produces the impression of "immense and potentially anarchic energy being brought—but only just—under control," 146.

12. The theme of parasitism, the major thematic element of *Bleak House*, is discussed in detail and traced through the analogies between the different episodes in Daleski, *Dickens and the Art of Analogy*, 159-65.

13. On "opting out" see Leavis and Leavis, *Dickens the Novelist*, 136.

14. J.H. Miller, *Charles Dickens*, 169.

15. In "*Bleak House*: The Agitating Women," Moers notes that "the masculine world in *Bleak House* has fatally slowed down, while the feminine world is alarmingly speeding up," 21. It seems, however, that the slowing down and the speeding up are effects of, respectively, obsessive hope and obsessive fear and that their relationship with gender is contingent.

16. In *Bleak House* the motif of "infection" combines the references to both disease and cure: on the one hand, the epidemic of what looks like smallpox breaks through the borderlines between the classes; on the other hand, the redeeming human sympathy is likewise often transmitted by way of contagion. On "contagion" as one kind of sympathy both described by and produced by Dickens's texts, see Sucksmith, *Narrative Art of Charles Dickens*, 119-24.

17. See Borges's explanation of the power of the recurrence of motifs in a work of fiction in terms of sympathetic magic; "Narrative Art and Magic," 209-15.

18. Part of the outrage aroused by Agatha Christie's *The Murder of Roger Acroyd* must have been caused by the fact that the "confidant" turns out to be the murderer: we sympathize with him throughout the novel, working under the delusion that our experience is parallel to and isochronic with his own; when this delusion is exposed we have a sense of having been double-crossed rather than legitimately outwitted. Prior to Agatha Christie Chekhov experimented with a similar device in "A Hunting Episode."

19. I agree with Gold, *Charles Dickens: Radical Moralism*, that tracing social evils to their roots in interpersonal relationships is a form of moral radicalism.

20. Nemo's advertisement in Krook's shop is written "in law-hand," like the letters Esther would receive from Kenge and Carboy's at Reading (49). It is not made clear whether Esther recognizes the handwriting itself or only its legal character.

21. Tulkinghorn's character and motivation are discussed in detail by Quirk, "Tulkinghorn's Buried Life."

22. The class struggle implications of this episode were first noted by Dyson, *The Inimitable Dickens*, 168. An interesting further discussion of the complexity of character portrayal in *Bleak House* can be found in Scott, *Reality*

and Comic Confidence, 61-121. In *Novel and the Police,* D.A. Miller notes Bucket's "amoral professionalization" (94) but does not recognize Bucket's strategy of sadistic procrastination: instead, he contrasts the Chancery's policy of delays with the expeditiousness of the Detective Police, whose coups strategy is represented by Bucket (74). This is one of the many minor yet symptomatic misreadings in Miller's essay on *Bleak House* (58-106). The essay discusses the power struggle between the various disciplinary institutions in the novel (including the novel itself); in a way Miller himself enters this struggle, and draws his readers into it. Despite the brilliant provocativeness of his general argument and separate points, the scope of the present work does not allow me to enter into polemic beyond noting that Miller's study has not escaped the dangers that lie in wait for New Historicism when its strategies are applied to great works of art instead of second-rate texts in which unconscious cultural presuppositions are not dwarfed by the authentic vision of the individual artist.

23. For this observation I am indebted to Smith, *Charles Dickens: Bleak House,* 31.

24. Cf. Zwerdling: "In the interstices of Dickens's magical solutions, he cannot help planting . . . grains of truth." "Esther Summerson Rehabilitated," 438.

25. Cf. also Smith, *Charles Dickens,* 31.

26. The term *mise en abîme* for a narrative enclave that reproduces the features of the whole work that contains it was first suggested by Gide, *Journal 1889-1939,* 41. Cases of *mise en abîme* are usually related to narratives within narratives but I apply this term also to descriptions of *fabula* details that can serve as metaphors for the narrative structure of the work as a whole. Different approaches to the problem are reflected in Ricardou, "L'histoire dans l'histoire," 171-90; Dällenbach, *Le récit spéculaire;* and Bal, *"Mise en abyme et iconicité."* The issues involved are subjected to an extensive critical scrutiny in Ron, "The Restricted Abyss."

27. See, for instance Broderick and Grant, "The Identity of Esther Summerson"; Axton, "The Trouble with Esther"; Leavis and Leavis, *Dickens, the Novelist,* 156; Zwerdling, "Esther Summerson Rehabilitated"; Daleski, "Dickens and the Proleptic Uncanny," 202-4; and Wilt, "Confusion and Consciousness in Dickens's Esther."

28. Items of this catalogue of spaces form one of the numerous rhythmic recurrences that testify to a high degree of organization in *Bleak House.* Another important set of recurrent motifs is related to the notion of rhythm itself as expressed in dance (keeping harmonious time), birthdays, and other references to timing; see Creevy, "In Time and Out." See also the discussion of the motifs that converge in Dickens's image of the inferno transpiring through the world of *Bleak House* in Hollington, *Dickens and the Grotesque,* 199-205.

29. See Bachelard, *The Poetics of Space,* 67-68. This is not to deny, however, that there are some sinister undertones in the novel's treatment of the motif of house; see, for instance, Connor's essay in a deconstructive reading of this novel, *Charles Dickens,* 59-88.

CHAPTER FIVE. *Emma:* "Double Dealing"—or Triple?

1. The references in the text of this chapter are to Austen, *Emma.*
2. See Duckworth, *Improvement of the Estate,* 149.
3. See also Harvey, "The Plot of *Emma,"* 51.
4. While Austen presents her heroines' education toward maturity, she also shows that the more energetic of her young ladies, Catherine Moorland, Marianne Dashwood, Elizabeth Bennet, and Emma Woodhouse, move toward situations in which they receive crushing blows that undermine their vitality and thus make them more suitable for the narrow roles that the proper ladies of their class are expected to perform. The more "sensible" of Austen's heroines—Elinor Dashwood, Fanny Price, and Anne Eliot—receive such blows very early in the novels, sometimes before the start of the action. Schopenhauer, the subtle analyst of the Will and the ways of its repression, could in this case say that the English novelist has been there before him. Yet there is usually no causal connection between the newly developed saintly virtuousness of an Austen heroine and its reward: the happy endings are brought along by coincidences that call for theoretical explanation—so much so that Leland Monk, for instance, suggests that Austen has planted hints that Frank Churchill has brought about his aunt's all too opportune death by a dose of poison; see "Murder She Wrote." Yet the deus ex machina peripeteia is rather one of Austen's antidotes to the illusions created by the novel's conventional form (see Booth, *The Company We Keep,* 432-35). The happy ending obviously depends on contingencies that tend to work out less well in the reality to which the novel refers.
5. In *Narrative and Its Discontents,* 3-106, D.A. Miller argues that the discontents, the mistakes, the waywardness, the flirtatiousness, the indecisiveness of Austen's heroines constitute the "narratable" material, whereas the exercise of common sense as well as happy conjugal choices are major threats to narratability. I disagree with some of Miller's points, but his discussion awakens layers of significance in episodes that had formerly received little or no critical attention.
6. See Duffy, *"Emma:* The Awakening from Innocence," 51.
7. Cf. also Berger, "The Rake and the Reader," 539.
8. In "Frankophobia in *Emma,"* 607-17, Hellstrom notes that the word "finesse" emphasizes Frank Churchill's frenchified character, also suggested by his first name, which comes into contrast with that of the steady Saxon George Knightley. Yet both the name Frank and the word "finesse" are polysemous and rich in connotations. Knoepflmacher suggests that the name is associated with a contemporary postage practice, the franking of letters. See "The Importance of Being Frank," 655.
9. See *Hoyle's Games: Containing the Rules for Playing Fashionable Games,* 6.
10. These are the meanings given by *Webster's Third New International Dictionary.*
11. See Tave, *Some Words of Jane Austen,* 29-30.
12. Burrows, *Jane Austen's Emma,* 64.
13. For a more extensive analysis of Emma's moral blindness, see ibid., 77.

14. See Barthes' discussion of catalysts *(catalyses)* and kernels (or cardinal functions) in "Introduction à l'analyse structural des récits," 9.

15. Cf. C.L. Johnson: "Austen attributes most of the moral unsteadiness in [*Mansfield Park*] not to any radical evil, but rather to radical mental laxity and inattentiveness." "The 'Operations of Time, and the Changes of the Human Mind,' " 33.

16. Rosmarin notes that "we are maneuvered into subscribing to Emma's insult on Box Hill"; see " 'Misreading' *Emma,* " 331. Rosemarin's article is likewise devoted to the "affective model" of interpretation: the reader is forced to reenact Emma's own complacency and subsequent mistakes. She rivets her model on our misdirected temporary sympathy with Emma's tactlessness rather than on the wrong surmise in the Churchill-Fairfax case—which is an important addition to the model proposed here. Many similar observations were made, independently and almost simultaneously, in Rosemarin's article and in the early version of this chapter.

17. "None of the comic characters communicates. They surround themselves with a web of words, but words which convey their own selfhood, their individuality, and make little or no impact upon the consciousness of others. The defect is an important detail to notice in a novel which focuses critically upon selfishness. It is a moral virtue to be ready to receive external evidence, which Emma does not always do. It is no less a virtue to be able to convey our thoughts to others, intelligibly and unequivocally. We live in a community, and our verbal style is the measure of our recognition of this." Butler, *Jane Austen and the War of Ideas,* 271.

18. Scott, *Waverley* (London, 1895), 405.

19. Booth, *Rhetoric of Fiction,* 154-55.

20. For this observation I am largely indebted to Burrows' *Jane Austen's Emma,* 64.

21. Chapman considers Austen's remark on Frank's good breeding an inadvertent slip and acquits her of "deliberately throwing dust into our eyes," *Jane Austen: Facts and Problems,* 206. Liddel, however, notes that "it is Emma who sees [Frank] as 'too well bred to hear the hint'; strictly speaking we should perhaps be told that it is her mental observation, but as we are hearing through her ears we can hardly feel cheated," *Novels of Jane Austen,* 100.

22. In *Middlemarch,* for instance, Eliot monitors inside views in order to withhold information about Mr. Bulstrode's guilty past. Unlike other characters, Mr. Bulstrode is presented strictly externally up to the point where his secret is revealed in a recognition scene.

23. In his argument against Booth's assertion that mystification is detrimental to the effect of *Emma*—see *Rhetoric of Fiction,* 255—Harvey observes that dramatic irony, which the absence of mystification would have considerably intensified, might have been much too heavy; see "The Plot of *Emma,*" 53-54. My purpose is to show why this does not happen on a repeated reading when the mystification is a matter of the past.

24. For a discussion of Austen's complex attitude to provincial society see Harding's "Regulated Hatred."

25. Austen's subtly subversive presentation of the "metatheatre of manners" is discussed in Tanner, *Jane Austen*, esp. 24-35.

26. On Austen's "cover stories" see Gilbert and Gubar, *Madwoman in the Attic*, 146-83.

27. See also Rosemarin, " 'Misreading' *Emma,*" 328-30, for a discussion of scenes and sentences that lend themselves "first to one interpretation, then to its revision, and then, frequently, to a revision of that revision" (328).

28. Letter to J. Edward Austen, 16 December 1816, in *Jane Austen's Letters*, 469. As Poovey suggests in her discussion of warnings voiced by Hanna Moore, the insecurity and the fear of failure must have been a greater deterrent to women who were dissatisfied with traditional roles than fear of seeming improper; see *The Proper Lady and the Woman Writer*, 34.

29. See Hellstrom, "Frankophobia in *Emma.*"

30. See Neil, "Between Deference and Deconstruction," 49. This is one of the numerous thought provoking remarks scattered through Neil's discussion of different approaches to the novel. Incidentally, Neil accounts for the name of Mr. Knightley's estate ("done-well" Abbey, 47) as an indication of the near-divinely correct Understanding attributed to this character on at least one level of the novel's structure of values.

31. "It was not a matter of decorum for its own sake: good manners and morals were seen as essential to the presentation of order in society. They alone could or should do what excessive laws, an often recalcitrant militia, and the absence of any properly organised police force were (it was felt) unable to do. It was as if the security and stability of the nation depended on good manners. To put it as bluntly as possible, good manners were no longer regarded merely as a seemly adjunct to the life-style of the upper classes: they became England's answer to the French Revolution." Tanner, *Jane Austen*, 27.

CHAPTER SIX. *Tom Jones:* "By Way of Chorus"

1. For a survey of attitudes to rhetoric in Ancient Greece, see, for instance, Murphy, "Origins and Early Development of Rhetoric."

2. Fish, "Aesthetics of the Good Physician," in *Self-Consuming Artifacts*, 1.

3. For an interesting discussion of Fielding's discomfort with the intellectual and literary context in which he found himself, see Hunter, "The Many Masquerades of Henry Fielding," 2-21, and "Some Models for Tom Jones," 118-40, in *Occasional Form*.

4. The nature and mechanics of these challenges are analyzed by Iser, "Reader's Role in *Joseph Andrews* and *Tom Jones*" in *Implied Reader*, 29-56. Empson was, it seems, the first to argue that *Tom Jones* builds up a coherent moral philosophy; see "Tom Jones." The most illuminating discussion of this ethical system and its relationship to the eighteenth-century debate is Harrison's *Henry Fielding's Tom Jones*.

5. Preston writes that the plot of this novel "exists in the reader's attention rather than in the written sequences. This means that its effect is epis-

temological rather than moral." *Created Self*, 114. Fielding's epistemology, however, is morally oriented.

6. A study of the way mystification necessitates the attribution of conflicting features to Miss Bridget and of Fielding's use of these conflicting features for a psychologically realistic creation of her complex character is to be found in Baker, "Bridget Allworthy."

7. Gardner, *On Moral Fiction*, 114-15.

8. Fielding's prefatory chapters and intrusive commentary have triggered critical controversy. Goldknopf, "The Failure of Plot in *Tom Jones*," for instance, suggests that the introductory chapters of *Tom Jones* are a compensation for the failure of the plot to form an adequate sense-supporting structure; whereas Iser, on the contrary, believes that the author-reader dialogue is one of the controls that prevents the subjectivity of the reader "from playing too dominant a part," bearing in mind that "it is the reader who produces the configurative meaning of the novel." *Implied Reader*, 46.

9. The parenthetic references in the text are of this chapter are to Fielding, *The History of Tom Jones, a Foundling*.

10. Bliss, who shows that the moral value of perceptiveness is thematized in *Tom Jones*, argues that the fact that we are still "with him" by the end of the novel is evidence "that there is goodness in his readers, hence in the world, and hence he is naturally justified in having the world of *Tom Jones* . . . exhibit its goodness by extricating Jones." "Fielding's Bill of Fare in *Tom Jones*," 242. This view, however, too readily identifies moral goodness with literary taste.

11. Leaving the reader work to do and trusting him to cope with it is one of the most frequently stated of Fielding's artistic principles in *Tom Jones* and elsewhere. See, for instance, his essay in No. 53 of *The Champion* (March 15, 1740), in Williams, *The Criticism of Henry Fielding*, 121-24.

12. This is essentially the technique of activizing perception as described by Gombrich in *Art and Illusion*, 174.

13. See Alter, *Fielding and the Nature of the Novel*, 194.

14. Iser likewise notes that the lesson in "prudence" that the reader receives from *Tom Jones* serves as a training for the reader's sense of discernment; see *Implied Reader*, 54.

15. Cf. the discussion of the *histor* in Scholes and Kellogg, *The Nature of Narrative*, 265-72.

16. "Metalepsis" is the intrusion of the extra-diegetic narrator (or narratee) into the diegetic universe; see Genette, *Narrative Discourse*, 234-36.

17. Cf. Sternberg's discussion of Fielding's omniscient narrative and informational distribution, *Expositional Modes*, 262-68; and Wright's comments on Fielding's comparison of life and the stage in *Henry Fielding: Mask and Feast*, 32.

18. For detailed discussions of the plot and the architectonics of *Tom Jones*, see Crane, "The Concept of Plot," 616-47; and Alter, *Fielding and the Nature of the Novel*, 99-139.

19. In his contributions to periodicals Fielding frequently attacked this and other corruptions of language. See Hartfield, *Henry Fielding and the Language of Irony*, 199.

20. On varieties of heteroglossia in the novel see Bakhtin, *Dialogic Imagina-*

tion, 301-31. Bakhtin discusses free indirect speech as one of the heteroglot techniques. On free indirect speech see also McHale, "Free Indirect Discourse." The reasons for the analytic attention that this device has recently enjoyed are discussed in Rimmon-Kenan, *Narrative Fiction*, 110-16.

21. The technique may be compared to the thickening of colors and intensification of motifs in the inset narratives in Hawthorne's *The House of the Seven Gables*, which bears distinct traces of Fielding's influence.

22. Cf. also Alter, *Fielding and the Nature of the Novel*, 40-43.

23. Paulson suggests that in *Tom Jones* the complexity of human motivation is both thematized and used as a structural principle, which distinguishes this novel from *Joseph Andrews*; see introduction to *Fielding: A Collection of Critical Essays*, 7-9.

24. In this respect it is interesting to compare Murry's discussion of Tom Jones's conduct in "In Defence of Fielding," Empson's derivation of Fielding's views from the action of *Tom Jones*, and Rawson's objection that these views are not hidden but actually stated; see Rawson, "Professor Empson's *Tom Jones*."

25. As Harrison has shown, Fielding differs from Shaftesbury and Butler in his belief in the necessity of a *prior moral commitment* to the good of others: "To be good hearted is to have made a commitment of will; a commitment to take other people's good as an ultimate goal of action. But to be goodhearted is equally to feel certain desires and to enjoy certain pleasures; it is because friends desire each other's good, for example, that they enjoy the pleasures of friendship. On this view, desire and enjoyment of certain sorts, far from being inconsistent with virtue, are part of the essence of virtue." *Henry Fielding's Tom Jones*, 113.

26. See Gadamer's discussion of the notion of taste in *Truth and Method*, 33-39.

27. Battestin, "Fielding's Definition of Wisdom," 191.

28. Cf. Booth: "For the reader with his mind on the main business . . . the narrator becomes a rich and provocative chorus." *Rhetoric of Fiction*, 217.

29. The placing of the novelist on the stage of the world that he has himself conjured up (since all the world was a stage before it became a filming site) is a "Strange Loop" phenomenon that "occurs whenever, by moving upwards (or downwards) through the levels of some hierarchical system, we unexpectedly find ourselves right back where we started." Hofstadter, *Gödel, Escher, Bach*, 10. Narrative levels in a work of fiction are an example of such a hierarchical system. Interesting in this connection is the strange loop that involves the "Hamlet" episode of *Tom Jones*. As M. Johnson has shown, while laughing at Partridge's naive responses to the performance of Shakespeare's play, Tom is blissfully unaware that his own predicament is a tragicomic version of Hamlet's story; see *Fielding's Art of Fiction*, 99-106.

30. See Nietzsche, "The Birth of Tragedy," 77, 80.

31. Observing that the chorus in Greek tragedy is "the symbol of the whole excited Dionysian throng," Nietzsche interprets the relationship between the stage *(scene)* where the action of the tragedy took place and the *orchestra* where the chorus was located in the following terms: "the scene, complete with the action, was basically and originally thought of merely as a

vision; the chorus is the only 'reality' and generates the vision, speaking of it with the entire symbolism of dance, tone, and words." Ibid., 65. Fielding's reliance on more technical stage conventions is discussed in Irwin, *Henry Fielding: The Tentative Realist* 103-9.

32. On the "shadow world" of *Vanity Fair* and its relationship with the "real" and the fictional worlds see Daleski, "Strategies in *Vanity Fair,*" in *Unities,* 3-17.

33. For this point I am indebted to Alter, *Partial Magic,* 97.

34. Nabokov, *Ada,* 528. I have analyzed some of these fiction-canceling techniques in "Nabokov and the Hawthorne Tradition," 323-49. Interesting examples of the canceled-character strategy are given in McHale, *Postmodernist Fiction,* 104-5.

CHAPTER SEVEN. *A Passage to India:* At an Angle to the Universe

1. On permanent gaps cf. also Rimmon, *Concept of Ambiguity,* 48-49 and Sternberg, *Expositional Modes,* 51.

2. Cf. also Rimmon, *Concept of Ambiguity,* 227-35 and my discussion of ambiguities in *Nabokov: The Mystery of Literary Structures,* 135-41.

3. All references in the text of this chapter are to Forster, *A Passage to India,* 39.

4. On manuscript versions of the scene, see June Perry Levine, *A Passage to India: Creation and Criticism,* 90-91; and Moffat, "*A Passage to India* and the Limits of Certainty."

5. Colmer discusses the dominant pattern of expectation and promise followed by disappointment and withdrawal as an expression of Forster's critique of Western liberal rationalism; see "Promise and Withdrawal in *A Passage to India.*"

6. See Sartre, *Literary and Philosophical Essays,* 84.

7. Throughout the novel and conversation of the Indians is dominated by what J.L. Austen calls the "perlocutionary" aspects of utterances and that of the English by the locutionary (see note 32, chapter 1). The tendency of each side to read the utterances of the other in the spirit in which its own are made is the cause of many misunderstandings.

8. Among the most interesting discussions of Forster's handling of language and his inquiry into the status and limitations of language in *A Passage to India* are Tinsley, "Muddle Et Cetera"; Orange, "Language and Silence in *A Passage to India*"; Herz, "Listening to Language"; Kazan, "Confabulations in *A Passage to India*"; and Dowling, "*A Passage to India* through 'The Spaces Between the Words.'"

9. Catachresis, or a catachretic gap, is a phenomenon that in a given language (and sometimes in all languages) can be expressed only by a metaphor or some other trope. The simplest case of catachresis in English is "to fall in love"—a notion that is expressed by one word in most other languages. As Furbank has noted, Forster's reference to the ineffable aspects of human experience is characterized by a half-humorous half-earnest following through

(extension) of the metaphors and sometimes by their realization, that is, by turning them into physical facts of the setting or the plot; see "Forster and the 'Bloomsbury' Prose," 165-66.

10. In "Structure, Symbol, and Theme," 947, Allen observes that "Adela's mind was 'blurred by the heat.' " The exact wording of the passage in the novel is as follows: "Simla next week, get rid of Antony, a view of Thibet, tiresome wedding bells, Agra in October, see Mrs. Moore comfortably off from Bombay—the procession passed before her again, blurred by the heat, and then she turned to the more serious business of her life at Chandrapore" (151). By saying that "the procession" rather than "Adela's mind" is "blurred by the heat," the narrator reduces our consciousness of the fact that Adela is affected by the heat. Besides, her mind does not seem to be blurred when she turns to the "more serious business" of planning her married life.

11. See, for instance, Kettle, *An Introduction to the English Novel*, 2:161.

12. We have seen analogous cautionary touches in *Emma* and *Tom Jones*, where the narrator's technique partly reenacts the conduct of a particular character. In *A Passage to India* the narrator sometimes also seems to imitate a certain character, namely the cautious Godbole.

13. See, for instance, Leavis, "E.M. Forster," 185; or Trilling, *E.M. Forster*, 126.

14. On some of these tendencies and their departure from the Romantic poetics see J. Beer, "*A Passage to India*, the French New Novel and English Romanticism." The difference between Forster's novels and the traditional English novels of manners and morals is discussed in Schwartz, "The Originality of E.M. Forster."

15. Daleski discusses the patterns of motifs in "Rhythmic and Symbolic Patterns," 266. See also Burke on several interesting cases of verbal echoes in *Language as Symbolic Action*, 232-37.

16. See Forster, *Aspects of the Novel*, 130-31.

17. Cf. Stone: "these enterings of images into the minds of different characters at different times, and without any obvious causal connections" are "the device whereby the collective unconscious manifests itself." "The Caves of *A Passage to India*," 22-23.

18. Cf. Allen, "Structure, Symbol, and Theme," 134. The supernatural in *A Passage to India*, should not, however, be understood as concretely as Hardy describes it in *Appropriate Form*, 79-80. According to Hardy, after Mrs. Moore's death, her spirit influences Adela's behavior at the trial.

19. The Marabar Hills "appear as a threatening denial of human aspiration: rising 'abruptly, insanely, without proportion,' they negate all ideals of harmonious relationships; and thrusting 'fists' above the soil, they image an enmity that is antithetical to the human hope expressed in the outstretched hand of friendship." Daleski, "Rhythmic and Symbolic Patterns," 266. This symbolic meaning of the hills determines their role in the development of the novel's theme of personal relationships. Other strands of meaning that readers distinguish in the novel grant the hills a spectrum of symbolic suggestions. For White they symbolize the "unity of negation." "*A Passage to India*: Analysis and Revaluation," 646, 648. Dauner in "What Happened in a Cave?" 266-67, regards them

as a symbol of the archetypal Great Mother. Hollingsworth interprets them as an allegory on Western culture in opposition to the Indian spirit. "*A Passage to India:* The Echoes in the Marabar Caves," 216-19. G. Beer notes, among other things, that it is the women who suffer in the Marabar caves and comments that, according to Lacan, women's psychosexual experience "forms the blind spot within Freud's symbolic system" and that Forster "images a blind spot in the caves." "Negation in *A Passage to India,*" 53. The list could be continued.

20. The case is put particularly strongly by Parry, who regards *A Passage to India* as Forster's "epitaph" to liberal humanism: "In search of other systems he had contemplated traditions to which ironically he had access because of the global space created and divided by imperialism, and if he withdrew from the sheer magnitude of the ambition to liberation nurtured within Indian philosophical modes, he had acquired a perspective on a transfigured tomorrow that made the social hope of his earlier fictions seem parochial. But as fascism, persecution, war and the repression of the colonial struggle brought force and violence near and made the 'not yet' seem even more distant, Forster retired to essays, criticism, biography and broadcasts, media in which it was still possible to reiterate an adherence to liberal values, an option unavailable in self-interrogating fictional texts." "The Politics of Representation," 42.

21. Crews has demonstrated how various world views are tested and found insufficient in *A Passage to India;* see *E.M. Forster: The Perils of Humanism,* 142-63.

22. At least one critic, Shusterman, interprets Godbole as the chief source of evil influence in the world of the novel; see "The Curious Case of Professor Godbole," 431. A diametrically opposite view—that the poet in Forster identified wholly with Professor Godbole—is argued by Drew, "The Spirit Behind the Frieze?" 81-103. Drew also presents very interesting explanations of the novel's various narrative details in terms of neo-Platonist philosophy in which Forster was interested and that bears significant affinities with Hinduism.

23. See, for instance, Shahane, "Forster's Inner Passage to India," 269-70, and Drew, "The Spirit Behind the Frieze?" 85-87.

24. Forster, *Aspects of the Novel,* 165.

25. Colmer maintains that "in exploring the ultimate mystery of life Forster assigns a subordinate role to all merely human relations." *E.M. Forster: A Passage to India,* 11. However, the opposite view, stating that the metaphysical issues are subordinated to the subtle analysis of human intercourse, may find support in the way Forster uses the extract from Walt Whitman's poem. "A Passage to India" serves not as an epigraph to the novel, but as its title, and as such it is primarily understood as referring to an actual journey, whereas the allusion to Whitman's attempts to reach out to the unknown is perceived as connotative.

26. White, "*A Passage to India:* Analysis and Revaluation," 642.

27. Forster, *Pharos and Pharillon,* 110.

CHAPTER EIGHT. *Absalom, Absalom!:* "Happen Is Never Once"

1. McHale discusses *Absalom, Absalom!* as one of the works in which there occurs a transition from the epistemological dominant of modernist

literature to the ontological dominant of post-modernism, *Postmodernist Fiction*, 6-11.

2. On writing and absence in *Absalom, Absalom!* see Krause, "Reading Shreve's Letters."

3. Some of the earlier studies, for instance, Longley, *Tragic Mask*, 214, accept Shreve's surmise rather uncritically.

4. All references in the text of the chapter are to Faulkner, *Absalom, Absalom!*.

5. This suggestion is made by Brooks in *William Faulkner: The Yoknapatawpa Country*, 316; yet Brooks also notes that Faulkner has wisely abstained from providing an unambiguous answer to this question.

6. The dialogue between Quentin and Henry reaches the words "to die" and is then played backwards step by step. This device can be compared to a palindrome or else to what musicologists call a "crab canon." Cf. Hofstadter, *Gödel, Escher, Bach*, 9, 198-204.

7. The most widespread view is that Bon is indeed Sutpen's part-Negro son and that Quentin "realizes" this on his visit to Sutpen's Hundred; see Goldman, *Twentieth Century Interpretations*, 11; and Guetti, *"Absalom, Absalom!: The Extended Simile,"* 103; and Swiggart, *Art of Faulkner's Novels*, 164. Both propositions of this hypothesis are strongly suggested by the text but never unambiguously sanctioned.

8. "Pseudo-diegetic" discourse is perceived as secondary-level narration (e.g., a story-within-a-story), yet turns out to be primary-level (diegetic) narration, economizing, as it were on one narrative level; see Genette, *Narrative Discourse*, 236-37; on "voice" and "focus" see note 39, chap. 1.

9. See also Lind, "The Design and Meaning of *Absalom, Absalom!*," 898. Hodgson suggests that the italicized soliloquy of Miss Rosa is presented not as directly heard but as remembered by Quentin; see "'Logical Sequence and Continuity,'" 107. It is problematic whether Quentin could be responsible for the intensely feminine sexual undersong that here seems to bring to the surface the subliminal consciousness of Miss Rosa; moreover, the alternation of Roman type and italics is used not only for distinction between speech and thought, as Hodgson suggests, but also for emphasis. In any case, our attempts to find the regularities in the narrative texture of the novel are attempts to determine the rules by which we must play the novel's reconstructive game upon joining it.

10. Irwin gives a striking but not wholly convincing psychoanalytic explanation of this similarity; *Doubling and Incest*, 110.

11. This term for a narrative within a narrative is used, with some reservations, by Barthes with reference to Balzac's "Sarrasine." *S/Z*, 90. In both *Absalom, Absalom!* and "Sarrasine," the subject matter of the nested narratives involves a considerable amount of imaginative activity on the part of the narrators because they have not witnessed all of the events that they report.

12. The affinity of Miss Rosa's speeches with the literary convention of the lovers discourse is discussed by Kaufman, "Devious Channels of Decorous Ordering," 183-200.

13. A view of the character in terms of his role in another novel is legitimate so far as *The Sound and the Fury* and *Absalom, Absalom!* are concerned,

though it may be dangerous elsewhere. Faulkner remarked that to him Quentin's character seemed consistent in both novels. *Faulkner in the University*, 247. Irwin's *Doubling and Incest* likewise cogently demonstrates that the two novels complement each other.

14. Sutpen rises to the position of the aristocracy much more quickly and violently but essentially in the same way as his fellow planters; see Millgate, *Achievement of William Faulkner*, 157.

15. The phenomenon of *paralepsis* is the opposite of that of *paralipsis* discussed in chapter 2. While *paralipsis* is the suppression of information of which the focal character is well aware, *paralepsis* consists of presenting more information than is authorized by the attribution of the focus. See Genette, *Narrative Discourse*, 195.

16. Clytie's role has been examined by Schmidtberger, "*Absalom, Absalom!*: What Clytie Knew," 255-63. This article represents precisely one of the ways in which the audience cues into the novel's game and resolves some of the apparent contradictions in its *fabula* material.

17. This has also been observed by Irwin, *Doubling and Incest*, 78; and Adams, *Faulkner: Myth and Motion*, 195.

18. Cf. my analysis of a similar technique of paraleptic projection in *Nabokov: The Mystery of Literary Structures*, 22-29.

19. See also Brooks, *Faulkner: The Yoknapatawpa Country*, 323.

20. For this observation I am indebted to Krause, "Reading Shreve's Letters," 158-59.

21. The word "renege" is also used to refer to Ellen's loss of the sense of reality (64) when carried away by Sutpen's illusions.

22. Thompson considers the main concern of *Absalom, Absalom!* to be with Quentin's character rather than with Sutpen's story. *William Faulkner: An Introduction and Interpretation*, 56. Faulkner himself expressly states that Sutpen is the protagonist of the novel, even though eventually the novel comes to tell "the story of Quentin Compson's hatred of the bad qualities in the country he loves." *Faulkner in the University*, 71.

23. On Shreve and Quentin's "use" of each other for their private intellectual purpose see also Kartiganer, *Fragile Thread*, 100-104.

24. Lind, "The Design and Meaning of *Absalom, Absalom!*," 904.

25. Kartiganer argues that, being "a literalist of the imagination," Sutpen never fully understands the arbitrariness of the symbols that he is supposed to act by in the Southern society; *Fragile Thread*, 90-91.

26. Poirier, "'Strange Gods' in Jefferson, Mississippi," 7.

27. His inability to recognize Bon can also be explained as a consequence of shame, since recognizing also involves being recognized. As Cavell notes in his discussion of *King Lear*, shame is the main motive for avoiding recognition, since it is "the specific discomfort produced by the sense of being looked at; the avoidance of the sight of others is the reflex it produces." Whereas guilt seeks to avoid discovery, under shame "what must be covered up is not your deed, but yourself." *Disowning Knowledge*, 49.

28. Cf. Swiggart, *Art of Faulkner's Novels*, 162.

29. Taking for granted Judith's awareness of Bon's parentage, Davis ex-

plains that Judith and Clytie rely too much on the "rapport of communal blood," which should, without special effort on their part, make Charles Etienne a Sutpen, one of them; they disregard, however, the essential otherness of the boy who also has other blood in his veins and whose first formative years have been passed in a totally different cultural environment; *Faulkner's "Negro,"* 159, 203-5.

30. See Swiggart, *Art of Faulkner's Novels*, 165-66.

31. The portrayal of Shreve is characterized by the same kind of verisimilitude as that of Quentin. His conduct seems to be uncannily well motivated, yet the motivation always remains ambiguous. For instance, we cannot tell whether his final provocation of Quentin is a cruel gesture—see Slatoff, *Quest for Failure*, 201—or whether it is his "final and supreme effort to get Quentin moving," Adams, *Faulkner: Myth and Motion*, 213.

32. Faulkner accepted a Virginia University student's suggestion that *Absalom, Absalom!* presents "thirteen ways of looking at a blackbird" and remarked that it is left for the reader to achieve the fourteenth vision—hopefully, the true one; *Faulkner in the University*, 273.

33. The effect of play is akin to the liberating effect of aesthetic experience. Huizinga, indeed, mentions that "The words we use to denote the elements of play belong for the most part to aesthetics, terms with which we try to describe the effects of beauty: tension, poise, balance, contrast, variation, solution, resolution, etc." *Homo Ludens*, 10.

34. See Kant, *Fundamental Principles*, 56.

CONCLUDING REMARKS

1. On the tension between the intrinsic interpretation of narrative fiction and interdisciplinary orientations see Gelley, *Narrative Crossings*, ix-xiv.

2. Augustine, *On Christian Doctrine*, 120, 123, and 138.

3. Schopenhauer, *The World as Will and Representation*, 1:18.

4. Schopenhauer, *The World as Will and Representation*, 1:363.

5. See Gadamer's discussion of the etymological roots of play *(Spiel)*, *Truth and Method*, 93-94. Gadamer denies the possibility of the aesthetic experience as based on Kantian disinterestedness, or "aesthetic differentiation." An absolute state of "aesthetic differentiation" is probably impossible, yet the alternation of self-consciousness with brief moments of aesthetic transport is an aesthetic phenomenon in itself.

6. See Nussbaum, *Fragility of Goodness*, 388.

7. Cavell, "Politics as Opposed to What?" 175, 176.

Works Cited

Adams, Richard P. *Faulkner: Myth and Motion*. Princeton: Princeton Univ. Press, 1968.

Allen, Glen O. "Structure, Symbol, and Theme in E.M. Forster's *A Passage to India*." *PMLA* 70 (1955): 934-54.

Alter, Robert. *Fielding and the Nature of the Novel*. Cambridge: Harvard Univ. Press, 1968.

———. *Partial Magic: The Novel as a Self-Conscious Genre*. Berkeley: Univ. of California Press, 1975.

Augustine, St. *On Christian Doctrine*. Trans. D.W. Robertson, Jr. New York: Bobbs-Merrill, 1958.

Austen, Jane. *Emma*. In *The Novels of Jane Austen*. Vol. 4. Text based on collation of early editions by R.W. Chapman. Oxford: Clarendon, 1948.

———. *Jane Austen's Letters to Her Sister Cassandra and Others*. Collected and ed. R.W. Chapman. Oxford: Clarendon, 1932.

Austin, John L. *How to Do Things with Words*. London: Oxford Univ. Press, 1962.

———. "Performative Utterances." In *Philosophical Papers*, ed. J.O. Urmson and G.J. Warnoch. London: Oxford Univ. Press, 1970.

Axton, William. "The Trouble with Esther." *Modern Language Quarterly* 26 (1965): 545-57.

Bachelard, Gaston. *The Poetics of Space*. Trans. Maria Jolas. Boston: Beacon, 1969.

Baker, Sheridan. "Bridget Allworthy: The Creative Pressures of Fielding's Plot." *Papers of the Michigan Academy of Science, Arts, and Letters* 52 (1967): 345-56. Reprinted in Henry Fielding, *Tom Jones*, ed. Sheridan Baker (New York: Norton Critical Editions Series, 1973).

Bakhtin, Mikhail. *The Dialogic Imagination*. Ed. Michael Holquist, trans. Caryl Emerson and Michael Holquist. Austin: Univ. of Texas Press, 1981.

———. *Problems of Dostoevsky's Poetics*. Ed. and trans. Caryl Emerson. Minneapolis: Univ. of Minnesota Press, 1984.

Bal, Mieke. "Mise en abyme et iconicité." *Littérature* 29 (1978): 116-28.

Barthes, Roland. "Introduction à l'analyse structural des récits." *Communications* 8 (1966): 1-25.

———. *S/Z*. Trans. Richard Miller. New York: Hill and Wang, 1974.

Battestin, Martin C. "Fielding's Definition of Wisdom: Some Functions of Ambiguity and Emblem in *Tom Jones*." *English Literary History* 35 (1968): 188-217. Reprinted in Fielding, *Tom Jones*.

————, ed. *Twentieth Century Interpretations of Tom Jones*. Englewood Cliffs, N.J.: Prentice Hall, 1968.

Beer, Gillian. "Negation in *A Passage to India*." In *A Passage to India: Essays in Interpretation*, ed. John Beer. Totowa, N.J.: Barnes and Noble, 1986.

Beer, John. "*A Passage to India*, the French New Novel and English Romanticism." In *E.M. Forster: Centenary Revaluations*, ed. Judith Scherer Herz and Robert K. Martin. London: Macmillan, 1982, 124-52. Reprinted in Beer, *A Passage to India: Essays in Interpretation*.

Beer, John, ed. *A Passage to India: Essays in Interpretation*. Totowa, N.J.: Barnes and Noble, 1986.

Benveniste, Emile. "Analytical Philosophy and Language." In *Problems of General Linguistics*, trans. Mary Elizabeth Meek. Coral Gables: Univ. of Miami Press, 1971, 231-38.

Berger, Carole. "The Rake and the Reader in Jane Austen's Novels." *Studies in English Literature* 15 (1975): 531-44.

Berthoud, Jacques. *Joseph Conrad: The Major Phase*. Cambridge: Cambridge Univ. Press, 1978.

Bleikasten, André. *The Most Splendid Failure: Faulkner's The Sound and the Fury*. Bloomington: Indiana Univ. Press, 1976.

Bliss, Michael. "Fielding's Bill of Fare in *Tom Jones*." *English Literary History* 30 (1963): 242.

Booth, Wayne. *The Rhetoric of Fiction*. Chicago: Univ. of Chicago Press, 1961.

————. *The Company We Keep: An Ethics of Fiction*. Berkeley: Univ. of California Press, 1988.

Borges, Jorge Luis. *Labyrinths*. New York: New Directions, 1964.

————. "Narrative Art and Magic." *Triquarterly* 25 (Fall 1972): 209-15.

Broderick, James H., and John E. Grant. "The Identity of Esther Summerson." *Modern Philology* 55 (1958): 252-58.

Brooks, Cleanth. *William Faulkner: The Yoknapatawpa Country*. New Haven: Yale Univ. Press, 1963.

Burke, Kenneth. *Language as Symbolic Action: Essays on Life, Literature, and Method*. Berkeley: Univ. of California Press, 1968.

Burrows, John Frederick. *Jane Austen's Emma*. Sydney: Sydney Univ. Press, 1968.

Butler, Marilyn. *Jane Austen and the War of Ideas*. Oxford: Clarendon, 1975.

Cavell, Stanley. *Disowning Knowledge in Six Plays of Shakespeare*. Cambridge, Cambridge Univ. Press, 1987.

————. *Must We Mean What We Say?* London: Cambridge Univ. Press, 1976.

————. "Politics as Opposed to What?" *Critical Inquiry* 9 (1982): 157-78. Revised version reprinted in *Themes out of School: Effects and Causes*. San Francisco: North Point, 1984.

Chapman, Robert William. *Jane Austen: Facts and Problems*. Oxford: Clarendon, 1948.

Chatman, Seymour. *Story and Discourse: Narrative Structure in Fiction and Film*. Ithaca: Cornell Univ. Press, 1983.

Cohn, Dorrit. *Transparent Minds: Narrative Modes for Presenting Consciousness in Fiction*. Princeton: Princeton Univ. Press, 1978.

Collins, Carvel. "Christian and Freudian Structures." *Twentieth Century Interpretations of the Sound and the Fury,* ed. Michael H. Cowan. Englewood Cliffs, N.J.: Prentice Hall, 1968. Reprinted from "The Pairing of *The Sound and the Fury* and *As I Lay Dying.*" *Princeton University Library Chronicle* 18 (Spring 1957): 115-19.

Colmer, John. *E.M. Forster: A Passage to India.* London: Arnold, 1967.

————. "Promise and Withdrawal in *A Passage to India.*" In *E.M. Forster: A Human Exploration,* ed. G.K. Das and John Beer. London: Macmillan, 1979.

Connor, Stephen. *Charles Dickens.* Oxford: Basil Blackwell, 1985.

Conrad, Joseph. *The Works of Joseph Conrad.* London: William Heinemann, 1921.

Coolidge, Archibald. *Dickens as a Serial Novelist.* Ames: Iowa State Univ. Press, 1967.

Cooper, Christopher. *Conrad and the Human Dilemma.* New York: Barnes and Noble, 1970.

Cowan, Michael H., ed. *Twentieth Century Interpretations of "The Sound and the Fury."* Englewood Cliffs, N.J.: Prentice Hall, 1968.

Crane, R.S. "The Concept of Plot and the Plot of *Tom Jones.*" *Critics and Criticism,* ed. R.S. Crane. Chicago: Univ. of Chicago Press, 1952. Reprinted in *Twentieth Century Interpretations;* and in Fielding, *Tom Jones.*

Creevy, Patrick J. "In Time and Out: The Tempo of Life in *Bleak House.*" *Dickens Studies Annual: Essays on Victorian Fiction* 12 (1983): 63-80.

Crews, Frederick. *E.M. Forster: The Perils of Humanism.* Princeton, New Jersey: Princeton Univ. Press, 1962.

Culler, Jonathan. "Fabula and Sjuzhet in the Analysis of Narrative: Some American Discussions." *Poetics Today* 1-3 (1980): 27-37.

Daleski, H.M. "Rhythmic and Symbolic Patterns in *A Passage to India.*" *Scripta Hierosolymitana* 62 (1966): 258-79.

————. *Dickens and the Art of Analogy.* New York: Schoken, 1970.

————. "Dickens and the Proleptic Uncanny." *Dickens Studies Annual: Essays on Victorian Fiction* 13 (1984): 193-206.

————. *Joseph Conrad: The Way of Dispossession.* London: Farber and Farber, 1977.

————. *Unities.* Athens: Univ. of Georgia Press, 1985.

Dällenbach, Lucien. *Le récit spéculaire: Essay sur le mise en abyme.* Paris: Seuil, 1977.

Das, G.K. and John Beer, eds. *E.M. Forster: A Human Exploration.* London: Macmillan, 1979.

Dauner, Louise. "What Happened in a Cave? Reflections on *A Passage to India.*" *Modern Fiction Studies* 7 (1961): 258-70.

Davis, Thadious M. *Faulkner's "Negro."* Baton Rouge: Louisiana State Univ. Press, 1983.

Dickens, Charles. *Bleak House.* Ed. George Ford and Sylvère Monod. New York: Norton, 1977.

Donovan, Robert A. "Structure and Idea in *Bleak House.*" *English Literary History* 29 (1962): 186-201.

Douglass, Paul. *Bergson, Eliot, American Literature.* Lexington: Univ. Press of Kentucky, 1986.

Dowling, David. *"A Passage to India* through 'The Spaces between the Words.' " *Journal of Narrative Technique* 15 (1985): 256-66.

Drew, John. "The Spirit Behind the Frieze?" In *A Passage to India: Essays in Interpretation,* ed. John Beer. Totowa, N.J.: Barnes and Noble, 1986, 81-103.

Duckworth, Alistair M. *The Improvement of the Estate: A Study of Jane Austen's Novels.* Baltimore: Johns Hopkins Univ. Press, 1971.

Duffy, Joseph M., Jr. *"Emma:* The Awakening from Innocence." *English Literary History* 21 (1954): 39-53.

Dyson, A.E. *The Inimitable Dickens: A Reading of the Novels.* London: Macmillan, 1970.

Eco, Umberto. *The Role of the Reader: Explorations in the Semiotics of Texts.* Bloomington: Indiana Univ. Press, 1979.

Ejkhenbaum, Boris. *"Kak sdelana 'Shinel' Gogolia"* and *"Illiuziya Skaza."* In *Texte der Russischen Formalisten,* vol. 1. Comp. Jurij Striedter. München: Wilhelm Fink, 1969, 122-58 and 160-66.

Empson, William. "Tom Jones." *Kenyon Review* 20 (1958): 217-49. Reprinted in Paulson, *Fielding;* in Battestin, *Twentieth Century Interpretations;* and in Fielding, *Tom Jones.*

Erlich, Victor. *Russian Formalism: History—Doctrine.* The Hague: Mouton, 1969.

Faulkner, William. *Absalom, Absalom!* New York: Random House, 1936.

———. *The Sound and the Fury.* New York: Random House, 1929.

Felman, Shoshana. *The Literary Speech Act.* Ithaca: Cornell Univ. Press, 1983.

Fielding, Henry. *The History of Tom Jones, a Foundling.* Ed. Sheridan Baker. Critical Editions Series. New York: Norton, 1973.

Fish, Stanley. "Literature in the Reader: Affective Sylistics." *New Literary History* 2 (1970): 123-62. Reprinted, with comments, in Fish, *Is There a Text in This Class?*

———. *Self-Consuming Artifacts: The Experience of Seventeenth-Centry Literature.* Berkeley: Univ. of California Press, 1972.

———. "Interpreting the Variorum." *Critical Inquiry* 3 (1976): 465-85. Reprinted in Fish, *Is There a Text in This Class?*

———. *Is There a Text in This Class? The Authority of Interpretive Communities.* Cambridge: Harvard Univ. Press, 1980.

Fitzgerald, F. Scott. *The Letters of F. Scott Fitzgerald.* Ed. Andrew Turnbull. New York: Charles Scribner's Sons, 1963.

Fontanier, Pierre. *Les Figures du Discourse.* Paris: Flammarion, 1977.

Ford, Ford Madox. *Joseph Conrad: A Personal Rememberance.* New York: Octagon, 1980.

Forster, E.M. *Aspects of the Novel.* New York: Harcourt, Brace and World, 1954.

———. *A Passage to India.* New York: Harcourt, Brace, 1924.

———. *Pharos and Pharillon.* New York: Knopf, 1923.

Freund, Elizabeth. *The Return of the Reader.* London: Methuen, 1987.

Furbank, P.N. "Forster and the 'Bloomsbury' Prose." In *E.M. Forster: A Human Exploration,* ed. G.K. Das and John Beer. Totowa, N.J.: Barnes and Noble, 1986, 161-66.

Gadamer, Hans-Georg. *Truth and Method.* London: Sheed and Ward, 1975.

Gardner, John. *On Moral Fiction*. New York: Basic, 1977.

Garrett, Peter K. *The Victorian Multiplot Novel: Studies in the Dialogal Form*. New Haven: Yale Univ. Press, 1980.

Gelley, Alexander. *Narrative Crossings: Theory and Pragmatics of Prose Fiction*. Baltimore: Johns Hopkins Univ. Press, 1987.

Genette, Gérard. *Narrative Discourse: An Essay on Method*. Trans. Jane E. Lewin. Ithaca: Cornell Univ. Press, 1980.

Gide, André. *Journal 1889-1939*. Paris: Gallimard, 1948.

Gilbert, Sandra M., and Susan Gubar. *The Madwoman in the Attic: The Woman Writer and the Nineteenth Century Literary Imagination*. New Haven: Yale Univ. Press, 1979.

Gillon, Adam. *The Eternal Solitary: A Study of Joseph Conrad*. New York: Bookman, 1960.

Ginzburg, Evgeniya. *Into the Whirlwind*, London: Collins/Harvill, 1967.

Gold, Joseph. *Charles Dickens: Radical Moralism*. Minneapolis: Univ. of Minnesota Press, 1972.

Goldknopf, David. "The Failure of Plot in *Tom Jones*." *Criticism* 11 (1969): 262-74. Reprinted in Fielding, *Tom Jones*.

Goldman, Arnold, ed. *Twentieth Century Interpretations of Absalom, Absalom!* Englewood Cliffs, N.J.: Prentice Hall, 1971.

Gombrich, E.H. *Art and Illusion: A Study in the Psychology of Pictorial Representation*. London: Phaidon, 1962.

Grenadier, M.E. "The Mystery and the Moral: Point of View in *Bleak House*." *Nineteenth-Century Fiction* 10 (1956): 301-5.

Grossvogel, David I. *Mystery and Its Fictions: From Oedipus to Agatha Christie*. Baltimore: Johns Hopkins Univ. Press, 1979.

Guerard, Albert. *Conrad the Novelist*. Cambridge: Harvard Univ. Press, 1958.

Guetti, James. "*Absalom, Absalom!*: The Extended Simile." In *The Limits of Metaphor: A Study of Melville, Conrad, and Faulkner*. Ithaca: Cornell Univ. Press, 1967, 69-108.

Gwynn, Frederick L., and Joseph L. Blotner, eds. *Faulkner in the University: Class Conferences at the University of Virginia*. Charlottesville: Univ. of Virginia Press, 1959.

Harding, D.H. "Psychological Processes in the Reading of Fiction." *British Journal of Aesthetics* 2 (1962): 133-47.

Harding, D.W. "Regulated Hatred: An Aspect of the Work of Jane Austen." *Scrutiny* 8 (1940): 346-62.

Hardy, Barbara. *The Appropriate Form: An Essay on the Novel*. London: Univ. of London Athlone Press, 1964.

Harrison, Bernard. *Henry Fielding's Tom Jones: The Novelist as Moral Philosopher*. London: Chatto and Windus, 1975.

Hartfield, Glen W. *Henry Fielding and the Language of Irony*. Chicago: Univ. of Chicago Press, 1968.

Harvey, W.J. "Chance and Design in *Bleak House*." In *Dickens and the Twentieth Century*, ed. John Gross and Gabriel Pearson. Toronto: Univ. of Toronto Press, 1962, 145-57.

———. "The Plot of *Emma*." *Essays in Criticism* 42 (1967): 48-63.

Hellstrom, Ward. "Frankophobia in *Emma.*" *Studies in English Literature* 5 (1965): 607-17.

Herz, Judith Scherer, and Robert K. Martin, eds. *E.M. Forster: Centenary Revaluations.* London: Macmillan, 1982.

———. "Listening to Language." In *A Passage to India: Essays in Interpretation,* ed. John Beer. Totowa, N.J.: Barnes and Noble, 1986.

Hewitt, Douglas. *Conrad: A Reassessment.* London: Bowes and Bowes, 1969.

Hodgson, John A. " 'Logical Sequence and Continuity': Some Observations on the Typographical and Structural Consistency of *Absalom, Absalom!*" *American Literature* 43 (1971): 97-107.

Hoffman, Frederick J., and Olga W. Vickery, eds. *William Faulkner: Three Decades of Criticism.* New York: Harcourt, Brace, World, 1960.

Hofstadter, Douglas R. *Gödel, Escher, Bach: An Eternal Golden Braid.* Harmondsworth: Penguin, 1980.

Hollingsworth, Keith. "*A Passage to India:* The Echoes in the Marabar Caves." *Criticism* 4 (1962): 210-24.

Hollington, Michael. *Dickens and the Grotesque.* London: Croom Helm, 1984.

Holub, Robert C. *Reception Theory: A Critical Introduction.* London: Methuen, 1984.

Howe, Irving. *William Faulkner: A Critical Study.* Chicago: Univ. of Chicago Press, 1975.

Hoyle's Games: Containing the Rules for Playing Fashionable Games. New York: Hurst, 1857.

Huizinga, Johan. *Homo Ludens: A Study of the Play Element in Culture.* Boston: Beakon, 1955.

Hunter, J. Paul. *Occasional Form: Henry Fielding and the Chain of Circumstance.* Baltimore: Johns Hopkins Univ. Press, 1975.

Irwin, John. *Doubling and Incest / Repetition and Revenge: A Speculative Reading of Faulkner.* Baltimore: Johns Hopkins Univ. Press, 1975.

Irwin, Michael. *Henry Fielding: The Tentative Realist.* Oxford: Clarendon, 1967.

Iser, Wolfgang. *The Act of Reading: A Theory of Aesthetic Response.* Baltimore: Johns Hopkins Univ. Press, 1978.

———. *The Implied Reader: Patterns of Communication in Prose Fiction from Bunyan to Beckett.* Baltimore: Johns Hopkins Univ. Press, 1974.

Jeliffe, Robert A., ed. *Faulkner at Nagano.* Folcroft, Pa.: Folcroft, 1970.

Johnson, Claudia L. "The 'Operations of Time, and the Changes of the Human Mind': Jane Austen and Dr. Johnson Again." *Modern Language Quarterly* 44 (1983): 23-38.

Johnson, Julie M. "The Theory of Relativity in Modern Literature: An Overview and *The Sound and the Fury.*" *Journal of Modern Literature* 10 (1983): 217-30.

Johnson, Maurice. *Fielding's Art of Fiction: Eleven Essays on "Shamela," "Joseph Andrews," "Tom Jones," and "Amelia."* Philadelphia: Univ. of Pennsylvania Press, 1961.

Kant, Immanuel. *Fundamental Principles of the Metaphysics of Ethics.* Trans. Thomas Kingsmill Abbott. London: Longmans, Green, 1946.

Karl, Frederick R. "The Significance of the Revisions in the Early Versions of *Nostromo.*" *Modern Fiction Studies* 5 (1959): 129-44.

Kartiganer, Donald M. *The Fragile Thread: The Meaning of Form in Faulkner's Novels*. Amherst: Univ. of Massachusetts Press, 1979.

Kaufman, Linda. "Devious Channels of Decorous Ordering: A Lover's Discourse in *Absalom, Absalom!*" *Modern Fiction Studies* 29 (1983): 183-200.

Kazan, Francesca. "Confabulations in *A Passage to India*." *Criticism* 29 (1987): 197-214.

Kettle, Arnold. *An Introduction to the English Novel*. New York: Harper and Row, 1960.

Kierkegaard, Sören. *Either/Or: A Fragment of Life*. Trans. David F. Swenson and Lillian Marvin Swenson. Princeton: Princeton Univ. Press, 1949.

Knoepflmacher, U.C. "The Importance of Being Frank: Character and Letter-Writing in *Emma*." *Studies in English Literature* 7 (1967): 639-58.

Krause, David. "Reading Shreve's Letters and Faulkner's *Absalom, Absalom!*" *Studies in American Literature* 11 (1983): 153-69.

Leavis, F.R. "E.M. Forster." *Scrutiny* 7 (1938): 185-202.

Leavis, F.R. and Q.D. Leavis. *Dickens, the Novelist*. London: Chatto and Windus, 1970.

Levine, June Perry. *A Passage to India: Creation and Criticism*. Lincoln: Univ. of Nebraska Press, 1971.

Liddel, Robert. *The Novels of Jane Austen*. London: Longman, Green, 1969.

Lind, Ilse Dusoir. "The Design and Meaning of *Absalom, Absalom!*" *PMLA* 70 (1955): 887-912. Reprinted in Hoffman and Vickery, *William Faulkner: Three Decades of Criticism*.

Lodge, David. *The Novelist at the Crossroads and Other Essays on Fiction and Criticism*. Ithaca: Cornell Univ. Press, 1971.

Longley, John Lewis. *The Tragic Mask: A Study of Faulkner's Heroes*. Chapel Hill: Univ. of North Carolina Press, 1957.

Lowery, Perrin. "Concepts of Time in *The Sound and the Fury*." In *English Institute Essays, 1952*, ed. Alan S. Downer. New York: Columbia Univ. Press, 1954, 57-82. Reprinted in Cowan, *Twentieth Century Interpretations*.

Maslow, Abraham H. *Motivation and Personality*. New York: Harper and Row, 1970.

McHale, Brian. "Free Indirect Discourse: a Survey of Recent Accounts." *Poetics and Theory of Literature* 3 (1978): 249-87.

———. *Postmodernist Fiction*. London: Methuen, 1987.

Miller, David Albert. *Narrative and its Discontents: Problems of Closure in the Traditional Novel*. Princeton: Princeton Univ. Press, 1981.

———. *The Novel and the Police*. Berkeley: Univ. of California Press, 1988.

Miller, Joseph Hillis. *Charles Dickens: The World of His Novels*. Cambridge: Harvard Univ. Press, 1958.

Millgate, Michael. *The Achievement of William Faulkner*. New York: Random House, 1966.

Moers, Ellen. "*Bleak House*: The Agitating Women." *Dickensian* 69 (1973): 13-24.

Moffat, Wendy. "*A Passage to India* and the Limits of Certainty." *Journal of Narrative Technique* 20 (1990): 331-41.

Monk, Leland. "Murder She Wrote: The Mystery of Jane Austen's *Emma*." *Journal of Narrative Technique* 20 (1990): 342-53.

Moser, Thomas. *Joseph Conrad: Achievement and Decline*. Cambridge: Harvard Univ. Press, 1957.

Murphy, James J. "The Origins and Early Development of Rhetoric." In *A Synoptic History of Classical Rhetoric*, ed. James J. Murphy. Davis, Ca.: Hermagoras, 1983.

Murry, John Middleton. "In Defence of Fielding." In *Unprofessional Essays*. London: Jonathan Cape, 1956, 9-52.

Nabokov, Vladimir. *Ada, or Ardor: A Family Chronicle*. New York: McGraw-Hill, 1981.

———. *King, Queen, Knave*. New York: McGraw-Hill, 1968.

———. *Lectures on Literature*. Ed. Fredson Bowers. New York: Harcourt, Brace, Jovanovich, 1980.

Neil, Edward. "Between Deference and Deconstruction: 'Situations' of Recent Critical Theory and Jane Austen's *Emma*." *Critical Quarterly* 29 (1987): 39-54.

Nietzsche, Friedrich. "The Birth of Tragedy." In *Basic Writings of Nietzsche*, ed. and trans. Walter Kaufmann. New York: Modern Library, 1968, 3-144.

———. *Untimely Meditations*. Trans. R.J. Hollingdale. Cambridge: Cambridge Univ. Press, 1983.

Nussbaum, Martha C. "Flawed Crystals: James's *The Golden Bowl* and Literature and Moral Philosophy." *New Literary History* 25 (1983): 25-50.

———. *The Fragility of Goodness: Luck and Ethics in Greek Tragedy and Philosophy*. Cambridge: Cambridge Univ. Press, 1986.

Orange, Michael. "Language and Silence in *A Passage to India*." In *E.M. Forster: A Human Exploration*, ed. G.K. Das and John Beer. London: Macmillan, 1979, 142-60.

Parry, Benita. "The Politics of Representation in *A Passage to India*." In *A Passage to India: Essays in Interpretation*, ed. John Beer. Totowa, N.J.: Barnes and Noble, 1986, 27-43.

Paulson, Ronald, ed. *Fielding: A Collection of Critical Essays*. Englewood Cliffs, N.J.: Prentice Hall, 1962.

Perry, Menakhem. "Literary Dynamics: How the Order of a Text Creates its Meaning [With an Analysis of Faulkner's 'A Rose for Emily']." *Poetics Today* 1 (1979): 35-64.

Poirier, Richard. " 'Strange Gods' in Jefferson, Mississippi." In *William Faulkner's Absalom, Absalom! A Critical Casebook*, ed. Elisabeth Muhlenfeld. New York: Garland, 1984. Reprinted from *William Faulkner: Two Decades of Criticism*, ed. Frederick J. Hoffman and Olga W. Vickery. East Lansing: Michigan Univ. Press, 1951, 217-43.

Poovey, Mary. *The Proper Lady and the Woman Writer: Ideology as Style in the Works of Mary Wollstonecraft, Mary Shelly, and Jane Austen*. Chicago: Univ. of Chicago Press, 1984.

Pratt, Mary Louise. *Toward a Speech Act Theory of Literary Discourse*. Bloomington: Indiana Univ. Press, 1977.

Preston, John. *The Created Self: The Reader's Role in Eighteenth-Century Fiction*. London: Barnes and Noble, 1970.

Pushkin, Aleksandr. *Eugene Onegin: A Novel In Verse*. 2 vols. Trans. from

Russian with commentary by Vladimir Nabokov. Bollingen Series. Princeton: Princeton Univ. Press, 1975.

Quirk, Eugene. "Tulkinghorn's Buried Life: A Study of Character in *Bleak
House.*" *Journal of English and Germanic Philology* 71 (1972): 526-35.

Rawson, C.J. "Professor Empson's *Tom Jones.*" *Notes and Queries* 6 (1959). Reprinted in *Henry Fielding's "Tom Jones": A Casebook*, ed. Neil Compton.
London: Macmillan, 1970, 173-81.

Ricardou, Jean. "L'histoire dans l'histoire." In *Problèmes du nouveau roman.*
Paris: Seuil, 1967.

Richards, I.A. *Principles of Literary Criticism.* London: Routledge and Kegan
Paul, 1926.

Rifaterre, Michael. "Describing Poetic Structures: Two Approaches to Baudelaire's 'Les Chats.'" *Yale French Studies* 36-37 (1966): 200-42. Reprinted in
Tompkins, *Reader-Response Criticism.*

Rimmon, Shlomith. *The Concept of Ambiguity—The Example of James.* Chicago:
Univ. of Chicago Press, 1977.

Rimmon-Kenan, Shlomith. *Narrative Fiction: Contemporary Poetics.* London:
Methuen, 1983.

Ron, Moshe. "The Restricted Abyss: Nine Problems in the Theory of *Mise en
Abyme.*" *Poetics Today* 8 (1987): 417-38.

Rosmarin, Adena. "'Misreading' *Emma*: The Powers and Perfidies of Inter-
pretative History." *English Literary History* 51 (1984): 315-42.

Sartre, Jean-Paul. "On *The Sound and the Fury*: Time in the Work of Faulkner." In
Literary and Philosphical Essays, trans. Annette Michelson. New York: Col-
lier, 1962, 84-93.

Saveson, John E. *Joseph Conrad: The Making of a Moralist.* Amsterdam: Rodolphi,
1972.

Schmidtberger, Loren. "*Absalom, Absalom!*: What Clytie Knew." *Mississippi
Quarterly* 32 (1982): 255-63.

Scholes, Robert, and Robert Kellog. *The Nature of Narrative.* New York: Oxford
Univ. Press, 1966.

Schopenhauer, Arthur. *The World as Will and Representation.* Trans. E.F.J. Payne.
New York: Dover, 1969.

Schwartz, Daniel R. *Conrad: Almayer's Folly to Under Western Eyes.* Ithaca: Cornell Univ. Press, 1980.

———. "The Originality of E.M. Forster." *Modern Fiction Studies* 29 (1983):
623-41.

Scott, P.J.M. *Reality and Comic Confidence in Charles Dickens.* London: Macmillan,
1979.

Searle, John. *Speech-Acts: An Essay in the Philosophy of Language.* Cambridge:
Cambridge Univ. Press, 1968.

Shahane, Vasant A. "Forster's Inner Passage to India." In *E.M. Forster: Centenary Revaluations*, ed. Judith Scherer Herz and Robert K. Martin. London:
Macmillan, 1982, 267-77.

Shalamov, Varlam. *Graphite.* Trans. John Glad. New York: Norton, 1981.

———. *Kolyma Tales.* Trans. John Glad. New York: Norton, 1980.

Shklovsky, Victor. "Art as Technique." In *Russian Formalist Criticism: Four Es-*

says, ed. Lee T. Lemon and Marion J. Reis. Lincoln: Univ. of Nebraska Press, 1965, 3-24.

Shusterman, David. "The Curious Case of Professor Godbole: *A Passage to India* Re-examined." *PMLA* 76 (1961): 426-35.

Slatoff, Walter J. *Quest for Failure: A Study of William Faulkner.* Ithaca: Cornell Univ. Press, 1960.

Smith, Grahame. *Charles Dickens: Bleak House.* Southampton: Camelot, 1974.

Sternberg, Meir. *Expositional Modes and Temporal Ordering in Fiction.* Baltimore: Johns Hopkins Univ. Press, 1978.

————. *The Poetics of Biblical Narrative: Ideological Literature and the Drama of Reading.* Bloomington: Indiana Univ. Press, 1987.

Stewart, George R., and Joseph M. Backus. "'Each in Its Ordered Place': Structure and Narration in 'Benjy's Section' of *The Sound and the Fury.*" *American Literature* 29 (1958): 440-56.

Stone, Wilfred. "The Caves of *A Passage to India.*" In *A Passage to India: Essays in Interpretation,* ed. John Beer. Totowa, N.J.: Barnes and Noble, 1986, 16-26.

Sucksmith, Harvey Peter. *The Narrative Art of Charles Dickens: The Rhetoric of Sympathy and Irony in His Novels.* Oxford: Clarendon, 1970.

Suleiman, Susan R., and Inge Crosman, eds. *The Reader in the Text.* Princeton: Princeton Univ. Press, 1980.

Swiggart, Peter. *The Art of Faulkner's Novels.* Austin: Univ. of Texas Press, 1962.

Tanner, Tony. *Jane Austen.* London: Macmillan, 1986.

Tave, Stuart M. *Some Words of Jane Austen.* Chicago: Univ. of Chicago Press, 1973.

Thompson, Lawrance. "Mirror Analogues in *The Sound and the Fury.* in *English Institute Essays, 1952,* ed. Alan S. Downer, New York: Columbia Univ. Press, 1954, 83-101.

————. *William Faulkner: An Introduction and Interpretation.* New York: Holt, Rinehart, Winston, 1967.

Thurley, Geoffrey. *The Dickens Myth: Its Genesis and Structure.* New York: St. Martin's, 1976.

Tinsley, Molly B. "Muddle Et Cetera: Syntax in *A Passage to India.*" *Journal of Narrative Technique* 9 (1979): 191-98. Reprinted in Herz and Martin, *E.M. Forster: Centenary Revaluations;* and in Beer, *A Passage to India: Essays in Interpretation.*

Todorov, Tzvetan. *The Poetics of Prose.* Trans. Richard Howard. Ithaca: Cornell Univ. Press, 1977.

Toker, Leona. "Between Allusion and Coincidence: Nabokov, Dickens, and Others." *Hebrew University Studies in Literature and the Arts* 12 (1984): 176-98.

————. "*Emma:* The Handling of a Surprise Gap." *Hebrew University Studies in Literature, Essays in Honour of A.A. Mendilow* 1982: 57-79.

————. "Nabokov and the Hawthorne Tradition." *Scripta Hierosolymitana* 32 (1987): 323-49.

————. *Nabokov: The Mystery of Literary Structures.* Ithaca: Cornell Univ. Press, 1989.

————. "Self-Conscious Paralepsis in Vladimir Nabokov's *Pnin* and 'Recruiting.'" *Poetics Today* 7 (1986): 450-69.

Tompkins, Jane P., ed. *Reader-Response Criticism: From Formalism to Post-Structuralism*. Baltimore: Johns Hopkins Univ. Press, 1980.

Trilling, Lionel. *E.M. Forster*. London: Hogarth, 1951.

Van Boheemen, Christine. *The Novel as Family Romance: Language, Gender, and Authority from Fielding to Joyce*. Ithaca: Cornell Univ. Press, 1987.

Vickery, Olga W. *The Novels of William Faulkner*. Baton Rouge: Louisiana State Univ. Press, 1959.

Wagner, Linda Welshimer. "Jason Compson: The Demands of Honor." *Sewanee Review* 79 (1971): 554-75.

White, Gertrude M. "*A Passage to India*: Analysis and Revaluation." *PMLA* 63 (1953): 641-57.

Williams, Ioan, ed. *The Criticism of Henry Fielding*. London: Routledge and Kegan Paul, 1970.

Wilson, W. Daniel. "Readers in Texts," *PMLA* 96 (1981): 848-63.

Wilt, Judith. "Confusion and Consciousness in Dickens's Esther." *Nineteenth Century Fiction* 32 (19): 285-309.

Wright, Andrew. *Henry Fielding: Mask and Feast*. London: Chatto and Windus, 1965.

Zwerdling, Alex. "Esther Summerson Rehabilitated." *PMLA* 88 (1973): 429-39.

Index